BLACK AFRICANS in the BRITISH IMAGINATION

BLACK AFRICANS IN THE BRITISH IMAGINATION

English Narratives of the
Early Atlantic World

CASSANDER L. SMITH

LOUISIANA STATE UNIVERSITY PRESS
BATON ROUGE

Published by Louisiana State University Press
lsupress.org

Copyright © 2016 by Louisiana State University Press
All rights reserved. Except in the case of brief quotations used in articles or reviews, no part of this publication may be reproduced or transmitted in any format or by any means without written permission of Louisiana State University Press.

Louisiana Paperback Edition, 2023

DESIGNER: *Mandy McDonald Scallan*
TYPEFACE: *Whitman*

Library of Congress Cataloging-in-Publication Data

Names: Smith, Cassander L., 1977– author.
Title: Black Africans in the British imagination : English narratives of the early Atlantic world / Cassander L. Smith.
Description: Baton Rouge : Louisiana State University Press, [2016] | Includes bibliographical references and index.
Identifiers: LCCN 2016012831| ISBN 978-0-8071-6384-9 (cloth : alk. paper) | ISBN 978-0-8071-6385-6 (pdf) | ISBN 978-0-8071-6386-3 (epub) | ISBN 978-0-8071-8199-7 (paperback)
Subjects: LCSH: English prose literature—16th century—History and criticism. | English prose literature—17th century—History and criticism. | Blacks—Race identity—Atlantic Ocean Region. | Africans in literature. | Colonies in literature. | Travel writing—Atlantic Ocean Region. | Travel writing—America. | Imperialism in literature. | Spain—Colonies—America—Race relations.
Classification: LCC PR830.A39 S65 2016 | DDC 820.9/3587000496—dc23
LC record available at https://lccn.loc.gov/2016012831

CONTENTS

ACKNOWLEDGMENTS ... vii

INTRODUCTION
Black Africans, a Black Legend, and Challenges of Representation ... 1

CHAPTER 1.
Points of Origin: *English Voyages to Guinea* ... 29

CHAPTER 2.
Reconstructing the Ethiop: *Sir Francis Drake and the Cimarrones of Panama* ... 58

CHAPTER 3.
Alliances Real and Imagined: *Thomas Gage and Black African Collaboration in New Spain* ... 85

CHAPTER 4.
Consuming Beauty: *Richard Ligon, Black African Women, and a Reciprocity of Power* ... 113

CHAPTER 5.
Locating Africa in the Americas: *George Best, Sir Walter Ralegh, and the Quandaries of Racial Representation* ... 140

AFTERWORD
Beyond the Mediation ... 175

NOTES ... 181

INDEX ... 219

ACKNOWLEDGMENTS

In a book that addresses the collaborative nature of early Atlantic literature, it is only fitting that I begin by acknowledging the collaborative energies that pushed this project to completion. To begin, I offer thanks to my colleagues at the University of Alabama, Tuscaloosa. I have been blessed to work with supportive, collegial scholars in UA's English Department, including especially encouraging department chairs, Catherine Davies and Joel Brouwer. The process of writing this book was much less daunting because of the daily camaraderie I experienced in the halls of Morgan and Rowand-Johnson. My thanks go in particular to Trudier Harris, who read earlier versions of several chapters and has been tireless in offering feedback and general advice about the profession—including a strategy for producing a book every two years. I will try to keep up! I thank, too, Phil Beidler and Sharon O'Dair. Like Trudier, they have been not just mentors but also advocates for my work. Phil helped me publish my first article and Sharon welcomed me into the community of Renaissance scholars at UA, even though I was trained as an early Americanist. I also thank my colleagues Michelle Bachelor-Robinson and David Deutsch, with whom I have spent countless hours writing, conversing, and watching the tenure clock tick tock. The time does, indeed, speed by. And I thank the women of AAWE (African American Women in English); the kind of support they have provided has been invaluable. To the graduate students in the group, I hope they will see this book as a testament to what they can do; indeed, my conversations with many of them helped me to nuance aspects of my argument. Also, I would like to acknowledge the support I received from UA colleagues beyond the English Department. Those colleagues include Utz McKnight, Jennifer Shoaff, Jennifer Purvis, Hilary Green, Jennifer Jones, Heather Miyano Kopelson, and Jenny Shaw.

I also owe a huge thank you to those in the English Department at Purdue University, where this project first took root. In particular, I thank Kristina Bross, who encouraged my intellectual pursuits back when I had no clue what I was thinking, how to articulate it, or why it even mattered. She is a model for the kind of scholar, teacher, and mentor I strive to be in the profession. I also thank Venetria Patton, whose expertise in nineteenth- and twentieth-century African American literature provided a valuable perspective that helped me understand the connections between my work and later approaches to African American studies. I am even more thankful for the manner in which Venetria reached out to me early on in my career and offered her mentorship and professional guidance. For their mentorship efforts, I thank also Christopher Lukasik and Ryan Schneider, who pushed me to think in more nuanced ways about race in early America. Sharon Solwitz, Charles Cutter, Susan Curtis, Shaun Hughes, and Emily Allen also deserve my gratitude for the avid interest and support they have shown in my work over the years.

In addition, this book has benefited from my intellectual engagement with scholars in a number of writing groups and scholarly communities. Those include UA's Americanist Group and the Early Atlantic Reading Group at Purdue. The book benefited greatly from my participation in two seminars, "Empire and Culture in the Early Modern English Caribbean," held at the Folger Shakespeare Library in 2010, and an NEH workshop, "European Encounters with the Early Americas," in 2011. I am grateful, too, to the members of the Society of Early Americanists and the Early Caribbean Society. Members of both organizations have embraced my work. Thanks especially to Katy Chiles, Joy Howard, Nick Jones, Sabine Klein, and Kelly Wisecup, who read and commented on chapters of the book. Among others who have encouraged my work are Nicole Aljoe, Ralph Bauer, Allison Bigelow, Philathia Bolton, Tara Bynum, Mary Fuller, Emily Garcia, Casarae Gibson, Miles Grier, Thomas Krise, Nicole Livengood, Megan Hughes Morton, Dennis Moore, Carla Pestana, Allison Hutton Poon, Karen N. Salt, David Shields, Laura Stevens, Elyssa Tardiff, and Hilary Wyss.

I owe a debt of gratitude, as well, to the Newberry Library, American Council of Learned Societies, Folger Shakespeare Library, National Endowment for the Humanities, and UA's Research Grants Committee. These organizations provided funding that allowed me to conduct research for the book.

Thanks go to *Studies in Travel Writing* and the Taylor and Francis Group for publishing an abbreviated version of chapter 5, which originally appeared as "'For They Are Naturally Born': Quandaries of Racial Representation in George Best's A True Discourse," in *Studies in Travel Writing* 17, no. 3 (2013). Thanks go also to the University of Alabama Press for publishing a version of chapter 2 that originally appeared as "Washing the Ethiop Red: Sir Francis Drake and the Cimarrons of Panama" in the essay collection *Race and Displace-*

ment: *Nation, Migration, and Identity in the Twenty-First Century* (University of Alabama Press, 2013).

I very much appreciate the efforts of the editors and staff at Louisiana State University Press, especially Alisa Plant, who remained enthusiastic and supportive from the beginning. I appreciate her patience, diligence, and professionalism. Thank you to the outside reader, whose feedback challenged me to be more precise.

I end my acknowledgments by thanking my family, whose unconditional support over the years has given meaning to everything I do. I am grateful to my parents, Mary and Thomas Davis, who nurtured my love for the humanities without worrying about whether I could get a job with a degree in English. This project is just as much their accomplishment as it is mine. I also thank my siblings, Michelle, Thomas, Alicia, Victoria, and Kevin, whose friendship and support are my lifeline. I have benefited, too, from an extended family, especially a host of aunts and uncles, who helped my parents shoulder the responsibility for my education from day one. You all make me proud of the stock from which I come. And speaking of extended family, I am grateful for the friendship of Kiffany Perlote, Elizabeth Rigaud, and Lamar Wilson. The trips, the lunch dates, the late-night phone conversations were vital components of the self-care I needed to maintain sanity. I owe a special thanks to Alberto Pérez-Huerta, who came along in the twenty-third hour to help this book cross the finish line. I am thankful for his patience and unwavering belief in the quality of this book and the importance of my research. Finally, I cannot end these acknowledgments without recognizing my ten inquisitive nieces and nephews, who are never afraid to ask the hard questions that challenge me to say more. This book is my effort to say more.

BLACK AFRICANS in the BRITISH IMAGINATION

INTRODUCTION

Black Africans, a Black Legend, and Challenges of Representation

This book examines the extent to which the physical presence of black Africans in the early Atlantic world disrupted English responses to Spanish imperialism.[1] It maps a course from sixteenth-century West Africa to seventeenth-century New Spain and traces the growing tension between Spain and England, fighting for imperial dominance in the Americas. Due to Spain's more lucrative start in 1492, England played catch-up, consequently finding itself responding to Spanish imperialism through a bevy of propagandistic literature designed to discredit Spain as a vile, inhumane empire, earning the latter nation the infamous moniker of "Black Legend."[2] English travelers to the Americas were key in producing some of the most widely circulated information about Spain's alleged brutalities.[3] In narratives about their encounters, those travelers often described the manner in which conquistadores burned, hanged, whipped—physically tortured—native populations to subdue and enslave them. The torture reportedly was so atrocious that one of Spain's own Dominican friars, Bartolomé de las Casas, advocated the use of sub-Saharan Africans as slaves to alleviate Native American suffering. Although he later regretted that prescription, Las Casas's remedy illustrates the kinds of racial ideologies (predicated on cultural and geographical distinctions) that were already forming throughout Europe and that would soon fuel the Atlantic slave trade. Black Africans were exported across the Atlantic in increasing numbers.

The growing presence of black Africans in the Americas created rhetorical conflicts for English priests, merchants, explorers, and privateers, who sought to understand those black Africans within racial and anti-Spanish discourses. Writers on occasion replaced Native Americans with black Africans as the victims of Spanish cruelty. In the material world beyond the texts, however, black Africans conducted themselves in ways contradictory to England's anti-Spanish rhetoric, complicating writers' efforts to articulate their experiences in accordance with ideology and political agendas. *Black Africans in the British Imagination* examines how and why those first English encounters with black Africans in the early Atlantic world produced moments of narrative crisis in which writers struggled to correlate the material details of their encounters with literary, rhetorical objectives. That struggle manifests itself in the texts as plot contradictions, ambiguities, and inconsistent characterizations, all forms of narrative compromise that undermine the narratives' larger critiques of Spanish empire. In identifying these moments of narrative compromise or disruption, *Black Africans in the British Imagination* ultimately reveals the extent to which black Africans, as historical presences, helped to shape the literary record of the early Atlantic world—not as passive constructions but as active participants. In short, *Black Africans in the British Imagination* performs three tasks: it reframes discussions about race and cross-cultural contact in the early modern period; it reexamines the political and religious tensions between Spain and England in the sixteenth and seventeenth centuries, approaching those tensions from the perspective of black Africans; and it uncovers the extent to which black Africans affected the literary production of the early Atlantic world by directly influencing writers' editorial and narrative choices. *Black Africans in the British Imagination* is part of the ongoing discussions in the growing field of Atlantic studies and even more specifically in black Atlantic and African diaspora studies. I join anthropologists, cultural critics, historians, and ethnographers who have examined the ways in which black diasporic communities helped to form the social, political, and material cultures of what we now call the early Atlantic world.[4]

Reality, Rhetoric, and Anti-Spanish Sentiment

In 1570 a Spanish official living in Panama City wrote a letter to King Philip II complaining about bands of "black outlaws" who were looting and attacking Spanish cities across the Panama isthmus. The official wrote:

> The matter which, in this kingdom, most urgently demands remedial action is the problem of dispersing the *cimarrones*, black outlaws in rebellion in its mountainous unpopulated interior. They are numerous and (such is their daring and audacity) they come forth upon the roads leading from this city to that of Nombre de Dios, kill travellers. . . . They threaten to burn these two towns and . . . frequently carried off

negresses at work. . . . Similarly, they carry off negroes sent out for firewood. . . . Wherefore no master dare punish his slave or even bid him do more than the slave may wish to do.[5]

Most striking about this complaint is that the official claims the Cimarrones were a threat physically, socially, and economically. They descended on Panama City and Nombre de Dios, settlements on opposite sides of the isthmus, with brazenness, and they were apparently brutal in their attacks. Perhaps most troublesome was that the Cimarrones stole away those enslaved—which strengthened their own numbers—and forced Spanish slave owners to modify their behavior, as "no master dare punish his slave" for fear that enslaved person would run off to join the Cimarrones. This official's complaints make vivid the active presence of Cimarrones on the Panama isthmus in the sixteenth century.

Given the antagonistic relationship between those black rebels and Spain, the English privateer Sir Francis Drake found ready allies when he arrived on the isthmus in 1572, intending to rob Spanish mule trains—caravans loaded with gold and silver. To execute that plan, he collaborated with a band of Cimarrones, led by a man named Pedro. Drake and Pedro stalked the isthmus for more than five months before seizing a silver-laden mule train en route to Nombre de Dios. Drake captured enough loot to fill the cargo holds of two frigates. In the narrative of this raid, *Sir Francis Drake Revived*, Drake articulates his collaboration with Cimarrones using anti-Spanish, liberation rhetoric. He represents them as refugees who "fled from the Spaniards their masters, by reason of their cruelty."[6] In Drake's heroic tale, the Cimarrones play the role of victims he must rescue from a tyrannical Spain. He evokes here the common imperial fantasy of English travelers to the Americas that the inhabitants of those regions, both Native Americans and black Africans enslaved to the Spanish, would welcome the English with open arms and support English efforts to usurp control of the Caribbean from Spain.

There is one particularly striking moment in the narrative, a moment that invites us to think more critically about the role black Africans played in English writers' efforts to create anti-Spanish propaganda. Drake, a handful of his sailors, and several Cimarrón guides, including Pedro, travel through the Panama jungle en route to intercept a mule train. One of the Cimarrones kills and dresses an otter for the men to eat. Drake hesitates before eating the meat. Upon seeing Drake's reaction, Pedro quips, "Are you a man of war, and in want, and yet doubt whether this be meat, that hath blood?"[7] In response, Drake chastises "himself secretly, that he had so slightly considered of it before."⁸ Ostensibly, this brief exchange is insignificant, only a couple of lines in which Drake illustrates the exotic dietary practices of the Cimarrones. He does not dwell on Pedro's censure, quickly moving on to descriptions of Cimarrón villages and customs.

Conventional historical and literary paradigms understand this kind of mediated moment, in which we get information about Pedro through the filter of Drake, as at most an act of ventriloquism, what Joyce Chaplin deems an "inaccurate and manipulative way" of representing Native American and black African presences.⁹ Similar to Chaplin, Stephen Greenblatt might say of the moment that it is "the recording of alien voices" that tells us more about the European writer than about his African (American) counterpart.¹⁰ Greenblatt defines alien voices as "the voices of those who have no power to leave literate traces of their existence."¹¹ In his influential essay "Invisible Bullets," Greenblatt excavates a "poetics of power" in Elizabethan England by examining English mathematician and scientist Thomas Harriot's *A Briefe and True Report of the New Found Land of Virginia*, Harriot's sixteenth-century account of his encounters with Algonquian communities in present-day North Carolina. According to Greenblatt, Harriot's narrative can tell us very little about the Native Americans with whom he interacted. He argues, "The recording of alien voices, their preservation in Harriot's text, is part of the process whereby Indian culture is constituted as a culture and thus brought into the light for study and discipline, correction, transformation. The momentary sense of instability or plenitude—the existence of other voices—is produced by the monological power that ultimately denies the possibility of plenitude."¹² In regard to the Algonquian people, Greenblatt separates the textual representations from their physical, historical referents. While acknowledging Harriot's interactions with actual Native Americans, Greenblatt deems those populations inaccessible through Harriot's narrative, their historical presences obscured by Harriot's mediating lens. In other words, we do not see the Algonquian people as they actually were; we see them as Harriot tells us they were.

A number of studies echo Greenblatt's idea about the power of mediation to shroud the other beneath a veil of discourse.¹³ Those studies, many of them published in the 1990s and concerned with European–Native American interactions, adhere to understandings of colonial encounters as discursive phenomena that are born out of an often tense relationship between rhetoric and material reality.¹⁴ While acknowledging the historical elements of colonial encounters, scholars engaged in colonial discourse analysis examine the degree to which language constitutes or obscures colonial realities, constructing cultural systems and circumscribing people's experiences within those systems. They focus on what the texts mean and in some cases how they struggle to mean it; that is to say, they emphasize the narrative disruptions that often characterize the writer's efforts to align rhetoric with reality. These narrative disruptions, or what Neil Whitehead calls texture, matter because such moments can point to "the relations between text and testimony," offering clues about the source material from which a writer crafts his or her narrative.[15] Reading with an emphasis on moments of rupture, as Kelly Wisecup notes, can lead us to "deeper literary histories" that "take account of how colonial literatures were actively shaped by Natives' and Africans' perspectives and actions."[16]

Like previous studies, *Black Africans in the British Imagination* meditates on the complex relationship between discourse and reality and the narrative dissonance that manifests itself as a consequence. My primary focus, though, is not on the power of language to make meaning out of colonial encounters. I emphasize instead the ways in which colonial encounters reveal language's limitations. More specifically, my interest in colonial texts centers on mediated moments and what those moments can tell us about how the texts function (or malfunction) discursively and about how the actual, physical interactions between Europeans and black Africans in particular helped to shape texts.[17] *Black Africans in the British Imagination* posits a method for reading black African representations beyond the mediation, an approach that nuances our understandings of black Africans as human agents in an early Atlantic world, broadens the conceptual parameters of African American literature, and challenges traditional notions of authorship as a solo enterprise.

Returning to Drake and Pedro's exchange, if we understand their encounter as a discursive phenomenon, which has a propensity to produce more Eurocentric conclusions, Drake assumes sole agency in the construction of Pedro's representation. Pedro becomes an object, a product of Drake's literary imagination. In the process, though, of constructing meaning, Drake, through his representation of Pedro, also reveals certain limitations in his ability to interpret the encounter. When Pedro challenges Drake about the otter meat, asking him, "Are you a man of war, and in want, and yet doubt whether this be meat, that hath blood," the moment is defined by contradictions, questions and other narrative disruptions that reveal themselves when we consider the moment from Pedro's perspective. Even as a mediated figure nestled at the margins of Drake's narrative, Pedro's disruptive effect comes through in two aspects. First, he challenges Drake's previous image of himself as a liberating demi-god among the Cimarrones. Elsewhere in the narrative Drake explains that the Cimarrones celebrate Drake's arrival and defer to him. In this moment, though, Drake seems to defer to Pedro with his silence, quietly chastising his own ignorance. Second, not only does Pedro's censure unsettle the representation of the Cimarrones as inferior to Drake, but it also unsettles Drake's very identity by casting doubt on his capabilities as a "man of war." Pedro's quip that Drake is a man "in want" could be a reference to the inadequacies of the Englishmen, who up until this point have relied on the Cimarrones for navigation, food, shelter, and war strategy. So, who, readers might ask, liberates whom? As the letter from the Spanish official above suggests, the Cimarrones were not simply victims of Spanish tyranny. They had been successfully fighting the Spanish for decades before Drake arrived. This moment in Drake's narrative is not a tidy, eloquent rhetorical move. It appears rather messy, ambiguous in its representation of both Drake and his Cimarrón counterpart.

A close-reading of Pedro's representation suggests the extent to which Drake's literary imagination was indebted to and challenged by interactions with his Cimarrón allies, whose mediated presences in the text both confirm and disrupt his deployment of Black Legend rhetoric. Put another way, the narrative disruptions matter for two reasons. First, they call into question Drake's authorial control. If Pedro's representation is the product of interactions that occurred outside the text, which the narrative disruptions suggest, then his mediation is the result of collaboration, not the sole product of Drake's rhetorical prerogative. Second, the disruptions illustrate that Pedro's very presence in the text (and by extension that of the Cimarrones) interferes with Drake's efforts to malign Spain's American activities. This prompts larger questions about how black Africans affected English uses of Black Legend rhetoric (and Hispaniphobia more generally) in the early Atlantic world.

What is at the heart of Pedro's criticism of Drake, and how might he be taking advantage of a Cimarrón-English alliance? Perhaps he condescends to the English privateer, teaching him about food sources in the Panamanian forest. Perhaps he processes Drake's reaction to the otter meat as a complaint, a display of ingratitude after all the Cimarrones have done to help Drake and his men survive. Drake explains that the Cimarrones "did us continually very good service . . . being unto us . . . guides in our way, to direct us; of purveyors, to provide victuals for us; of house-wrights, to build our lodgings. . . . Yea, many times when some of our company fainted with sickness or weariness, two symerons [sic] would carry him with ease between them."[18] Perhaps the most pressing question of all is why Pedro aligns with Drake, who seems as much a liability as an asset. We cannot know the answers. The details of Pedro's life have been long lost to us. The void, though, made apparent by these questions reminds us that Pedro existed beyond the text, and that existence, I will argue more specifically in chapter 2, was crucial in the materialization of his representation inside the text. *Black Africans in the British Imagination* identifies a number of moments where black African mediations disrupt the narratives in which they appear. Such moments are crucial because they suggest that black Africans as actual, physical presences played a much more active and contentious role in the shaping of English imperial agendas and in early English Atlantic literature. As we begin to see in Drake's narrative, representations of black Africans were the product of complex textual negotiations and accommodations that we can trace through English efforts (and the struggles inherent in those efforts) to manipulate black Africans rhetorically in service to anti-Spanish propaganda.

Although there is disagreement about how, why, where, and when Spain's image as the Black Legend began, most scholars agree that Spain's own Las Casas and his advocacy for Native Americans was central in solidifying the image. In his 1542 *Brevísima Relación de la Destrucción de las Indias* Las Casas describes a Native American genocide. "At a conservative estimate," he claims, "the despotic and diabolical behaviour of the Christians has, over the last forty years, led to the unjust and totally unwarranted deaths of more than twelve million souls, women and children among them, and there are grounds for believing my own estimate of more than fifteen million to be nearer the mark."[19] He outlines the methods of this genocide: "There are two main ways in which those who have traveled to this part of the world pretending to be Christians have uprooted these pitiful peoples and wiped them from the face of the earth. First, they have waged war on them: unjust, cruel, bloody, and tyrannical war. Second, they have murdered anyone and everyone who has shown the slightest sign of resistance, or even of wishing to escape the torment to which they have subjected him."[20] He describes gruesome acts of burnings, hangings, dismemberment, dog attacks, and so forth. He characterizes the Indians as noble savages, living in peace and harmony before the intervention of Spanish conquest. In a direct address to the then-prince Philip, Las Casas describes Native Americans as "naturally so gentle, so peace-loving, so humble and so docile."[21]

Las Casas catalogs the violence not only to showcase Spanish brutality and savagery but also to illustrate the severity of the problem. He seeks reform. He tells Prince Philip in the prologue, "It would constitute a criminal neglect of my duty to remain silent about the enormous loss of life as well as the infinite number of human souls dispatched to Hell in the course of such 'conquest,' and so resolved to publish an account of a few such outrages . . . in order to make that account the more accessible to Your Highness."[22] Although Las Casas imagined his work addressing a national crisis, the text soon took center stage in a continental debate about empire and conquest. The Dutch were the first to translate and propagate Las Casas's narrative, in 1578. They highlighted the text's descriptions of brutality to argue for their own suffering as a Spanish colony. In 1583 the French and the English published translations.

For England specifically, as E. Shaskan Bumas points out, the rhetoric "tended to partake largely of religious discourse, implying in and of itself the lack of religion on the part of the Spaniards, who were, after all, mere Catholics."[23] England linked Catholicism with reports of Spanish savagery in the New World, transforming its own fledgling imperial project into a spiritual imperative to rescue America's natives. The earliest translation of Las Casas's narrative into English bears out England's propagandistic intent. The title page alone implicates Spain. Whereas Las Casas's title page focalizes victimization, the Indies, and the region's destruction, the English translation emphasizes the perpetrator, "Spanish Colonie or Brief Chronicle of the Actes and Gestes of the Spaniardes." In the preface to the translation, the writer, James Aliggrodo, emphasizes Spain's "barbarousnesse," claiming that "so great and excessive have their trecherie been, that the posteritie shall hardly thinke that ever so barbarous or cruell a nation have bin in the worlde."[24] Casting religious judgment on the Spanish, calling them "wicked," the writer urges his fellow Englishmen to "think upon God's judgements: and refraine from their wickedness and vice."[25] Samuel Purchas included Las Casas's text in his seventeenth-century collection of travel narratives. Over the next centuries, the account was central in England's war of words with Spain. Las Casas's narrative joined a bevy of pamphlets, epistles, political tracts, and travel narratives published in London.

Reconsidering the Race Debate

English writers' efforts to manipulate anti-Spanish rhetoric were complicated by the growing presence of black Africans in the Americas, who were key in English deployment of anti-Spanish rhetoric and in English discourses about human difference. There is an ongoing debate in early modern studies regarding the origins of our modern concept of race as the delineation of power based on biological fictions of human difference. At issue is what Europeans meant when they employed the term *race* in the sixteenth and seventeenth centuries. At what point did race come to mean what it means today? The nature of blackness and its immutable qualities have baffled the Western world for centuries. Especially in English Renaissance literature, the question of whether an Ethiopian could be washed white was a prevailing motif, the answer to which was always *no*.[26] The motif signified the futile or irrational. It also mediated discussions of beauty and cultural difference. If the Ethiopian's blackness was immutable, was the same true of fair skin? Scholars today disagree about the extent to which these kinds of contemplations of somatic (and cultural) differences reflect our modern thinking about racial difference. Do such discussions point to the existence of racism, culturally pervasive beliefs that result in the oppression and degradation of people who share particular corporeal features? Or were discussions of race in the early modern era less systematic and therefore less resonant aspects of larger social structures that determined people's quality of life? In short, how powerful was *race* as an organizing ideological principle in the early modern world?

Some historians and literary scholars emphasize the continuity between early modern and modern concepts of race. Although most do not apply terms like *racism* and *racist* to the early modern period, they recognize that even then race was a powerful, coherent idea that denoted human differences as inherent and inheritable. Joyce Chaplin, for example, argues that as early as the sixteenth century the English elevated themselves above others based on differences in lineage and the body. "Long before the eighteenth century," she maintains, "English colonists articulated assessments of bodies as superior and inferior, particularly in response to disease. . . . The body was the site for the construction of identity."[27] Because Indians died in such large numbers due to diseases brought over by the English, colonists deemed them weaker and therefore inferior. According to Chaplin, they maintained a belief that "certain corporeal traits were specific to certain lineages. Racial identity was a logical if unintended outgrowth of English views of corporeal differences among the peoples (including Indians and Africans) in early America."[28]

In many respects, Chaplin's approach harkens back to and makes current Winthrop Jordan's 1968 thesis from *White over Black*. He argues that black Africans were marked for enslavement in America because of preconceived racial notions that Englishmen carried with them across the Atlantic. "From the first," Jordan argues, "Englishmen tended to set Negroes over against themselves, to stress what they conceived to be radically contrasting qualities of color, religion, and style of life, as well as animality and peculiarly potent sexuality."[29] Black Africans' skin color was especially important. According to Jordan, "In England perhaps more than in southern Europe, the concept of blackness was loaded with intense meaning. . . . Black was an emotionally partisan color, the handmaid and symbol of baseness and evil, a sign of danger and repulsion."[30] Black Africans, then, became the embodiment of evil. Focusing on race in Spanish American colonies, Barbara Fuchs argues that systems of racial classification did assume certain "essentializing" qualities early on, a result of the culture's emphasis on blood purity. She asserts that "what began in Spain as religious and cultural intolerance gradually became, over the course of the sixteenth century, an essentializing obsession with genealogy and blood. . . . This ideology, honed and exacerbated over the same decades in which the Spanish were carrying out their conquest of the New World, translated into a system of white/Spanish privilege in the colonies."[31]

On the other side of this debate are those who emphasize the radical changes that racial ideologies undergo over time. For these scholars, race gained its modern-day power during the Enlightenment era when Europeans sought more systematic engagements with the world through the observation, accumulation, and organization of knowledge to arrive at essential truths. Roxann Wheeler argues that before the Enlightenment, racial terminology was fluid, unstable and when used in reference to humans, denoted cultural differences, especially dress and religion—differences that were not inextricably bound to the body. She maintains that our modern concept of race—one emphasizing skin color and other biological, innate traits—emerges with the Enlightenment when "the ideology of human variety broadly changed from being articulated primarily through religious difference, which included such things as political governance and civil life, to being articulated primarily through scientific categories derived from natural history that featured external characteristics of the human body—color, facial features, and hair texture."[32]

Likewise, Ruth Hill argues that race was a less rigid and less pervasive guiding principle in early modern Spanish culture. She points out that the term *casta*—based on a combination of factors including the somatic, language, and geography—more closely conveys the system of differentiation that organized social hierarchies in traditional Spanish cultures.[33] Hill points out that the culture's obsession with blood purity, or *limpieza de sangre*, which might suggest an emphasis on biological, hereditary features, was the product of figurative, not literal contemplations. Skin color functioned more as a metaphor for cultural or ethnic difference. Both Wheeler and Hill's approaches are an effort to, in Wheeler's words, "encourage a more precise periodization of when race and colonialism, as well as race and slavery, became intimately codependent and when other factors, such as political and economic issues, predominated."[34] From their perspective, to ignore the nuances and instabilities in terminology before the eighteenth century is to engage in anachronistic scholarship that fosters misunderstanding about the time period's rhetoric and politics.[35]

I align myself with those who emphasize continuity between early modern constructions of race, as unstable as those constructions might have been, and modern constructions. The pliant nature of discourses centered on human difference in earlier eras does not illustrate that race did not operate in Europe and the Americas before the Enlightenment.[36] Race, to use Jonathan Burton and Ania Loomba's words, has always been "an amalgam of contradictory, unstable, evolving ideas" that can be better understood "within a history of discriminatory *practices*."[37] All of this is to say that race was and continues to be experiential, not only discursive or theoretical. From the perspective of those black Africans enslaved and in other ways exploited in Renaissance Europe or modern America and all points in between, the *effect* of race, however we choose to understand it as a discourse or theory, was and remains an oppressive aspect of life.[38]

Furthermore, *Black Africans in the British Imagination* extends the contours of the early modern race debate by posing a different set of questions. Rather than asking what Europeans meant when they used "race" in the early modern period, I ask questions about how black Africans, as active presences in the early Americas, interfered with Europeans' efforts to represent race and how this interference manifests itself in the texts. For whatever reasons—granted those reasons and their articulations do change over time—black Africans were marked for uniquely degrading treatment, making them especially vulnerable to forms of discrimination—the most egregious example of which manifested itself in the transatlantic slave trade.

Re-Presenting the Ethiop in America

As the transatlantic slave trade grew, it was not long before English writers in the Americas began representing black Africans, both enslaved and free, in service to anti-Spanish rhetoric. The kind of Spanish cruelty that Las Casas and then English writers initially noted were perpetrated against Native Americans, they then found reflected in Spanish treatment of black Africans. Textually, black Africans functioned alongside or replaced Native Americans as victims of Spanish cruelty. Miles Phillips, for example, during his nearly decade-long captivity on the Spanish Main in 1567, writes that both groups "hate and abhorre the Spaniardes with all their hearts" and "daily lie in waite to practise their deliverance out of that thraldome and bondage, that the Spaniardes doe keepe them in."[39] In the case of Drake's Panama narrative, black Africans become the native population, the victims seeking refuge with the English.

The English, when imagining their imperial project as a more humane, more Christian alternative, naturally assumed that the victims of Spanish cruelty would not only welcome them but also supply resources—in the form of knowledge, weapons, shelter, and so forth—that would aid English efforts to usurp control of the Caribbean, in particular, from Spain. In his *Discourse Concerning Westerne Planting*, Richard Hakluyt wrote of those black Africans that had allied with Drake in Panama that they would, along with "a fewe hundrethes of [the English], trained upp in the late warres of Fraunce and Flaunders, bringe great things to passe, and that with greate ease."[40] These English assumptions played out in representations of black Africans that rendered them, more so than Native Americans, as pugnacious and hostile toward all things Spanish. The English imagined they could harness that aggression and anti-Spanish sentiment toward their own ends, transforming black Africans into cooperative servants of England.

Even as English travelers to the Americas sought to represent black Africans (and Native Americans, I argue in chapter 5) within familiar anti-Spanish—and racial—discourses, outside the texts English-African interactions contradicted English assumptions. There was a significant divide between the rhetoric of English-African cooperation and the reality of such relationships. As Michael Guasco points out in his study of sixteenth-century Anglo-Afro encounters in Spanish America, such alliances were on the one hand "desirable because, in an Atlantic world largely governed by the Iberian powers, Africans could prove to be the difference makers between the success or failure of England's transatlantic enterprises," but on the other hand those imagined alliances "bore only limited resemblance to how most English mariners encountered, interacted with and exploited Africans in the sixteenth-century Atlantic world."[41] For Guasco, this rhetorical conflict centered on England's ambivalence about the moral or ethical contours of slavery, not wholly in favor of its implementation but not wholly committed to rescuing black Africans from lives of perpetual servitude. In fact, Guasco argues, the English viewed black Africans "through the same prism [as commodities]" as the Spanish.[42] Both nations "were equally interested in exploiting the peoples and resources of the Atlantic world to their own advantage."⁴³ I would point out, though, that black Africans were motivated by the same kind of self-interest and often agreed to alliances based on mutual benefit, not coercion. This meant that the English could not take for granted or see as inevitable black African cooperation in their American exploits. While Guasco notes the inconsistency between reality and rhetoric, I examine the effect of that inconsistency on the narratives English travelers wrote about their encounters with black Africans.

My approach advocates a way of reading early Atlantic texts that gives primacy to mediated figures, which opens up those texts to new interpretative possibilities while also expanding ongoing discussions about the cultural and historical significance of black Africans in the early Americas. The project is inspired by those in postcolonial theory, cultural anthropology, African American history, and whiteness studies. It began as a meditation on Gayatri Spivak's decades-old question regarding mediated, colonized figures in Western culture: "Can the subaltern speak?"⁴⁴ And here speech is metonymic, referring to any physical act that conveys a message externally. For Spivak, the answer to this question centers on the notion of comprehension and the subaltern's access, or lack thereof, to Western discourses. Can mediated figures act in such a way that their actions are understood as they intend those actions to be understood? Can a mediator ever accurately convey a subaltern's speech? In this sense, the subaltern is made legible—or illegible—by a mediator. What is more, according to Spivak, once a subaltern figure finds a voice—gains access to dominant discourses—he ceases to be a subaltern. For me, however, it is not an issue of comprehension or accuracy. We will never know what a figure like Pedro intended in his interactions with Drake. We cannot know how his narrative would read if he were writing or speaking himself. And yet, we should not consider him as merely a silent, irrecoverable figure. To do so is to ignore the very fact that he acts, whether or not his actions are comprehended fully by those listening or watching—or in the case of my project here, writing and reading. Even if the mediator misunderstands the act, the act is itself a form of empowerment. Miscommunication, like communication, is bilateral.⁴⁵ What does this (mis)communication mean, then, for the text in which it appears?

To help answer this question, I rely on the work of Myra Jehlen, whose approach to colonial discourse analysis emphasizes the importance of material realities in shaping colonial discourses. A number of discursive studies identify a certain 'disruptive' quality in colonial texts.⁴⁶ Jehlen's approach expands the analysis by not only contemplating the disruptions but arguing that the disruptions offer vital clues about the interactions among human actors in the Americas. Although we might not be able to answer questions about what "really" happened in those encounters, Jehlen argues that moments of narrative disruption matter because they reflect the writer's response to the "force of the other he is describing" and allow "us to hear the other's resisting voice."[47] *Black Africans in the British Imagination* takes up Jehlen's challenge to read colonial contact literature "in a way that uncovers the agency of the colonized even though the texts one is reading are virtually always and only the colonizers' narratives."[48] With this approach, I aim to broaden the temporal and geographical frameworks of what we traditionally define as early African American literature.

The Black Atlantic and African American Literature

In 1993 Paul Gilroy insisted that we approach black cultural production from more transnational perspectives, understanding African American literature, for example, as a hybrid form arising out of the circulation of black African bodies and ideas through the Atlantic's watery routes.[49] Since then, a number of literary studies have situated the origins of African American literature in a wider eighteenth-century black Atlantic world.[50] *Black Africans in the British Imagination* builds on this broader conceptual framework by demonstrating the ways in which black diasporic populations—from the very beginning of English expansion into the Americas—shaped the literature being written all around them in locations such as Panama, Guiana, Guinea, even the Arctic northwest. Currently, there are two default approaches to the study of black African mediations in early American and African American literature. Either we do not consider the mediations at all or we read them as stagnant metaphors. The first approach is the result of assumptions that those of African descent were not relevant in literature produced about the Americas until 1760 with publication of the first autobiographical/slave narratives and poems from figures such as Phillis Wheatley, Briton Hammon, and Olaudah Equiano.[51] The representations of black Africans prior to 1760 are largely discounted because they, like Pedro in Drake's narrative, appear as minor figures in the narratives of European explorers, missionaries, merchants, and so forth—despite the fact that mediation is a defining feature of early African American literature. *Black Africans in the British Imagination* draws our attention to forms of mediation that predate Hammon, Wheatley, and Equiano. In the pages that follow, I examine the literary works of sixteenth- and seventeenth-century Englishmen such as Drake, Sir Walter Ralegh, and Richard Ligon, and I offer a re-orientation to those works. Rather than examine the narratives for what they divulge about the writers' experiences and literary imaginations, as so many scholars do, I make prominent the mediated presences of those black Africans who reside at the narratives' margins. From the periphery, they disrupt the narratives, offering important clues about the writer's encounters with black Africans outside the texts and the extent to which those encounters helped to shape the texts.

The second default approach shaping early American and African American literary studies also is embedded in assumptions; when we do consider the mediated presences of black Africans in early American texts, we assume that the mediated figures are symbolic presences that European(-American) writers created and manipulated to achieve particular discursive goals. Cultural studies of race in early America reflect this second approach. Toni Morrison, in the 1990s, was among the first literary scholars to draw attention to the ways in which African Americans performed symbolic needs for Euro-American writers.[52] Morrison challenges literary scholars to think more seriously about what she terms the Africanist presence.[53] She urges scholars to examine American literature for its deployment of blackness as a metaphor to define whiteness. Other literary studies have followed and have extended Morrison's argument by also examining the ways in which black writers, such as Frederick Douglass, reacted to and in other ways engaged racial ideologies.[54]

While such scholarship has been vital in recognizing the import of race in the early formations of American (and African American) literature, the scholarship tends to emphasize black Africans as racial metaphors in the minds of Euro-Americans to which African American writers later respond in their own literature. I want to expand the story of black African participation in early American literature by looking beyond the reactionary intent that we typically ascribe to African American writers. Those earliest black Africans whose lives were recorded in contact narratives function as formative, not reactive, forces. Rather than stagnant metaphors, their mediations were the product of complex textual negotiations and accommodation that anticipated the kinds of collaborative processes that produced those as-told-to accounts of enslaved black Africans beginning in the eighteenth century. Although Drake's representation of Pedro does not illustrate a black literary consciousness, it does offer insight into how black Africans negotiated their lives in the early period and the ways in which their efforts to negotiate helped shape the literary record of the early Atlantic world. As such, they are crucial to studies of early African American, American, and, more broadly conceived, Atlantic literature.

The historical presence of black Africans produced for the writers discussed in this book a series of narrative crises, or ethical dilemmas, usually at the level of characterization or plot.[55] While this book is not a project about early modern readership, it does consider text as performing a social function that implicates implied readers in the author's narrative choices. It is, to evoke Wayne Booth's understanding of ethical criticism in narrative, an examination of "the encounters between a story-teller's ethos with that of the reader or listener."[56] Ethical dilemmas arise, then, when English writers endeavor to cohere the material details of their expeditions with the expectations of those implied readers back home. In chapter 1, I discuss how these readers' expectations were created, in part, by early English voyages to West Africa. English merchant William Towerson led three voyages to Guinea, on the coast of West Africa, between 1555 and 1558. The Portuguese, who had claimed a monopoly on Guinea trade since the mid-fifteenth century, deemed English activity in the region as piracy. They readily attacked English ships spotted in Guinea waters, and they attempted to inflict harsh penalties on those coastal Guinea towns that engaged the English in trade. In his narratives about those voyages, Towerson constructs himself as a liberator who travels through the region protecting Guinea inhabitants from the *tyrannous* Portuguese. This representation lends political credence to the English presence in Guinea and conveys a moral imperative through which Towerson can identify himself (and his commercial enterprises) in England's quickly expanding overseas trade networks. The problem, though, with his commercial and rhetorical goals is that his interactions with black Africans in Guinea contradict the rhetoric, manifesting itself in the narrative as episodic interruptions that suggest his Guinea counterparts were politically powerful and savvy traders from whom the English, ironically, on occasion needed protection. His experiences become so confrontational and unstable that after his third voyage he abandons efforts to establish trading posts in Guinea. Towerson's narratives are seldom discussed within the context of early American and Atlantic studies because the cultural encounters occur in Guinea and do not involve directly English participation in the Atlantic slave trade. I bring these texts into my study of the early Atlantic world to illustrate how black Africans were represented early on as mediating presences to define a fledgling English imperial project. Not incidentally, Towerson represents the Portuguese in the same vein that later English writers would represent Spain. And black Africans are constructed as both victims and allies. The liberation, anti-Spanish rhetoric on which Drake relies to justify his piracy, perhaps owes its genesis not only to Las Casas's accounts of Spanish atrocities but also to Towerson's accounts of Portuguese oppression in Guinea. Towerson's text is also important because it anticipates the ways in which black Africans will later disrupt English efforts to represent black Africans as victims of Spanish cruelty in the Americas.

I end this first chapter with a brief discussion of John Hawkins's *A True Declaration of the Troublesome Voyage,* Hawkins's account of his third slaving expedition that traveled from England to Guinea to the Caribbean in 1568. In *A True Declaration,* he describes his efforts to liberate an African town from its oppressive neighbors to the north in exchange for slaves. The alliance falls apart when his African allies fail to deliver the promised slaves. His story of liberation mutates into a story of deception and failure. The deception and failure become more pronounced when Hawkins continues his voyage to the Caribbean, where the Spanish, under the guise of a truce, attack his fleet at the port of San Juan de Ulúa. In describing the misfortunes of this voyage, Hawkins articulates in similar language the perfidy of both Guineans and Spaniards, a juxtaposition designed to "darken" the character of his Spanish rivals. He manipulates black Africans as a textual tool to condemn Spanish activity and character in the Americas, providing a model for his distant cousin Sir Francis Drake. A close-reading of Hawkins's representations of black Africans illuminates how and why Drake designs, executes, and articulates his exploits in Panama in 1572–73.

In chapter 2, I examine the problems inherent in Drake's efforts to replicate Hawkins's rhetoric. Those problems center on an active black African presence whose actions interfere with Drake's literary imagination. Like Hawkins, Drake describes collaboration with black Africans, this time a band of Cimarrones (or fugitive slaves), to steal gold and silver from the Spanish who controlled Panama in the sixteenth century. Also like Hawkins and Towerson, Drake presents himself as a liberator, helping those Cimarrones find freedom—never mind that the Cimarrones had already liberated themselves before Drake's arrival. In Drake's hands, the liberatory discourse and rhetoric of alliance that were initiated in Towerson and Hawkins's narratives take on new political significance as he constructs his narrative to condemn Spanish empire and sanctify English imperial activity. To that end, he portrays the Cimarrones as oppressed natives suffering under the cruel hand of Spanish tyranny. Despite his references to the Cimarrones as victims, they appear just as often in the narrative as aggressors, who have resisted successfully Spanish rule for decades. In fact, the efficacy of their resistance prompted Drake's desire for alliance. The Cimarrones, then, are not simply passive victims of

Spanish cruelty. They are also combatants, waging guerilla warfare against the Spanish. In essence, the Cimarrones disrupt Drake's anti-Spanish rhetoric by denying him a victim, an object of Spanish cruelty. Several historical studies have examined the relationship between Drake and his Cimarrón allies. Those studies, however, relegate the Cimarrones to the status of servants who work *for* Drake. This chapter offers a textual analysis of the alliance that challenges the historical assumptions of a hierarchical relationship between Drake and the Cimarrones. A close-reading of Drake's narrative illustrates that the allied forces work together. In fact, the alliance guides certain generic features, compromising Drake's narrative design. The rhetorical disruptions in Drake's narrative anticipate the ways in which black Africans will disrupt English political strategies in the next century.

Despite the disruptions that emerge from an against-the-grain reading of Drake's text, his understanding of black Africans as victims of a Spanish Black Legend and therefore useful allies stimulated English imperial desires, leading England to construct political policies that would factor prominently black African cooperation in their efforts to conquer Spanish America in the seventeenth century. In chapters 3 and 4, I examine the narrative problems and political failures that result, in part, from English fantasies about black African cooperation. Almost a century after Hawkins's initial alliance with black Africans and in the shadow of Drake's exploits in Panama, Englishman Thomas Gage, who was a Catholic priest-turned-spy, traveled through New Spain (in portions of present-day Mexico and Guatemala). In 1648 he published a lengthy narrative of his experiences interacting with native communities, enslaved black Africans and maroons, and Spanish creoles. The text is essentially a scouting report, informing the English about the feasibility and necessity of invading and occupying New Spain. Occupation is all the more feasible, according to Gage, because of black African enmity toward Spain. In chapter Three, I argue that a trope of black African alliance that began with Towerson and Hawkins and transformed with Drake re-appears in Gage's text, guiding but also complicating his representation of black Africans. Gage indulges what by 1648 had become more fantasy than reality that black Africans in New Spain would be ready-made weapons for England in its confrontation with Spain in the West Indies. The fantasy is often undercut by his descriptions of how black Africans deceive or attack him, without regard for his national identity or the hostility between the two European powers. Gage's descriptions of his interactions with black Africans contradict the narrative's larger rhetoric of alliance and Spanish cruelty. Gage's narrative is central to this study as it does more than illustrate black Africans' disruptive presence in English anti-Spanish rhetoric. His narrative also speaks to the political consequences of the rhetorical disruptions. Gage's narrative was published on the eve of Oliver Cromwell's 1655 Western Design, England's master plan to invade the Spanish Caribbean. Gage's (and by extension Drake's) insistence that black Africans would be resources in that invasion, guided Cromwell's plans. The campaign failed miserably. Not incidentally, those accounts published in the wake of the botched campaign expressed their surprise (and terror) that black African slaves took up arms alongside the Spanish to repel English forces. Black Africans behaved in the opposite manner from what Gage had predicted just seven years before. In Gage's text, then, narrative disruptions correlate with and anticipate the disruptive effect of black Africans on the ground in the Caribbean in 1655.

While chapter 3 examines the ways in which literary rhetoric precedes (and fuels) political strategy and expectations, chapter 4 examines the reverse dynamic, addressing the ways in which Richard Ligon's 1657 *True and Exact History of Barbadoes* represents black African women to cohere with larger political designs. Although the Western Design had failed a couple of years prior to publication of Ligon's narrative, his text nonetheless is an effort to promote English settlement in the Caribbean. To that end, Ligon constructs Barbados (and the Caribbean at large) as a commercial space brimming with possibilities for consumers. As proof of the region's bounty, he offers two anecdotes of his encounters with beautiful black African women on the Cape Verde island of Santiago—en route to Barbados. Through representations of these women, Ligon illustrates the kinds of novelties English investors can enjoy in the Caribbean. They are potential products. So long as Ligon encounters the women at the level of observation, they function without problem in a rhetorical schema that privileges a white, male, imperial gaze. For Ligon, the Caribbean and its myriad resources are readily available for English consumption. What is more, that consumption comes with imperial stakes as Ligon's narrative joins a host of other pamphlets designed to lure would-be English settlers to Barbados—and Jamaica, the only territory the English was able to wrestle from Spain in 1655.

At one point in his narrative, Ligon decides it is not enough to observe these beautiful black women in Santiago. He wants interaction. He initiates a kind of romantic dialogue with them, transforming into a suitor. Once he interacts with the women, the racial myths that had defined the women give way to other modes of representation. In general, Ligon describes enslaved black African women as monstrous bodies hunched over in sugar fields with babies strapped to their backs that they nurse even while they work. Their productive and reproductive potential becomes part of the consumptive rhetoric with which Ligon sells Barbados to his readers. The women Ligon encounters in Santiago, though, are not fertile bodies valuable for both their labor and reproductive capabilities; in fact, only one of the women is actually enslaved—to the island's Portuguese governor—and her labor does not produce tangible, material goods. Rather than producers, these women are, themselves, consumers. Through various exchanges of flirtation and courtship, they procure expensive and exotic goods from Ligon. The women Ligon encounters in Santiago disrupt the narrative's larger discussion of Barbados as a potentially rich base from which the English can usurp control of the Caribbean from Spain. Their mediated presences in Ligon's narrative subvert a consumptive paradigm that renders black African women elsewhere in the text as objects. Importantly, their representations suggest a more complex relationship between black Africans and systems of production/consumption in the early Caribbean as not just producers but also consumers of material goods.

The final chapter examines two texts: George Best's *A True Discourse* (1578) and Sir Walter Ralegh's *Discovery of the Large, Rich and Beautiful Empire of Guiana* (1595). Here, the book's argument shifts slightly to focus on narratives that describe encounters with native populations in the Americas. Both texts are early responses to Spanish imperialism and rely on the same expectations and language of earlier English narratives that describe encounters with black Africans in Guinea. I argue specifically that Best and Ralegh employ racial rhetoric to contemplate and order human difference and lend credibility to their imperial visions in the Arctic and South America. That rhetoric, however, maintains a disruptive quality in both texts because the writers attempt to align ideas about sub-Saharan Africa with their encounters with native peoples. The purpose of this chapter is to extend the book's argument and the stakes by illustrating the ways in which English encounters with black Africans complicated representations of not only black Africans in the Americas but also Native Americans. In the chapter, I emphasize two points: First, even in texts with no specific black African presences, ideas about black Africans and sub-Saharan Africa shape English anti-Spanish propaganda. Second, these texts suggest that European conceptions of native peoples was not the product of a bilateral movement of ideas and encounters between the Americas and Europe, but the product of a wider triangular Atlantic experience that shapes and disrupts the texts, undermining English rhetorical efforts to strategize against an expanding Spanish empire. The book ends with an afterword that addresses the role of mediation and authorship in early African American literary studies.

My methodology depends a great deal on textual analysis—the examination of characterization, plot, discourse and language, and narrative structure. This strategy is central in highlighting the dissonance in the texts but cannot alone explain how and why that dissonance occurs. To address questions of *how* and *why,* I position the texts and the authors within cultural and historical contexts by adopting a more interdisciplinary approach, engaging the work of those in ethnography, material culture, race studies, and history, in particular. The last strategy I employ is speculation, re-creating the narratives from the perspective of the black African figures, a move that emphasizes the dissonance and the silence of those figures at the margin. I am motivated by a similar strategy historian Wendy Anne Warren employs in her work to recover the experience of a black enslaved woman who complained of being raped in Englishman John Josselyn's 1674 journal recounting his travels in the Massachusetts Bay Colony. The episode occupies only a small paragraph in Josselyn's journal, but Warren, through speculative and circumstantial evidence re-creates the likely details of the woman's life.[57] Warren is unable to offer specific, irrefutable conclusions. She argues, though, that tiny moments in historical documents provide rich opportunities for historians to gain a deeper understanding of the histories of African Americans and women in America.[58] Like Warren, I believe in the importance of speculative analysis. Again, I speculate with caution, understanding that it is impossible to truly re-create black African lives that have been rendered inaccessible by the gloss of mediation. I insist on the speculation, cobbled together from details that creep into the narratives, because this method is the best reminder we have of those black Africans who lived beyond the texts and the effect their lives had on the literature. The speculation reminds us that black Africans lived—they breathed, ate, cried, sang, loved and hated. They plotted and manipulated, sought political power, allied with neighbors. Although we will never be able to recover the specific details of their lives, early Atlantic literature fortuitously logs clues about how they negotiated those lives.

Beyond the Mediation

People of African descent were long ago actively attempting to define and redefine themselves in the Americas. Literature written in and about the early Atlantic world inevitably and contentiously chronicles that effort, and I suggest a way of reading the literature that makes visible the importance of those historical presences. This move is similar to conversations already under way in early Native American studies where scholars have worked to recover Native American voices in the early American textual archive.[59] Those studies recognize that "the presence of Indian peoples in the land that is now the United States has been of profound significance to the shaping of American literature—not only to texts that overtly engage this presence, but to the whole body of literature produced in a nation itself produced by encounter."[60] In other words, Native Americans were central to early American literature not just as symbols but also as physical presences whose actions directly affected how and what European writers included in their texts.

Black Africans in the British Imagination, in part, models this methodological turn in early Native American studies. I insist on a reading of black African representations that at once respects the power of mediation but that also pushes the limits of mediation. Indeed, Greenblatt's point is well taken that "alien voices" are "utterly bound up" and "contained politically" by the rhetorical purposes and involvement of the European writer that constructs those mediations.[61] However, approaching mediation as an impenetrable wall "codifies an agnosticism," as Ed White warns, about those nonwriting populations who appear in the literature but do not speak for themselves.[62] The problem of engaging non-European perspectives in early Atlantic texts is not necessarily a lack of evidence but rather of the critical apparatuses we have implemented to prevent us from seeing the evidence. That is to say, if we read colonial contact texts and "lament the meager evidence of an examination" of other cultures, as White argues, "this is partly because prevailing theoretical assumptions render that evidence invisible."[63] Despite White's warnings and current trends in early Native American cultural studies, the idea persists that mediated figures in early colonial texts are valuable mostly for what they divulge about European discursive mechanisms.[64] The idea is especially prevalent in early African American literary studies, where scholars have ignored textual representations of black Africans before the eighteenth century. *Black Africans in the British Imagination* is the first study to comment on the literary significance of these representations in the seventeenth- and eighteenth-century Atlantic world and in doing so calls for a broader approach to the study of African American literature.

The critical apparatus that underpins *Black Africans in the British Imagination,* grounded in the triangulated strategy of textual analysis, perception, and speculation, does not make transparent black African figures in early Atlantic literature. It problematizes the process of mediation, making more pronounced, more visible the disharmonies and discontinuities that manifest themselves in mediated moments. The goal is not simply to highlight traces of black African presences in the literature but to emphasize the ways in which black Africans helped to shape that literature in at least one context—English anti-Spanish propaganda. Such an approach is not without its limitations and obstacles. First, no matter how we engage the texts, we cannot ignore the power of mediation. "The voices of the other," in Greenblatt's words, "do not reach us in pure or uncontaminated form—as if such a condition were ever possible."[65] Consequently, the rhetorical goals and imagination of the European writer are central to analysis. Second, by and large black Africans are absent in the literature written in and about the early Atlantic world. In those instances when European (-American) writers do not disregard their presences, those figures appear in the literature as mostly snippets, one- or two-line references. The figures appear long enough to interrupt the narrative flow and then, inexplicably, disappear. All too often, we overlook such references; on occasion, we note the interruption, then move on. Analysis of such sparse textual material demands a meticulous eye that senses (or perceives) rather than sees. The analytical experience is akin to detecting the trace of bay leaf in a stew long after the cook has removed the leaf from the pot. Even without the physical leaf, circumstantial evidence in the form of taste and smell allows us to sense the leaf's effect on the dish. I note that this kind of sensory reading gets even more complicated when we encounter black African figures who are represented in different ways by different authors in different time periods—as is the case with Pedro. After initially appearing in Drake's narrative, he re-appears in several seventeenth-century texts, including a 1659 opera by William Davenant.[66] He undergoes layers of mediation and narrative transformation, underscoring the impossibility of recovering the actual lives and experiences of mediated figures. For sure, a sensory reading of mediated moments cannot overcome the power of mediation. It does, however, help us to contextualize and become more attuned to the silences and erasures that characterize such moments.[67]

Because of the power of mediation and the limited textual evidence, a third limitation is that I offer no unified narrative that neatly ties the black African representations together in this project. The ways in which the presences interrupt the narratives manifest themselves differently in each chapter. My explanations for how and why the disruptions occur and what they mean change from chapter to chapter. However, they all produce forms of narrative compromise. I evoke both meanings of *compromise,* as a factor that undermines the integrity of a structure or system and as collaboration, a series of concessions between two parties. Consider again Pedro's effect on Drake's narrative. He is a subversive presence that undermines Drake's rhetoric, and his representation is the product of negotiation. Based on circumstantial evidence that appears in the text, Drake's experiences outside the text inform and circumscribe his literary imagination.

These limitations notwithstanding, *Black Africans in the British Imagination* offers three general conclusions: narrative disruptions are a defining feature of black African representations in early Atlantic literature; those representations and their disruptive qualities redefine authorship as collaboration and complicate discussions about the role of mediation in early African American literature; and black Africans mattered as both material and literary presences that complicated English efforts to design, articulate, and justify their imperial projects in Spanish America. *Black Africans in the British Imagination* conceives of early Atlantic literature as multicultural texts shaped by encounter. They register the important material presences of black Africans, whose engagements with the early Atlantic world leave literary and sociopolitical traces.

A Note on Terminology

Throughout the book, I rely on some key terms. The first of these is "race," which I understand in a neutral sense as a form of articulating and categorizing mankind into groups. Race matters because the writers discussed in this book bring to their encounters with black Africans in the Americas a host of assumptions based on prior notions of human difference. Some of those assumptions they confirm through interactions; some they do not. In the early modern era, the justifications for racial categorizations, indeed the categories themselves, fluctuated, depending on a number of factors related to geography, wealth, biblical exegesis, culture, family lineage, and somatic features. The sixteenth century was key in the development of English understandings about human difference.[68] Proto-ethnographic descriptions of black Africans' cultural and physical differences assumed new significance with the growth of the Atlantic slave trade. As Chaplin notes, race as we know it today is the product of the Atlantic world in which practical issues about labor needs and commodities that new world developments created combined with European thinking about disease and the body (specifically the belief that black bodies were hardier) to form structures of human exploitation.[69] Underpinning this racial development were previous associations between skin color and labor that combined with new ideas about human difference to create what Sujata Iyengar terms a "mythology of race" in Renaissance England. Before the sixteenth century there was a common association between people with 'suntanned' or burnt skin and outdoors work. "With the establishment of plantations in Barbados," as Iyengar points out, "this residual connection between skin color and outdoor, manual work . . . becomes an emergent myth linking dark skin and other physical features to an inherited destiny to slave labor on the one hand and to species difference on the other."[70] Chaplin and Iyengar remind us of the stakes involved in English discussions of racial difference beginning in the sixteenth century. When Drake and others narrate their encounters with black Africans in the Americas, then, the observations are not neutral but attached to political, social, and economic goals. I address the ways in which racial considerations inform and complicate their rhetorical choices. At the point where a writer's observations about human difference combine with derogatory rhetoric intended to malign and oppress particular groups, I use the term "racism."

Another related but distinct term is "blackness discourse." Race and racism, as reflected in the texts discussed throughout this book, may or may not privilege skin color and other physical features as defining markers of racial difference. Sir Francis Drake, for example, emphasizes instead behavior, dress, and dietary habits. Sir John Hawkins, in chapter 1, emphasizes culture and morality. I use "blackness discourse" in reference to the kinds of conversations occurring in early modern England, Spain, and the Americas that linked the term "black" and all its negative connotations, with people of African descent. Throughout the pages that follow, I refer often to the work of Kim Hall and Winthrop Jordan, who both note that the color "black" early on carried a religious significance. It denoted evil and sin, and the description of a person as "black" was a commentary on moral character. It was not necessarily a distinct racial marker. By the end of the sixteenth century, however, the word's usage transformed just as the geopolitical boundaries of Europe transformed. 'Black' more often became a literal somatic descriptor for those people who descended—or who looked like they descended—from the sub-Saharan regions of Africa. Inside the figure of the sub-Saharan African, the religious and the somatic combined. There are important nuances to note in how the writers discussed in this book participated in racial discourses. I account for differences in time, politics, gender, and geography in how the writers represent black Africans in their texts.

When deciding on what to call those African-descended people I study in this project, I considered several terms: African American, black, Negro, people of color, African, mediated figures, none of which fully conveys the social, political, geographical, and ideological import of the figures they signify. Ultimately, I chose the term "black African" for several reasons. To explain my use of "African" first: for sure it is a nebulous marker that stands in for what we cannot know about the specific regions on the continent to which the figures in this study are linked. It is an unknowingness that results from what Orlando Patterson calls natal alienation, a strategy employed by slave masters whereby the slave is physically removed from his birthplace, his ancestry, cut off from his birthright and any semblance of a social order. This in essence kills the slave's sense of a communal self and renders him only in relationship to his slave master. He undergoes a social death.[71] Despite the limitation of the term "African," I use it as a reminder that the figures in this project had common geographical and cultural origins that contributed to their enslavement in the Americas. "African" and the natal alienation it evokes also explain why it became necessary for black Africans to renegotiate identities and social networks in a new landscape. I use the term ultimately not to emphasize social death but rebirth. Not every black African came to the Americas as a slave, and even among the many who did, some experienced moments of triumph, forged new social connections, like the Cimarrones in Panama. I insist on coupling "African" with "black" for two reasons. First, it is a reminder of how important somatic features were in the kinds of ideologies Europeans developed to categorize and denigrate those hailing from the sub-Saharan regions of Africa, especially in the seventeenth century with the rise of the Atlantic slave trade and the link between race and labor. Second, the term differentiates the figures I study from their tawny-skinned North African counterparts, who were more often described as Moors, Arabs, or Muslims, and not as frequently subjected to slavery in the Americas. This is not to say that all North Africans were lighter-skinned or did not suffer enslavement. For consistency's sake, "black African" also refers to those people of African descent who were born in the Americas, who would more customarily be labeled African American.

I designate the scope of my project as "early Atlantic" and see the body of texts I discuss as early Atlantic literature with the understanding that "Atlantic" would not have been a specific construct for the writers I examine. In Atlantic studies, scholars continue to grapple with ways of defining the Atlantic world in geographical and ideological terms. I find David Armitage's articulation especially useful. He defines the Atlantic as more than a specific geographical region framed by the four continents that border the Atlantic Ocean. It is also the

> product of successive waves of navigation, exploration, settlement, administration, and imagination. It did not spring fully formed into European consciousness any more than "America" did, though it could certainly be found on maps—and hence in minds—two centuries before the full extent and outline of the Americas would be. It was European invention not because Europeans were its only denizens, but because Europeans were the first to connect its four sides into a single entity, both as a system and as the representation of a discrete natural feature.[72]

In thinking about the Atlantic world as a "European invention," Armitage reminds us of the political stakes involved in how and why Europeans traveled through the Atlantic and articulated those travels in narratives. *Black Africans in the British Imagination* points out the ways in which the physical presence of black Africans complicated those political stakes. I will note that I could just as well label this project as early American given that the conceptual framework of early American studies has become increasingly more circum-Atlantic, especially in the last fifteen or so years. Indeed, all the texts I discuss here with the exception of those in the first chapter are widely taught in early American studies courses. Ultimately, I prefer "Atlantic" because I see this book as an extension of what Gilroy began in 1993 with his understanding of the black Atlantic as a cultural zone connected by water routes and the circulation of black bodies and ideologies. So if we think about the black Atlantic as Gilroy does, as a "counterculture," I interrogate the ways in which that counterculture informed the literary and sociopolitical climate of the early Atlantic world.

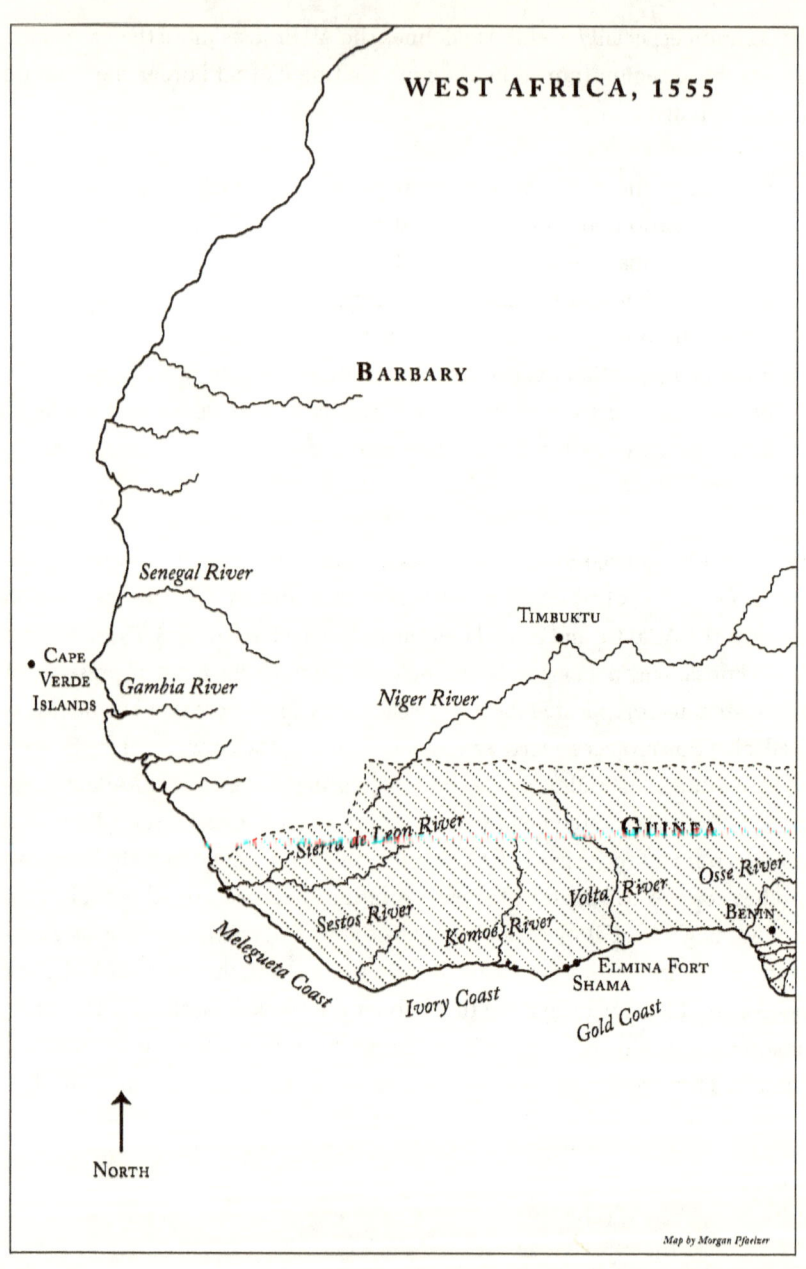

CHAPTER 1

Points of Origin: *English Voyages to Guinea*

In this first chapter, I discuss early English encounters with West Africa, examining the significance of those encounters in terms of how English travelers articulated their experiences later in the Americas. The discussion centers on the travel accounts of William Towerson and John Hawkins. Towerson was a sea merchant who made three profitable trade voyages to Guinea in 1555, 1556, and 1558. Virtually obscure in 1555, he was four years into a seven-year apprenticeship with a London skinner, Miles Mording, when he assumed the role of sea captain.[1] He proved himself a capable trader and seaman as he returned from each of his three voyages with profitable cargos. Scholars seldom discuss Towerson's voyages within the context of early American and Atlantic studies, presumably because the travels occur as a bilateral move between England and West Africa. In addition, Towerson did not participate, at least directly, in the Atlantic slave trade. Rather, his expeditions were significant, as J. D. Alsop notes, because they transformed the Guinea trade into a "profitable sector of England's developing long-distance commerce."[2]

Towerson was emblematic of what Alsop calls a new kind of London elite, one comprised of men born of modest means who were lured to London, where they secured apprenticeships. Those apprenticeships gave them access to maritime trade from which they built their fortunes financially and socially. Towerson, Alsop argues, "provides an informative illustration of the rise of an exceedingly obscure individual through participation in the West African trade of the 1550s and his subsequent integration into an Elizabethan commercial elite heavily involved in overseas trade and exploration."[3] Alsop points to the commercial and social consequences of Towerson's early Guinea voyages. I emphasize the cultural, specifically literary, consequences.

Towerson's voyages are unique in that he left behind three full narratives detailing each of his expeditions. The English undertook a number of voyages to West Africa in the second half of the sixteenth century. For most of those voyages we are left with only fragments and truncated secondhand accounts, the majority of which Richard Hakluyt cobbled together in his *Principal Navigations*.[4] Towerson's narratives, by contrast, provide an especially rich quantity of material from which to examine the rhetorical features of early accounts of English voyages to Guinea.[5] Specifically, Towerson's narratives are shaped by political and commercial imperatives to validate English overseas trade in a region where Portugal had already claimed a monopoly. To avoid charges of piracy, Towerson insisted he conducted trade with sovereign Guinea nations who were not subject to Portuguese rule. What is more, he claimed that those nations welcomed trade with the English as the Portuguese were an oppressive presence in the region. He attempted to build trade alliances with Guineans by positioning himself as a liberator. He promised them exotic wares—and protection.

In his interactions with prospective Guinea traders, some of whom are especially adept at manipulating international trade politics, Towerson discovers what Drake will learn twenty years later in Panama—the difficulty of representing as oppressed people with a clear sense of autonomy and political ambitions of their own. This difficulty creates a series of ruptures in Towerson's narratives. Those ruptures matter because they provide textual traces or circumstantial evidence that suggests black Africans actively engaged Europeans on the coast of Guinea, their actions directly affecting the shape of Towerson's narratives. Also, through those ruptures we see more clearly the vital but contested role black Africans played in an English imperial imagination that sought to justify England's overseas conduct through moralizing and liberatory paradigms.

In short, the mediated presences of black Africans in Towerson's narrative disrupt a victim/tyrant binary through which Towerson attempts to portray the Portuguese. This disruption, in turn, challenges Towerson's own self-image as a more benevolent European force, denying him the justificatory language that would sanctify English trade in Guinea. Towerson's ventures—and the narratives they produced—helped to set the rhetorical stage for English-black African interactions later in the Americas, providing an early illustration of how the material presences of black Africans challenged the representational strategies English writers deployed to articulate national and imperial identities.

A decade after Towerson's voyages, John Hawkins employed a similar rhetorical strategy in his pamphlet "A True Declaration of the Troublesome Voyage," the account of his third slaving expedition to Guinea and the Caribbean. Hawkins was the second son of William Hawkins, who was one of the first English traders to participate in an Atlantic triangular trade when he stopped along the Sestos River in Guinea in the 1530s to trade English goods for ivory en route to trading destinations along the east coast of South America. John Hawkins undertook three Atlantic voyages in the 1560s. Like his predecessors, Hawkins saw Guinea as a region brimming with resources—not gold, spices, and ivory but people whom he could enslave. He captured black Africans along the Melegueta Coast, mostly in Sierra Leone, then sold them to buyers in the Spanish-controlled Caribbean. While all three voyages effectively initiated England's entrance into the Atlantic slave trade (although it would still be several decades before the English participated fully), the most significant was the third voyage because it produced political and rhetorical consequences that aided in the deterioration of English-Spanish relations in the Americas and produced a series of narratives designed to stir English Hispanophobia.

Like Towerson, Hawkins embodies a liberatory persona in the descriptions of his interactions with Guineans. On that third voyage, he was approached by a Guinean king in present-day Sierra Leone seeking an alliance to protect his town from a neighboring enemy. Hawkins supplied resources, manpower, and eventually his own martial strength to liberate the king and his subjects. For his troubles, Hawkins expected to secure a cache of slaves taken from among the prisoners of war. According to Hawkins, the king deceived him by stealing away in the dead of night with the entire lot of prisoners, leaving Hawkins with nothing. This deception mirrored Hawkins's interactions with a Spanish viceroy weeks later at the Spanish port of San Juan de Ulúa in Mexico. After the men agreed to share the port, Hawkins claimed that the viceroy reneged on the agreement, attacking Hawkins's ships and destroying his fleet. Hawkins and only a fraction of his men survived.

In the account Hawkins writes of his ordeal, he mediates the perfidy of the Spanish viceroy through his interactions with the Guinean king, and his text replaces the anti-Portuguese sentiment of Towerson's narratives with an anti-Spanish one. As part of this book's larger project, Hawkins's narrative matters for three reasons. First, it works in conjunction with Towerson's narrative to illustrate that black Africans very early on played a key role in how England sought to articulate its overseas enterprises. Whereas Towerson's narratives, though, are marked by certain narrative disruptions, Hawkins's text does not reflect the same kind of narrative dissonance. He avoids the potentially disruptive effect of black African presences by fictionalizing key material details of his encounters in Guinea. As I will discuss shortly, Hawkins changes the *facts* when constructing his narrative to ensure that the plot more closely aligns with his rhetorical aims, a strategic move that itself illustrates the ways in which the material presences of black Africans worked in tandem with English writers' literary imaginations to produce texts. Second, Hawkins's narrative illustrates the ways in which English encounters with sub-Saharan Africa affected how English writers articulated their experiences specifically in the Americas. Third, the narrative stands as a rhetorical transition between Towerson and Drake, an early formulation of those representational patterns that Drake (and others) will adopt several years later in New Spain—where the material presences of black Africans will undermine Drake's self-construction and his articulation of England's imperial project. Together, Towerson's and Hawkins's narratives illuminate those patterns of interaction and representation—created through early Guinea-English encounters—that black Africans later challenge in the Americas.

Imagining Africa: Towerson's Travel and Literary Predecessors

I begin the discussion here with Towerson's narratives by examining first those travel accounts of his predecessors to contextualize his rhetorical strategies. Then I discuss the political and social landscape of Guinea in the 1550s before providing a close-reading of Towerson's texts. In 1555, the English scientist and translator Richard Eden published a collection of travel narratives designed to herald the overseas achievements of Spain and encourage the English to pursue their own overseas agenda.[6] The collection, titled *Decades of the Newe Worlde or West India*, highlighted Spanish activity in South America and the Caribbean and early English voyages to the northeast—Muscovy (Russia) and Cathay (China).[7] At the end of his collection, Eden added two accounts of Englishmen's travels in 1553 and 1554 to the Guinea region of West Africa. The narratives provide readers with two of the earliest English eyewitness accounts of the region and are reprinted in 1589 in Hakluyt's massive *Principal Navigations*. For Eden (and Hakluyt), the voyages are vital accomplishments, illustrative of the breadth of England's commercial activity and overseas travel. Both voyages come on the heels of successful trading expeditions to Barbary in North Africa in 1551 and 1552 and are part of England's efforts to expand its trade reaches into faraway locales such as the Mediterranean, East Indies, and Russia.[8] In fact, shortly after initiating travel and trade to West Africa and in the same year that Eden published his collection, the English formed the Muscovy Company. Not incidentally, some of the same London investors backed trade ventures to both Russia and Guinea.[9]

The first of those Guinea voyages departed England in 1553 with two ships and a pinnace under the leadership of Thomas Wyndham, who had led the voyages to Barbary in the two years prior.[10] Accompanying Wyndham as second in command, or "petycapitaine," was Antonio Anes Pinteado, a Portuguese ex-patriot with experience of the West African coastline.[11] The venture suffered several disasters. Due to poor leadership (Pinteado and Wyndham bickered constantly) and illness, a voyage that began with 140 sailors returned with barely forty men. The voyage did manage to yield valuable commodities, including 150 pounds of gold and tons of pepper. The profits prompted a second voyage the next year under the leadership of merchant and investor John Lok. After some twenty weeks, Lok returned to England with a bounty of African goods, including gold, spices, and ivory. In the wake of this second voyage, Eden catalogued the commodities gained as "foure hundredth pounde weyght and odde of golde of xxii carrattes and one grayne in finenesse. Also xxxvi buttes of graynes: and abowt two hundredth and fiftie elephantes teethe of all quantities."[12]

Equally important as the material gains, those first two voyages revived for English readers classical ideas about the continent of Africa and its inhabitants. Eden's account of Lok's voyage, in particular, has been a popular go-to text for scholars seeking to understand early English attitudes toward black Africans.[13] He bookends his narrative of Lok's voyage with historical and proto-ethnographic descriptions of Africa and Africans. He describes the continent, the sub-Saharan region in particular, as a land of monstrous races (cannibals and headless men), anomalous geographic features, such as water spouts that originate in the sky and fall into the sea, and lascivious women, who "contracte no matrimonie, neyther have respect to chastitie."[14] He continues, "Many thynges more owre men sawe and consydered in this vyage worthy to bee noted wherof I have thought good to put sum in memory that the reader maye aswell take pleasure in the varietie of thynges as knowledge of the hystorye."[15]

Eden's narratives of those first English voyages inform later English travelers' thoughts and accounts, including those of Towerson, who mimics Eden's monstrosity rhetoric. He notes, for example, that along the St. Vincent River, on the Melegueta Coast the people "race" their skin "with divers works," and the "men and women goe so alike, that one cannot know a man from a woman but by their breastes, which in the most part be very foule and long, hanging downe low like the udder of a goate" (367).[16] Farther along the St. Vincent, he encounters another town of people where he describes the inhabitants as "wilde and idle," and women's breasts are "exceeding long" so that "some of them will lay the same upon the ground and lie downe by them" (369).[17] The observations *appear* neutral, detached conclusions about foreign, exotic cultures, but those observations are far from inconsequential. They point to an emerging racial discourse that will in time transform with the growth of the Atlantic slave trade from considerations of cultural practices and mores to considerations of bodily difference.[18]

Both Towerson and Eden perpetuate these monstrous images from medieval travel predecessors, such as Leo Africanus and John Mandeville, who regale readers with stories about monstrous races that reside at the edges of the habitable world.[19] The link between the foreign and the monstrous dates back to the classical period when thinkers such as Pliny the Elder, who in "Book Seven" of his *Natural History,* cataloged a series of monstrous races that occupied faraway nations, mostly in Asia and Africa.[20]

Importantly, the racial rhetoric in Towerson's narratives is complicated by a greater political expediency that demands he represent the humanity, as opposed to a presumed monstrosity, of black Africans. To refute Portuguese claims that he is a pirate, Towerson legitimizes his trade by humanizing Guinea communities as self-governing trade partners struggling to conduct trade under the yoke of a Portuguese tyrant. Consider, for example, his description of an encounter in the town of Hanta (or Ahanta) on that second voyage. The residents of the town complain to Towerson "that there were five Portugall shippes at the Castle and one pinnasse, and that the Portugals did much harme to their Countrey, and that they lived in feare of them, and we told them againe, that we would defend them from the Portugals whereof they were very glad" (399). He makes similar promises to residents in Shama several days later. He writes:

> Then wee departed and went to Shamma [sic] and went into the river with five boates well appointed with men and ordinance, and with our noises of trumpets and drummes, for we thought here to have found some Portugals but there were none: so wee sent our Negros on shore, and after them went divers of us, and were very well received, and the people were very glad of our Negros, specially one of their brothers wives, and one of their aunts, which received them with much joy and so did all the rest of the people, as if they had bene their naturall breth-

ren: we comforted the captaine and told him that hee should not feare the Portugals, for wee would defend him from them: whereupon we caused our boats to shoote off their bases and harquebusses, and caused our men to come on shore with their long bowes and they shot before the captaine, which he, with all the rest of the people, wondred much at, specially to see them shoot so farre as they did, and assayed to draw their bows but could not. When it grew to be late, we departed to our ships, for we looked every houre for the Portugals (399).

Towerson's articulation of this scene at Shama is striking. An emotional energy pervades the moment as Towerson's black African mediators reunite with the inhabitants of the town. The joyous reunion exists alongside the town leader's fears of a Portuguese attack. The English, too, are anxious, even as they descend on the town like guardian angels. Notably, the emotional energy gives way to a display of cultural supremacy when Towerson demonstrates English technology, specifically weaponry, which the town leader and "all the rest of the people wondred much at."[21] Here, Towerson shows rather than merely tells the people at Shama that he can defend them against the Portuguese, that he is in fact a great liberator. Throughout the second narrative, especially, Towerson portrays himself as enjoying a warm reception on the coast. He regales readers with examples of people who risk life and limb to trade and interact with him. One man is so eager to trade with the English that he braves rough seas to get to the English ship, but, according to Towerson, "the land-wash went so sore that it overthrew his boat" (397). The man drowns. At another town, Towerson claims, the town's leader greets him at sea with tears of joy. Towerson writes that the man "seemed to be the gladdest man alive, and so did all the companie that knew mee" (404). In contrast to the Portuguese, Towerson's presence does not evoke fear, anxiety, and hostility among Guineans. Rather, he appears a great comforter to the people, ushering in joy and excitement wherever he goes. Moments like this aid in representing English commercial activity abroad in more humane, ethical terms. This will become a more urgent imperative when the English expand across the Atlantic and seek to define themselves in opposition not to Portugal but to Spain.

On the Ground: The Social and Political Logistics of Guinea-English Trade

By the time Towerson arrived on the Guinea coast in 1555, African towns had been trading with the Portuguese for nearly a century.[22] The Portuguese, in fact, had set up a fort along the coast, São Jorge da Mina, or El Mina for short. The French had been in the region since the 1530s. As they navigated the waterways, then, Towerson and his crews were on constant guard for competing French and Portuguese fleets. The Portuguese, especially, were aggressive about protecting their monopoly on Guinea trade, secured in part through the 1494 Treaty of Tordesillas. The treaty split up those newly encountered lands in the Atlantic Basin south of Europe along a vertical demarcation a little less than four hundred leagues west of the Cape Verde Islands. Thanks to Columbus's voyages, Spain claimed exclusive rights to those lands west of the line, including the Caribbean. Portugal claimed lands to the east, including all of Guinea and the Cape Verde Islands.

On both his second and third voyages, Towerson engaged Portuguese ships in battle near El Mina. The Portuguese condemned Towerson as a pirate conducting illegitimate trade. In 1557, a Portuguese official stationed in Guinea lamented the consequences of English (and French) "piracy" in the region. In a letter to Portugal's Queen Catherine, the official wrote, "If our Lord the King would send a fleet each year so that it could be securely defended against the pirates who come here and do not allow trade to be pursued, as they did this year, much money could be gained at this trading-post. But as this coast is not guarded from the pirates, none at all can be gained, on account of the very cheap goods they trade with the blacks."[23] Back in 1554, after Lok's voyage, the Portuguese Crown appealed to England's Queen Mary to deter English trade in Guinea on the grounds that it violated papal bulls and infringed upon Portugal's right of first discovery.[24]

The English responded by asserting their own right to trade in open markets. In 1555, London merchants said of English trade in Guinea, "Our factors landed not in anie place where the said king [of Portugal] had anie fortresse, towne, garrison or governaunce or anie officer or other person, that did forbid them."[25] Furthermore, according to the London merchants, English traders conducted trade only with those who "came to them in their shippes," and they "refused to use anie traficque until they wer infourmed by [Guinea traders] that they wer no subjects to the King of Portugall."[26] As I argue shortly, this political tension between Portugal and England becomes vital in how Towerson represents his interactions with black Africans in his narratives about the voyages.

Towerson's encounters with the French were equally complex and tense, fluctuating between tolerable and hostile.[27] When he encountered French ships on his second voyage, the fleets formed a trade alliance, agreeing to travel together and sell their goods at the same fixed prices to maximize gains against their Guinea counterparts. The agreement fell apart a month later when Portuguese ships attacked the allied fleet, causing French and English ships to abandon each other, scrambling for survival. It did not help the English-French alliance that Guinea traders preferred French goods to English, especially cloth. According to Towerson, "The Negros perceived the difference in cloth betwixt ours and that which the Frenchmen had, which was better, and broader then ours. . . . I perceived that being there where [the French] cloth was sold, I should do no good" (404). By the end of the second voyage, Towerson abandoned the partnership and took measures to undermine Guinea's French trade through various acts of intimidation. For example, when the French fleet's vice admiral proposed to travel alongside the English to trade just outside of Shama, Towerson refused. He fired on the ships, forcing the French to flee.

In addition to navigating and sometimes initiating hostile encounters with other European nations, Towerson also reckoned with experienced African traders, who approached the English with a savvy and shrewdness that Towerson often found off-putting. He complained about the 'unreasonable' demands of Guinea traders. Even after the English and French fixed their prices on that second voyage, Towerson often walked away from the trade negotiations empty-handed, despairing, "we could not give them the halfe of that which they demaunded" (399). At other times, Africans showed little interest in English goods because they had access to higher quality products from the French or because they had brokered trade alliances with the Portuguese. At the end of his third voyage, when Towerson failed to entice the town leader at Shama to trade, he attributed the failure to the fact that the leader had become "subject to the Portugals," and he burned the town (426).

European interest in sub-Saharan Africa had its roots in classical theories that linked extreme temperatures with the formation of precious metals. Aristotle, for example, theorized that gold was created in extremely hot zones. Specifically, he postulated that the sun's effect on the earth caused the earth to exhale in a sense, and that exhalation could be vaporous (or moist) in nature or smoky (dry). Gold was created when a vaporous exhalation, containing moisture, got trapped beneath the earth's surface and formed into a malleable substance. He called this process "concoction," a kind of physical ripening. "For when concoction has taken place," he argued, "we say that a thing has been perfected and has come to be itself. It is the proper heat of a thing that sets up this perfecting."[28]

Following Aristotle's theory, the African continent, which the equator dissects, should have contained vast quantities of gold. The theory seemingly found confirmation in certain medieval travel texts, containing more fiction than fact, describing gold-rich kingdoms near the equator in Africa, India, and later the Americas. One of those accounts, *The Travels of Sir John Mandeville*, was a popular item among English travelers, including Martin Frobisher and Sir Walter Ralegh, whose expeditions I discuss in chapter 5. Africa had its own version of El Dorado in the historical city of Timbuktu, the seat of power for the fourteenth-century Mali Empire existing just north of present-day Ghana. Led by the Muslim ruler Mansa Musa, the empire's wealth assumed a mythical status, resulting in large part from the exaggerated accounts of Muslim traders who visited the region and took back reports to North Africa and Europe. According to legend, Mansa Musa was so rich that during a pilgrimage to the Holy City of Mecca, his lavish spending and acts of charity created massive inflation in the cities he passed along the way.[29] Another account describes Mansa Musa as having "many plates and scepters of gold, some whereof weigh 1300 poundes: and he keepes a magnificent and well furnished court."[30] Stories of golden kingdoms, not prospective slaves, first lured the Portuguese to the African West Coast, where they sought to "tap supplies of Guinea gold closer to their sources as a means of compensating for . . . shortages in Lisbon."[31] When that first English crew arrived in 1553, they found a wealth of trading possibilities with African settlements willing to swap gold and spices for English cloth and metal goods.

European gold fever helped create on the West African coast an international trade community—albeit unstable—where black Africans met European merchants in encounters characterized by shifting power dynamics and competing interests. The Atlantic slave trade and images of European slavers who raided the Gold Coast for slaves have dominated conceptions of African-European interactions in the early modern period. Texts like Olaudah Equiano's slave narrative *The Interesting Narrative* reify such conceptions. In the sixteenth century, though, diplomacy, not raids, more often characterized encounters. It is important to note the kinds of motivation that fueled Africans' decisions to trade with Europeans. As John Thornton reminds us, it was not about a scarcity of resources in West Africa. Too often, especially in modern times, we view West Africa as a region in need, wanting and lacking. In the sixteenth and seventeenth centuries, Africans already produced the kinds of goods Europeans exported. This included cloth, metals, and jewelry. African-European trade, Thornton argues, did not develop to "make up for shortfalls in production or failures in quality of the African manufactures.

Rather, Africa's trade with Europe was largely moved by prestige, fancy, changing taste, and a desire for variety."[32] In other words, African traders in the 1550s often sought European goods because they were exotic, novelties—the same kind of motivation that drove English interest in elephant heads and tusks that they could put on display in their homes.[33] All of this is to say that Towerson was forced to finesse his interactions in Guinea. Recognizing the autonomy and agency of those black Africans with whom Towerson interacted is essential to understanding the rhetoric and narrative ruptures that characterize Towerson's accounts of his voyages.

Signifying Encounter: Political and Literary Convergences

Textual analysis of several key moments in Towerson's narratives suggests a disharmony between material reality and Towerson's rhetorical aims. Two moments from the first narrative embody this tension. In both moments Towerson narrates the English's hostile encounters with Guinean and Portuguese allied forces, whose union is fueled ironically by a common anti-English sentiment. In the first moment, Towerson encounters a Guinea trader who recently escaped captivity at El Mina. With this trader, Towerson swaps forty-two baskets and dishes for some three ounces of gold dust. The terms of trade please Towerson as it "was the best reckoning that we did make of any basons" (381). After detailing the trade exchange, Towerson provides backstory on the trader:

> This fellow, as farre as we could perceive, had bene taken into the castle by the Portugales, and was gotten away from them, for he tolde us that the Portugales were bad men, and that they made them slaves if they could take them, and would put yrons upon their legges, and besides he told us, that as many Frenchmen or Englishmen, as they could take (for he could name these two very well) they would hang them; he told us further, that there were 60 men in the castle, and that every yeere there came thither two shippes, one great, and one small carvell, and further, that don John had warres with the Portugals, which gave mee the better courage to goe to his towne, which lieth but foure leagues from the castle." (382)

This former captive supplies Towerson crucial information regarding the defenses at El Mina and possible trade alliances Towerson can establish in the surrounding area. Towerson accepts the man's information at face value perhaps because the moment helps him establish the Portuguese as imperial villains. The Guinea trader finds asylum among the English. After concluding their business, Towerson writes that the man "came aboord our shippe without feare" (382). On the surface, this moment performs crucial rhetorical work. It provides experiential testimony of Portuguese cruelty. It also establishes a contrast between the Portuguese and the English, who do not seek to enslave Guinea inhabitants but conduct fair trade. Recall that with this trader Towerson engaged in trade that provided the *best reckoning* for his wares. He believes the exchange fair. The trader apparently does, too, as evidenced by the fact that he goes on to trade with several other members of Towerson's crew.

A key transition occurs after the man boards the English ship and refers to an episode that occurred the year before. In Lok's 1554 voyage to Guinea, his crew kidnapped five black Africans and brought them back to England. This Guinea trader, who apparently knew about the kidnappings, calls Towerson to answer: "As soone as he came [aboard], he demaunded, why we had not brought againe their men, which the last yeere we tooke away, and could tell us that here were five taken away by Englishmen: we made him answere that they were in England well used, and were there kept till they could speak the language, and then they should be brought againe to be a helpe to Englishmen in this Countrey; and then he spake no more of that matter" (382). Now, the very tenor of the writing shifts, and the man no longer appears a sympathetic victim and refugee. Instead, he is an angry inhabitant who, "as soone" as he is aboard ship, "demaunds" answers about the welfare of his countrymen. The trader's actions also shift Towerson's stance as he moves from judging the Portuguese to defending the English. Towerson assumes his answer appeases the trader because the man "spake no more of that matter," and they travel east of El Mina to the town of Don John.[34] As a mediated presence, this Guinea trader challenges Towerson's understanding of himself (and England) as ally and liberator. As the trader reminds us, the English engage in activity quite similar to that of the Portuguese by capturing black Africans. His representation, designed to embody Portuguese cruelty, ironically, also confirms English cruelty, undermining Towerson's efforts to differentiate Portuguese and English activity in Guinea.

This narrative tension makes sense if we read the exchange against the grain, an approach that reminds us of the material world referent whose actions provided the source material from which Towerson constructed the moment. If what Towerson says about the Guinea trader's background is correct, then the trader has reason to be wary of both the Portuguese and the English, and this becomes a scene in which that trader pits European factions against each other. Consider the following: This trader presumably possesses some measure of resourcefulness as suggested by the fact he escapes imprisonment at El Mina. Also, he apparently understands something of the sociopolitical and economic climates along the Guinea coast. He engages in trade with Towerson that satisfies both sides, and he supplies Towerson with political intelligence regarding the areas surrounding El Mina. He tells Towerson exactly what Towerson wants to hear—that the Portuguese are bad men and a threat not only to black Africans but to the French and English, who could be hanged if caught by the Portuguese. His information inflames tensions. In addition, he encourages Towerson to seek out an alliance with the Guinea ruler Don John, whose town is "but foure leagues from the castle," based on the principle that the enemy of an enemy is a friend (382).

At first glance it appears that Towerson and the trader both understand the Portuguese as villains. Perhaps, too, the trader seeks to manipulate English resources to attack the Portuguese fort—retaliation for the Portuguese having held him captive. This reading of the trader's motives, though, is complicated by his actions once he boards Towerson's ship and demands answers about the whereabouts of his five friends. His change in demeanor suggests that he views the English as villains, too, not as allies in a fight against a common foe. Textual evidence implies that the Guinea trader is no simple victim cowing from the harsh treatment of the Portuguese and seeking asylum with the English. His interactions with Towerson are much more active and manipulative, but to what end? Perhaps we get the answer in what happens next in the narrative.

Recall the Guinea trader's insistence that Towerson travel four leagues east to Don John's Town, presumably to create a trade alliance as protection from the Portuguese. Towerson follows his advice. The English arrive just off the shore at Don John's Town in the afternoon on January 8, 1555/56, where they sit in their ships for three hours waiting "to see if any man would come" to trade (383). No one comes, an odd reception (or lack thereof) given the Guinea trader's insistence that Don John residents would welcome them eagerly. To induce trade, the Englishmen transfer their wares to smaller boats and move closer to the shore. One man approaches the boats, assuring them that residents of the town want to trade but cannot until their town leader returns. The English wait all the next day. On the third day, they begin trading wares for gold, but the transactions are cut short when a Portuguese force appears just over a hill and attacks the English.[35] The Portuguese are accompanied by inhabitants from the town, including Don John's son, who "conspired with the Portugales" against the English. The allied forces push the English back to their ships (385).

Towerson says of the black Africans' role in the attack, "the Negroes more for feare then for love stoode by [the Portuguese] to help them; and when we saw that the Negroes were in such subjection unto them that they durst not sell us anything for feare of [the Portuguese], we went aboord" (385). Towerson does not consider that the town's residents and the Portuguese willingly collaborate. The residents coax Towerson to shore, and they stall trade negotiations for three days while they await the arrival not of the town leader but of their armed Portuguese allies. Towerson does not acknowledge what very well could have been a Guinea-Portuguese alliance because, as Hair notes, "it was in the English interest to assert that the local African polities were in no sense allies of the Portuguese, since this enabled the English to limit the area of Portuguese effective occupation and to claim that their own trading was no direct challenge to Portuguese rights."[36] In other words, a Guinea-Portugal alliance would indict Towerson as an interloper and delegitimize England's presence in West Africa. So Towerson vilifies Portugal and objectifies the residents of Don John's Town. At stake, Towerson believes, are massive stores of gold. He muses when arriving at a town next to Don John (Don John de Viso), "The most part of the golde that comes thither comes out of the countrey, and no doubt if the people durst for feare of the Portugals bring forth their gold, there would be had good store: but they dare not sell anything, their subjection is so great to the Portugales" (386).

This scene, in which Towerson represents black Africans as objects of Portuguese oppression, seemingly leaves no space to recognize them as active, thinking subjects. If we only read this series of events, though, from Towerson's perspective, we miss the much more complex energies fueling his encounters with the residents of Don John—and even more so with that Guinea trader. Remember that the trader goads Towerson toward Don John's Town at the same time that he demands to know the whereabouts of his countrymen. He assures Towerson of a warm reception at the town, and maybe he is sincere in his suggestion. Perhaps prior to the trader's captivity at El Mina, the Portuguese and residents of Don John were at war, just as he claims. Perhaps they arrived at a truce, unbeknownst to the trader, while he was imprisoned. Maybe, too, Towerson's explanation regarding the five captured men mollifies the trader.

Equally plausible is that the trader has manipulated Towerson. Portugal and Don John's Town were not at war during the time of Towerson's voyage. However, their relationship was ambivalent, as suggested by letters sent from the governor administrator at El Mina back to Portugal's regent Queen Catherine. In those letters, the governor, more than a bit perturbed, describes Don John as self-interested and devious. He complains, "I have found out through spies that [Don John] and his son-in-law, and the people of the king of Comane, traded more than 30,000 pesos. Whenever [English and French] pirates come they will do this and will not forbid trading, because self-interest and the profit they gain count for more than whatever this fortress can give them in bribes."[37] Irritated though he might be, the governor's tone does not suggest war is imminent. In fact, elsewhere in the letters, the governor describes Don John as an ally who helps the Portuguese maintain peace in the surrounding towns.[38] Given this historical context, it seems that the trader quietly leads Towerson's men into an ambush. Once he arrives at Don John's Town, Towerson does not mention the Guinea trader again. He does not acknowledge the possibility that he has been manipulated. However, there are enough narrative inconsistencies in the encounter for readers to interpret counter-narratives and alternative ambitions for Towerson's black African counterparts. Ultimately, that Guinea trader's presence hovers over the moment like a ghost.

The scene at Don John's Town illustrates Towerson's rhetorical strategy to represent the English as legitimate traders and liberators. The scene also undermines that representation. When we read the moment against the grain, black Africans appear not as hapless victims who need rescue from a tyrannous Portugal but as calculating participants in complex trading relationships. The kinds of inconsistencies that manifest themselves in Towerson's representation and that of his would-be Guinea allies appear again in a second, parallel, scene. Two days after leaving Don John's Town, Towerson and his men continue traveling east, along the coast. He comments on the landscape, which is dotted with high, wooded hills and red cliffs. There are several small towns but few rivers. The people mostly speak the same language as residents at Don John's Town, and they have a rudimentary command of Portuguese. As Towerson travels along, he notes that the towns grow in size, "wherein were greater houses then in the other townes" (386). People come down to the shore to watch them pass. At one point, several inhabitants wave a white flag at Towerson's ships, inviting him to trade. When Towerson sets anchor and heads toward the shore in a smaller boat, loaded with trading goods, the people do not approach him. Towerson interprets their reaction as fear "because . . . foure men were taken perforce the last yeere from this place" by men on Lok's voyage (387). The reaction from residents here echoes the wariness of the Guinea trader in the previous scene, again challenging Towerson's efforts to render the English in a more benevolent light. Towerson concedes trading failure and heads back to his anchored ship. Shortly after, though, more inhabitants come to the shore, again waving a white flag. This time the town leader comes down to the shore, too, and sends a boat toward Towerson that "would not come neere us, but made us signes to come againe the next day" (387). The would-be traders appear cautiously inviting. Their hesitation contradicts moments elsewhere in the narratives where Towerson describes the people's eagerness to interact with him. Remember the trader who drowns in a choppy sea while swimming toward Towerson's ships or others who weep with excitement upon seeing the English. At one point, he manages to coax men aboard his ship, and he offers gifts—cloth, food, and bowls—they can take back to their town leader.

Despite the people's hesitation to actually engage Towerson, their white flags encourage him. That next day he moves to shore, where he waits for hours for people to appear with their wares—but to no avail. When he attempts to leave, the inhabitants come "running downe with a flagge to wave us againe" (387). Despite the people's inexplicable behavior, which might not be so inexplicable given events at Don John's Town, Towerson lingers. Several of the town inhabitants approach Towerson ashore and offer him items, including a hen, and promise him that "within two houres the marchants of the countrey would come downe and buy all that we had" (388). Towerson gives the men copper to take back to the town leader. After exchanging goods, the inhabitants propose the exchanging of hostages (or pledges), not an uncommon gesture in these kinds of encounters. Towerson does not hesitate to the terms, writing "we, willing to doe so, put one of our men in their boate, but they would not give us one of theirs, so we tooke our man againe" (388). Towerson does not ponder the inhabitants' refusal to reciprocate in the hostage exchange. Rather, he and his men "there tarried for the marchants" (388). It would seem that his patience has paid off shortly afterward when the town leader appears, accompanied by an entourage.[39] He does not, however, approach Towerson's boat. Rather, he assumes a perch nearby under a tree. At that point, Towerson and his men "perceived a great many of them to stand at the end of a hollow way, and behind them the Portugales had planted a base, who suddenly shotte at us" (388). Towerson quickly navigates his boat back to their ship amid gunfire from both the Portuguese and Guineans. They survive the attack and prudently decide to leave. Towerson writes, "Then we went aboord to goe from this place, seeing the Negroes bent against us, because that the last yeer M. Gainsh [on Lok's voyage] did take away the captain's sonne and three others from this place with their golde, and all that they had about them; which was the cause that they became friends with the Portugales, whom before they hated" (388).

This is another representation of Guinea-Portugal alliance that disrupts the binary through which Towerson characterizes the English as liberators and the Portuguese as oppressors. This time he attributes the alliance to the English's own faulty reckoning with the inhabitants of the town. As in the previous scene, here Towerson understands the Guineans as objects or victims of an oppressive regime, the English. The moment becomes a cautionary tale. Lok's mistake has proved costly for Towerson and the English because not only are they prevented from achieving alliances of their own, but also their actions foster cooperation between Guineans and Portuguese. Not incidentally, on his second voyage Towerson will bring back several of those kidnapped men, his attempt to improve England's image in the region.

The very fact that Towerson offers this cautionary tale in his narrative speaks to the active engagement of black Africans on the Guinea coast. This is not a region where the English—or the Portuguese—can raid towns or kidnap inhabitants at will. The Guineans with whom Towerson interact do not sit back as passive victims, awaiting protection or liberation from European forces. By all appearances, the townspeople manipulate Towerson, those white flags of welcome a ploy to prolong his stay on the coast. If we follow the counter-narrative, they marshal the resources of the Portuguese to exact revenge on the English for kidnapping their relatives. The most telling and most chilling image is that of the town leader sitting under a tree atop a hill watching the assault, poised as a god-like figure overseeing the attack below.

Towerson's difficulties constructing himself as a liberating force and black Africans as victims might explain why he all but abandons the rhetoric in the narrative of his third voyage. The rhetoric would have been especially difficult to maintain given the unusual hardships he encountered on that third voyage. For starters, the crew departed later than usual, not until after January of 1557/58, which meant that by the time they arrived on the Guinea coast, traders had already exchanged their supplies of gold dust for wares from the French. Towerson was able to salvage some trade but only because he adopted a more aggressive strategy. He raided French ships and Guinean towns. Adding to the voyage's difficulties, illness swept through the crews on Towerson's three ships, reducing his manpower so drastically that he sunk one of the ships. He lost another ship at sea. A greatly diminished and weakened crew hobbled back to England in October 1558 aboard the one remaining ship and a small pinnace.

The narrative of that third voyage offers few details about Towerson's interactions with Guinean traders. He emphasizes more his violent clashes with French and Portuguese ships. The few scenes that do recount his encounters with Guinean traders represent Towerson's struggles to maintain those alliances he had established on his second voyage. Despite his earlier promises of liberation and protection that seemed to open up markets, Towerson repeatedly finds Guinea inhabitants hostile and unwilling to trade on his third voyage. Consider his reception, for example, at the town of Hanta. Remember in the narrative of his second voyage, Towerson writes that the residents of this town lived in fear of the Portuguese, who "did much harme to their countrey" (399). Because the people lived in fear, Towerson claims, he promised them that the English "would defend them from the Portugals whereof they were very glad" (399). Again, this scene aligns with Towerson's liberatory rhetoric. But something happens in those approximately twelve months between Towerson's second and third voyages. When he returns in 1558, the town residents treat Towerson and his men "very ill" (426). "Neither the captaine nor the Negros durst traffike with us," Towerson writes, "but intised us from place to place and all to no purpose" (425). He is vague about the ploys town residents enact to entice, or toy with them, but we can imagine that their stunts would have been similar to those employed by residents at Don John's Town on that first voyage. Interestingly, Towerson concedes some measure of agency on the part of Hanta residents, rather than attributing their cold reception to Portuguese tyranny.

The "joy" Towerson says Hanta residents exhibited upon accepting his promises of protection a year earlier has faded. What caused the change? Perhaps the Portuguese did employ oppressive tactics to coerce Hanta residents into an alliance. Maybe a member of Towerson's crew or another Englishman committed some act of treachery that gravely offended the town, causing residents to sever ties with the English. As Eden notes about Guinea inhabitants, they are "very wary people in theyr bargenynge, and wyl not lose one sparke of golde of any value. They use weyghtes and measures, and are very circumspecte in occupying the same. They that shall have to do with them must use them gently for they wyl not trafike or brynge in any wares if they be evyll used."[40] Were Hanta residents *evyll* used by the English in 1558? Or did they simply renegotiate their alliances to accept more favorable terms from the

Portuguese? Whatever the reason(s) for the change in reception, it speaks volumes about the volatility of the political and commercial climate along the Guinea coast during Towerson's travels. That volatility—fueled by black African agency—circumscribes Towerson's narrative efforts.

A new mood, one of resignation, informs this third narrative. This is nowhere more apparent than in the descriptions of his final encounter with residents at Shama, which had been a vital trading post for Towerson on his first and second voyages. His return in 1558 parallels the reception he got several days earlier at Hanta: "We tooke our boat and pinnesse, and manned them well, and went to the towne of Shamma [sic], and because the Captaine thereof was become subject to the Portugals we burned the towne, and our men seeking the spoile of such trifles as were there found a Portugals chest, wherein was some of his apparel, and his weights, and one letter sent to him from the castle, whereby we gathered that the portugall had bene there of a long time" (426). Recall that Shama is the same town where, on Towerson's second voyage, residents marveled at English weaponry and, according to Towerson, sought asylum. The alliance from the year before seems to have vanished. This moment is most striking, then, because of what it does not say. Towerson makes no effort to coax the people at Shama to trade. He does not assume the liberator role or remind them of their trade alliance from the previous year, and he does not attempt to dazzle them with another display of English technological power. Instead, the writing turns impatient and lacks detail. Only three actions comprise the sequence of events: they man the boats; they arrive at the town; and they burn it. He does not offer details about his reception, or lack thereof. Maybe they shoot at his ships, as those in other towns had done on previous voyages? Perhaps they toy with him in a manner similar to those at Don John's Town. It might even be the case that they leave the town upon Towerson's arrival.

It is ironic that Towerson decides to burn Shama. As illustrated throughout this chapter, Towerson often encountered hostile towns in which people denied his trade overtures, most recently at Hanta. His actions here suggest that he had a specific set of expectations. His burning of the town seems more personal, born of frustration perhaps. The hurried pace, the concise prose suggests Towerson's anger, targeted at his former allies, who behave in a manner contradictory to Towerson's previous rhetoric. He does revert back to a familiar paradigm in one regard. He declares that the town leader, the *captaine,* has fallen under the subjection of the Portuguese. Again, he assumes that Shama residents are oppressed victims with little agency in shaping their commercial and political lives. This is a final attempt to represent implicitly English overseas trade in Guinea as humane and legitimate. Given Towerson's previous experiences in the region, we cannot take for granted that Shama's rejection of the English in this moment indicates their subjugation to the Portuguese.

Based on what Towerson tells us, we can ascertain that the material details of his encounters in Guinea have changed. This means the kind of narrative he can construct must change also. Usually, when Towerson encounters a town aligned with the Portuguese, the residents' actions follow this pattern: They lure Towerson to the beach with promises of trade. They employ various guises to stall his stay on their coast. After several days, a joint force of Guinean and Portuguese soldiers stage an attack. Town residents appear crafty and devious. Notably, Towerson's experiences at Shama on his final visit diverge from the pattern. It seems that residents reject him immediately and directly, without any of the tricks and ploys—and without the Portuguese martial support. There is no armed Portuguese presence that Towerson can point to as visual proof of Portugal's militant control over the town. A Portuguese man's storage chest, containing a few articles of clothing and other trinkets, provides the only evidence to suggest a Guinean-Portuguese alliance. Presumably, in rejecting Towerson, Shama residents act on their own behalf.

Like those living in Hanta, Shama residents deny Towerson his usual narrative of liberation and alliance. Although he assumes that the Portuguese have threatened Shama leaders into an alliance, we should not mimic that assumption. In light of the counter-narratives that appear throughout Towerson's texts that suggest black Africans acted independently of their European counterparts, we can infer that the shift in attitude among Shama residents was advantageous to them and voluntary, not coercive. We can infer also that the material presences of black Africans guided Towerson's narrative choices, impeding his efforts to construct himself—and by extension England—as a benevolent force. Towerson's Guinea ventures end here, but the liberatory rhetoric through which he struggles to articulate a space for himself, and for England, in overseas commerce does not.

The Aftermath: Hawkins in Guinea and America

Based on the financial successes of those 1550s voyages, Englishmen continued planning and conducting voyages to Guinea over the next decade.[41] In 1561 John Lok planned to return to Guinea to oversee the construction of an English fort on the Gold Coast, east of El Mina. This voyage was based, in part, on news Towerson brought back from his second voyage that the king of a rich, large kingdom on the Gold Coast invited the English to build a fort there to foster trade.[42] Lok aborted his plans, though, complaining about the poor quality of ships, turbulent weather, and rumors of an armed Portuguese fleet waiting to attack. English ships traveled to Guinea throughout the 1560s and then sporadically through the remainder of the century. The travels of most interest for the purposes of this book's larger argument were those organized and carried out by the privateer and slave trader Sir John Hawkins.

Hawkins led three voyages to Guinea in the 1560s, the most consequential of which was the third voyage, which set sail for Guinea in October of 1567 with a fleet of six ships anchored by a seven-hundred-ton flagship, the *Jesus of Lubeck,* which Queen Elizabeth herself provided. More than four hundred men manned the fleet. Based on the profitable outcomes of his voyages in 1562 and 1564, Hawkins expected similar success. What he got instead, in his own words, was a series of "troublesome" events. The troubles began when they arrived on the Guinea Coast and struggled to capture and enslave inhabitants. On previous voyages, Hawkins was able to commandeer Portuguese ships or raid coastal towns to build up a slave cargo. On this third voyage, though, he encountered Guinea inhabitants who aggressively resisted his efforts. After a failed raid of one town near Cape Verde on the coast, Hawkins lost eight men and nearly died himself from poisoned arrow wounds. When January arrived and they still had not collected a substantial number of captives, not more than 150 of the estimated five hundred he sought, Hawkins turned his attention to gold, intending to make his a conventional Guinea gold voyage. Before he could pursue the new objective, though, he found himself embroiled in a civil war when a Sierra Leone king sought his aid to defeat a neighboring town. In exchange for Hawkins's help, the king promised Hawkins his choice of slaves from among the anticipated prisoners of war. Hawkins accepted the alliance. They assaulted the town by both sea and land. They burned the town to the ground and captured nearly nine hundred men, women, and children. Afterward, according to Hawkins, the king reneged on his promise, escaping in the dead of night with his own warriors and the majority of the prisoners. Despite the struggles in Guinea, Hawkins managed to secure about five hundred black Africans as captives and departed the Guinea coast.

As in previous voyages, Hawkins managed to unload the majority of his enslaved cargo at various stops in the Caribbean. The most significant event during the Caribbean leg of his venture occurred after he had concluded his business and set a course for England. His fleet of ships encountered a severe storm near Florida and sought a safe harbor to repair ships damaged in the storm. He landed at the island of San Juan de Ulúa in the Gulf of Mexico. The island and its harbor were a major staging area where armed Spanish fleets arrived once a year to transport to Spain the gold and silver farmed out of American mines. Unfortunately for Hawkins, he arrived at the harbor during that transport season. Officials at San Juan de Ulúa were daily expecting the arrival of the armed fleet, which meant that the harbor was abuzz with people and activity. Hawkins seized the island, holding hostage some one hundred Spanish sailors and officials. That next morning the anticipated Spanish fleet arrived. Aboard the flagship was a newly appointed viceroy of New Spain, Martín Enríquez. Initially, so as to prevent war, Hawkins released most of the men he held as prisoners, and he and Enríquez compromised to share the harbor. Days later, Enríquez attacked Hawkins's fleet. In the ensuing battle, Hawkins lost three of his original ships, including the Queen's *Jesus*. One ship, led by a young Sir Francis Drake, fled back to England, leaving Hawkins to rescue stranded sailors and navigate the last ship, badly damaged and overcrowded, back home alone.[43] He sustained a heavy loss in goods and men. One hundred and thirty men were killed in the battle at San Juan de Ulúa; fifty-two were taken prisoner.[44] Then, in the retreat from San Juan de Ulúa, Hawkins deposited another hundred men or so on a beach (Tampico) off the Mexican coast to relieve the strain of an overcrowded ship. Those men did not fare well. Most of them surrendered to the Spanish and faced imprisonment, forced conversion, or execution. Including the men he lost in Guinea and those who died from illness on the voyage home, Hawkins returned to England with fewer than fifteen men, from a journey that began with more than four hundred.[45]

Hawkins's expeditions represent a transition in English voyages to Guinea because Hawkins positioned Guinea as an intermediary stop, a point in a larger trade triangle, illustrating for the English the profitability of the Atlantic slave trade.[46] His voyages also did much to fuel hostilities between the Spanish and English. Shortly after he returned, Hawkins published a pamphlet of the events from that third voyage, "A True Declaration of the Troublesome Voyage of M. John Hawkins to the Parties of Guynea and the West Indies, in the Yeares of Our Lorde 1567 and 1568." In the pamphlet, he vilified Spain and sought royal support for financial restitution and the release of those taken prisoner at San Juan de Ulúa. To further press his suit, he testified about the events before England's High Court of Admiralty, established to arbitrate maritime disputes. Hawkins claimed huge financial losses resulting from the destruction of ships, weapons, supplies, trade goods, and other cargo that included some fifty enslaved men and women.[47] Hawkins's narrative, then, was not simply a report compiled for the benefit of investors or overseas merchants who wanted to expand England's trade reaches. The political and financial stakes were much higher, feeding into the quickly deteriorating relations between Protestant England and Catholic Spain.[48]

It is especially telling that in a text designed to fuel English passions against the Spanish, Hawkins employs a rhetorical strategy that figures prominently his interactions with black Africans in Sierra Leone. A close-reading of the text reveals the ways in which his encounters in Guinea emphasize Spain's treachery in the Americas. More specifically, in "A True Declaration of the Troublesome Voyage," Hawkins represents his voyage to Guinea as a foreshadowing of the troubles he will experience in San Juan de Ulúa. Foreshadowing manifests itself in the descriptions of his interactions with the king in Sierra Leone, a man who works as an African cognate for the viceroy Enríquez. Hawkins's encounter with the Guinea leader comes at a moment when he and his crew are especially vulnerable. The men are sick and risk getting sicker because of "the late time of the yeare" (sig. A iii, recto).[49] In addition, they have failed to secure a cargo that would warrant a trip across the Atlantic. Facing death and debt, Hawkins and his men "in consultacion" decide to head to the Gold Coast and there "obtain some gold for our wares" so they may at least break even (sig. A iii, recto). These details speak to Hawkins's mental state. Not incidentally, the details are juxtaposed with the town leader's proposition. "But even in that present instante," Hawkins writes, "there came to us a Negro sente from a Kynge oppressed of other kings his neyghboures desiring our aide, with promise that as many negrose as by these wars might be obtained aswell of his part as of ours sholde be at our pleasure whereupon we concluded to geve ayde" (sig. A iii, recto). The town leader's offer of an alliance is a saving grace that delivers Hawkins from his current struggles. Note that Hawkins represents the town's residents in terms quite similar to those used by Towerson; they are victims, "oppressed of other kings," not the Portuguese but other Guineans. Hawkins, even in his abject state, transforms into a liberator.

On January 15, 1567/68, Hawkins sends 120 of his men to help attack his "alyes adversaries" in a town of eight thousand (sig. A iiii, verso). They lose the battle and send a request to Hawkins for more manpower and resources. Hawkins goes himself, recognizing that "the good success of this enterprise might highly further the commodity of our voyage" (sig. A iiii, verso). Of this second battle, Hawkins writes:

I went my self and with the help of the king of our side assaulted the towne bothe by land and sea and very hardly with fyre (their houses beinge covered with drie palme leves) obtained the town, and put the inhabitants to flight where we toke 250 persones men women and children and by our frende the king of oure side there was taken 600 prisoners whereof we hoped to have had our choyse: but the Negro (in which nacion is seldome or never found troth) ment nothing lesse, for that night he removed his camp and prisoners, so that we were fayne to content us with those few which we had gotten our selves. (sig. A iiii, verso, recto)

Rhetorically, the passage renders Hawkins as fully invested in the alliance, so much so that the diction foregrounds the actions of the English and positions the Guinea allies as an auxiliary force *that helps* in the assault. He writes in terms of "our side" and refers to his ally as "frende," ultimately an ironic marker. Their opponents are rendered more or less inconsequential in the face of English land and sea might, which Hawkins does not deploy fully but "very hardly with fyre." Hawkins's investment in the alliance magnifies the duplicity of his false ally at the end of the scene. Interestingly, though, he does not dwell on the deception. He registers frustration and maybe a bit of annoyance, but he dismisses it as the usual behavior of one who comes from a culture in whom is "seldome or never found troth." In other words, any moral outrage Hawkins might feel is tapered by his expectations of black Africans. Those expectations, according to Kenneth Andrews, reflect the nature of Guinea-English interaction. Hawkins's sentiment, Andrews maintains, "would have been echoed by many an English Guinea trader, not because these English had preconceived ideas about black men, wide-eyed wonder being rather their typical state of mind, but because the particular conditions of their relationship with the Africans naturally bred mistrust" on both sides.[50]

Andrews's point here is well taken that we should be careful not to read racism into Hawkins's understanding of black Africans. The viewpoint, instead, is a product of encounters that were often unpredictable and unreliable. This is not to say, however, that the moment is not racially significant. Hawkins deems the town leader's actions as representative of the whole. He participates in a normalizing discourse that, according to Mary Louise Pratt, defines a group of people based on the actions of one. The nation of Negroes, to which Hawkins refers, is reduced to what Pratt would call an "iconic *he* (= the standard adult male specimen)," represented in this case by the town leader. This "iconic he" becomes "the subject of verbs in a timeless present tense [that] characterize anything 'he' is or does not as a particular event in time, but as an instance of a pregiven custom or trait. . . . Particular encounters between people get textualized, then, as enumerations of such traits."[51] Hawkins's reflection on the town leader's actions, and by extension the actions of black Africans, encodes difference. Guineans are untrustworthy in opposition to the English, who keep their promises. That difference, perhaps grounded in culture and contact as Andrews claims, resonates in discourses about the body that are already unfolding in the sixteenth century.[52]

The deliberate nature of Hawkins's rhetoric in this moment manifests itself even more clearly when compared to other accounts of the same moment. Three men traveling with Hawkins, one unnamed, produced narratives of the third voyage. Two, perhaps all three, sailed aboard the flagship alongside Hawkins and were among the hundred men Hawkins set down on an island during his retreat from San Juan de Ulúa. The first was Miles Phillips, only about thirteen at the time of the voyage. After more than a decade in Spanish custody in Mexico, he escaped back to England in 1582. Hakluyt published his account in *Principal Navigations* in 1589. The second was Job Hortop, who served as a gunner on the flagship. He published his account as a pamphlet in 1591, after which Hakluyt reprinted it in his second edition of *Principal Navigations* in 1599/1600. Regarding the third anonymous account, to which scholars refer as the "Cotton manuscript," historians speculate that its author was a trader, ship's officer, or a gentleman traveler on the voyage. The manuscript, not published until the twentieth century, offers the most detailed account of Hawkins's third voyage.[53]

With the exception of Phillips's, the narratives diverge significantly from Hawkins's rendition of the battle in Sierra Leone.[54] Neither Hortop nor the Cotton manuscript describes the Guinea king as duplicitous in the battle's aftermath.[55] Rendering the episode in only a couple sentences that imply rather than detail an alliance, Hortop recounts that Hawkins "valiantly tooke the towne" after which the English "tooke & caried thence for traffique to the *West Indies* 500. Negroes."[56] Most of the other prisoners of war, some seven thousand according to Hortop, were driven into the river and drowned. The Cotton manuscript does corroborate Hawkins's account by detailing his alliance and referring to the allied forces as "frendes." The account also confirms that the Guinea allied forces abandoned camp in the middle of the night. However, according to the Cotton manuscript, they sent a message to Hawkins explaining the reason for their departure—a king's son had died in the battle—and inviting him to come to their new location "and there they wolde make readye negros for him."⁵⁷ The narrative implies that the king(s) made good on the promise, noting that "with the negros the kinges sent and them the generall took and others that he had in the rivers by trafique, we had nowe abowt 470 negros in all."⁵⁸ These accounts portray Hawkins's encounter in Sierra Leone as fruitful, the alliance successful. The implication, based on information gleaned from the accounts of Hortop and the Cotton manuscript, is that Hawkins changes the details of his encounters with his Guinea ally to more closely match the treachery he experienced at San Juan de Ulúa. When faced with material details that do not align with his rhetorical aims, Hawkins—it appears—changes those details, a move that allows him to avoid the kind of narrative disruptions that will characterize the accounts of his English successors, Drake in particular.

Hair determines that Hawkins's accusation of Guinea duplicity was "largely unjustified."⁵⁹ It is unjustified, perhaps, but it is not inexplicable if we understand it as a rhetorical flourish designed to give meaning to his experiences at San Juan de Ulúa. Hawkins ends the discussion of his *failed* Guinea alliance with a bit of graciousness, finding a measure of contentment with the captives they secure. There is no such measure of graciousness in his description of events at San Juan de Ulúa. In the Americas, a false alliance escalates into full-blown treachery that demands redress. Hawkins begins the discussion by detailing the English's abject state, which harkens back to their circumstances in Sierra Leone; they desperately seek a port where they can make repairs to their weather-beaten ships. They try Florida but find "no place nor Haven" because the waters there are too shallow (sig. A vi, verso). With a new storm setting in, they travel three days west and are "inforced to take for [their] succour" the port at San Juan de Ulúa (sig. A vi, verso). At this point, the writing in the narrative turns self-conscious and defensive as Hawkins explains how and why he seizes three Spanish ships and takes hostage one hundred men "which passingers we hoped should be a meane to us the better to obtayne vittualles for oure money, and a quiet place for the reparinge of oure fleete" (sig. A vii, verso). Here, he notes his peaceful intentions, finding a "quiet place" and seeking supplies they can buy, not take. The seemingly aggressive acts of seizing ships and men are born of necessity, not malice. To further prove this, he mentions that twelve Spanish ships are at port loaded with gold and silver, all of which he sets "at libertye, withoute the taking from them the weight of a grote" (sig. A vii, verso). He also sends a message to officials in Mexico City informing them of his presence and requesting supplies. He refers to himself and crew as "frends of Kinge Phillipe," articulating the same kind of relationship he had with the Guinea town leader (sig. A vii, recto).⁶⁰

When the thirteen-ship Spanish fleet carrying the incoming viceroy of New Spain arrives at the port the next day, Hawkins strives for an alliance of a different sort—a truce. Over the course of three days, Hawkins negotiates with Enríquez, Hawkins requesting supplies and time to fix his ships, the viceroy requesting access to the port, which Hawkins has blocked off. They settle into an uneasy peace, as Hawkins notes, "the captaines of eache parte and inferior men of their partes promis[ed] greate amytie of all sides, which even as with all fidelitie was ment of our part the spainyardes ment nothing lesse of their partes" (sig. B ii, recto). Just as in his Guinea alliance, Hawkins emphasizes his sincerity. He intends to uphold the terms of this new agreement, but for the second time on the same voyage, he enters into an alliance with what he characterizes as a dissimulating partner. Not incidentally, Hawkins portrays Enríquez's insincerity by mimicking the diction with which he describes the intentions of the Guinea town leader. Both men "ment nothing lesse" than to deceive Hawkins. The events at San Juan de Ulúa, however, are not a simple deception masterminded by a "Negroe in whome is seldom or never found troth." His descriptions of the attack that ensues as a result of Enríquez's deception are much more extreme, Hawkins much more vehement. He describes Enríquez's actions as treason, and the Spaniards are enemies to whom his men must beg for mercy, a mercy "whyche," Hawkins proclaims, "I doughte was verye lytell" (sig. B v, verso).

Again, Hawkins's manipulation of diction and perspective are more pronounced when compared to Hortop's version of events.⁶¹ Hortop's account does corroborate Hawkins's sincerity in his dealings with Enriquez, describing Hawkins as "bearing a godly and Christian minde, voyde of fraude and deceit."⁶² He describes the Spaniards in contrast as "faithlesse."⁶³ However, Hortop, with rhetorical aims of his own, seems less invested in portraying the English as victims of a Spanish attack. While confirming the viceroy's deception, Hortop makes it clear that what unfolded at San Juan de Ulúa was, in fact, a battle, not merely an attack that left the English battered and broken. To that end, he catalogs the damage inflicted upon both sides. He notes, for example, that although the Spanish sunk the general's "ship called the *Angel*, and tooke the *Swallow*: the Spaniards Admirall had aboue threescore shot through her: many of his men were spoyled: foure other of their ships were sunke."⁶⁴ In one of the more vivid moments from his text, Hortop describes Hawkins's valor:

> Our Generall couragiously cheered vp his souldiers and gunners, and called to . . . his page for a cup of Beere, who brought it him in a siluer cup, and hee drinking to all men willed the gunners to stand by their Ordinance lustily like men. He had no sooner set the cup out of his hand, but a demy Culuerin shot stroke away the cup . . . which nothing dismaid our Generall, for he ceased not to incourage vs, saying, feare nothing, for God, who hath preserued me from this shot, will also deliuer vs from these traitours and villaines.[65]

For Hortop, the English are not pitiful victims of Spanish treachery but brave combatants. In all, Hortop claims, 540 Spaniards died in the battle, compared to 130 English.[66] Hawkins includes no details about his efforts to rally the troops or about Spanish casualties, which would have undermined the much more commiserative tone of his text.[67]

As Hortop's narrative (and the Cotton manuscript discussed earlier) illustrates, Hawkins had at his disposal a wealth of details from which to craft his narrative. In a text that is designed to condemn Spain and help him recover men and money from a disastrous encounter in the Americas, he relies on his interactions with black Africans in Guinea. This rhetorical move is all the more remarkable because certainly Hawkins did not need a Guinea counterpart to articulate his anti-Spanish sentiment. In 1569, relations between Spain and England were already such that he could have convinced English readers of the viceroy's "evil" deeds without mentioning his encounters in Sierra Leone. That he uses the same language, the same mode of representation, the same tone to discuss both events tells us something about the importance of black Africans in the political discourse of the day. For Hawkins, they are a viable literary and political tool used to sharpen, through mimicry, anti-Spanish rhetoric. Paralleling events also allows Hawkins to extract some measure of pity from readers and justify his ultimate lamentation, with which he ends the narrative, that "if all the miseries and troublesome affayres of this sorowefull voyadge shoulde be perfectlye and throughlye written, there shoulde need a paynfull man with his penne, and as greate a tyme as he had that wrote the lives and deaths of the martyrs" (sig. B viii, verso).[68]

In his narration of the troublesome incidents that comprise his third voyage, Hawkins employs a representational strategy similar to that of Towerson, whereby black Africans are rendered as agents; the actual actors are the European forces fighting for supremacy of Atlantic trade routes.[69] Hawkins extends this representation to the Caribbean and turns anti-Portuguese sentiment into an anti-Spanish one. Importantly, he relies on his interactions with a black African town leader in Sierra Leone to articulate his experiences with a Spanish viceroy, helping to fuel England's growing suspicion and animosity toward Spain. Several years later, his distant cousin, Sir Francis Drake, will employ a similar strategy to articulate his exploits on the Panama isthmus. Drake's efforts, though, are complicated by his representations of black Africans that muddle more than vilify Spanish character. This first chapter illustrates the tropes and patterns that emerge in narratives of early English voyages to Guinea. Subsequent chapters examine the ways in which these tropes and patterns inform and strain the narrative strategies of five English travelers to the Americas, beginning with Sir Francis Drake.

CHAPTER 2

Reconstructing the Ethiop
Sir Francis Drake and the Cimarrones of Panama

While John Hawkins traveled back and forth to London seeking restitution and the release of his sailors from Spanish custody after the events at San Juan de Ulúa in 1568, a very young Francis Drake developed and executed his own form of retaliation—pillaging Spanish settlements on the Panama isthmus. In January each year, the Spanish organized caravans of mules to carry cargoes of gold and silver and other goods from locations on the Pacific side of South America (mainly in Peru and Chile) up to Panama City. Then, by land the caravans cut across the isthmus, traveling to the port town of Nombre de Dios. There, just as at San Juan de Ulúa, the cargo was transferred to heavily armed ships and transported across the Atlantic Ocean to Spain.

Drake's plan was to seize Nombre de Dios and raid the town's storehouse. When that plan failed, he decided to intercept mule trains as they crossed the isthmus. Based on the recommendation of a slave informant, Drake aligned his efforts with a group of Cimarrones, former slaves who had run away from their Spanish masters and built settlements in the Panamanian mountains and jungles. Cimarrones had been waging guerilla warfare against the Spanish for years before Drake arrived. They, themselves, had attacked Spain on more than one occasion in the very manner Drake proposed. Together, Drake and the Cimarrones waited and watched. They finally spotted a caravan outside of Nombre de Dios in April 1573. A mixture of Englishmen, Cimarrones, and a few Frenchmen, who had stumbled onto the scene a month earlier, all descended upon an outmatched envoy of Spanish commissaries and slaves, quickly ridding the mule caravan of nearly all it carried. Despite heavy losses, including two of his brothers, Drake escaped Panama with tons of valuables to fill English coffers and avenge his and Hawkins's, if not the nation's, pride.[1]

This book began with a brief introduction of the narrative that relates Drake's activities on the Panama isthmus, *Sir Francis Drake Revived*. Here, I continue the discussion, emphasizing the ways in which Drake's articulation of his ventures in Panama mirrors that of his travel predecessors in Guinea and results in a series of narrative conflicts, mostly at the level of characterization. In a sense, Hawkins's and Towerson's narratives open an imaginative space for Drake's text. *Sir Francis Drake Revived* performs much of the same rhetorical work as Hawkins's *Troublesome Voyage*—vilifying Spain and articulating Drake's own outrage about the events off the coast of Mexico. He specifically references San Juan de Ulúa in the narrative. Also like Hawkins's, Drake's narrative positions black Africans as a prominent feature of the rhetorical landscape. For Hawkins black Africans reflect the negative character traits of the Spanish and, importantly, magnify Hawkins's role as victim. In Drake's narrative, black Africans occupy the role of victim, and he renders himself a hero, arrived in Panama to rescue Cimarrones. In this way, Drake evokes Towerson, who portrayed himself as a liberating force protecting Guinea traders from Spain's Catholic brethren in Portugal. In Drake's narrative Hawkins's anti-Spanish rhetoric combines with Towerson's liberation rhetoric to create an amalgam that scholars might more readily recognize as a discourse of the Black Legend.[2]

The Black Legend was about oppositions: Catholicism versus Protestantism; Spain versus England (and other Protestant nations); Europe versus America; good versus evil. Native Americans were at the heart of that discourse. Descriptions and images of their broken, abused bodies circulated throughout Europe as proof of Spain's corruption.[3] Their victimization fueled moral imperatives for other European nations to rescue America's native inhabitants. There was no moral imperative, no discourse without a victim. By the time Drake penned his narrative in 1592, Spain's image had already blackened thanks to the translation of Las Casas's *Brevísima Relación* into English almost a decade before and the narratives of Drake's fellow sailors Miles Phillips and Job Hortop, discussed in the previous chapter. That Drake's narrative reflects a discourse of the Black Legend, then, is not surprising. Nor is it surprising that he supplants Native Americans with black Africans as the victims of Spanish cruelty. Towerson had already established precedence in his portrayal of Guinean-Portuguese relations. This chapter emphasizes instead the narrative consequences inherent in Drake's rhetorical choices.

In vilifying Spain, Drake revels in an English, Protestant identity.[4] Importantly, that identity gains its meaning from the presence in his narrative of that group of Cimarrones through whom Drake renders himself in opposition as a liberator come to free them and weaken Spain's hold on the Caribbean.[5] Drake's text extends Toni Morrison's argument about nineteenth- and twentieth-century American literature and the ways in which that literature employed a symbolic "Africanist presence," designed to more clearly delineate constructions of whiteness (or in the case of Drake, Englishness) and monitor certain social, political, and cultural structures.[6] The black Africans who populate Drake's narrative reflect Morrison's theory—but with one key distinction. The Africanist presence for Drake had an actual, historical referent, a population of autonomous black Africans whose actions in the material world outside the text conflicted with Drake's rhetorical goals. If we can believe the reports of Spanish officials living on the Panama isthmus in the sixteenth century, the Cimarrones were not simply victims of Spanish tyranny. Indeed, Drake's narrative suggests as much.

A close-reading of *Sir Francis Drake Revived* reveals a number of inconsistencies in Drake's representation of himself and of black Africans, evident in moments like the exchange between Drake and the Cimarrón leader Pedro that I discuss in this book's Introduction.[7] I read those inconsistencies as suggestive of the ways in which Drake's rhetorical imaginings were circumscribed by the actual, physical presence of black Africans. The inconsistencies do not make transparent the physical presences of black Africans or allow us to claim with certainty particular historical understandings about the true nature of Drake's interactions with the Cimarrones. The inconsistencies do, however, demand that we pause in our reading and approach Drake's angle of vision with more circumspection. Put another way, Drake's interactions with black Africans strain the limits of his rhetorical imagination. In his efforts to portray them as victims of Spanish cruelty—in line with Black Legend discourse—Drake also renders them an autonomous body that resists rather than surrenders to Spanish oppression. They disrupt Drake's narrative by denying him a victim, which destabilizes the anti-Spanish rhetoric.

Plotting Revenge: The Personal as Political

Drake is perhaps most famous for his 1577 circumnavigation of the world; he was only the second explorer to accomplish such a feat, and unlike his predecessor, Magellan, he lived to tell the story. In the decade leading up to his circumnavigation, Drake struggled among his English peers to gain respect, resulting, in part, from the events at San Juan de Ulúa. Drake commanded

Hawkins's fifty-ton *Judith*. In the battle's immediate aftermath, Drake made the controversial decision to flee back to England, ignoring Hawkins's command that he help rescue stranded sailors and relieve Hawkins's overcrowded ship. In his narrative, Hawkins accused Drake of having "forsoke vs in oure greate miserie."[8] In the subsequent years and based on his early raids in the Caribbean, Drake garnered a reputation as a pirate, a rogue. The Spanish dubbed him *El Draque*. That 1577 circumnavigation, as John Parry states it, "proved to be the turning point of Drake's career. By means of this voyage he graduated, one might say, from slightly disreputable though successful slaver and pirate to famous privateer-explorer . . . respected admiral and ultimately a folk hero and a national legend."[9] After his circumnavigation, Drake led a number of attacks (or more precisely, raids) on Spanish holdings in the Caribbean and even at Cádiz on the southern coast of Spain. In 1588, he served as vice admiral for the English fleet that defeated the Spanish Armada.

By the time he died in 1596, Drake's biographers had a great deal of fodder from which to construct a national hero. As England's imperial energies grew more fervent at the turn of the seventeenth century, they looked to the memory of Drake for inspiration. He became his own kind of mythology, as Richard Frohock notes. He was such a popular figure, Frohock argues, because English historians could readily construct "his exploits as an example of what might be achieved in America."[10] Within the context of Drake's mythology, his raids at Nombre de Dios are characterized as a minor excursion, a prelude to more significant escapades. Hodgkins, for example, argues that Drake's liberatory persona begins not in Panama in 1572 but in California seven years later when Drake becomes England's white legend, a presence offering kinder, gentler treatment to America's natives. In 1579, during his famed circumnavigation, Drake arrived off the coast of what is today San Francisco, where he encountered the Miwok. The Miwok, Drake's men claimed, treated them like gods, presenting them gifts, offering land, and begging the English to heal them. During the English's three-week stay, Drake and his men proselytized to the natives while trying to convince them that the English were not gods. The Miwok elevated Drake to chieftain, and he claimed the territory for England, naming it Nova Albion [New Britain]. According to Hodgkins, this encounter brought "together in unique combination many elements crucial to England's imperial imagination."[11] Those elements included images of indigenous populations as "helpless natives needing liberation from . . . sinister European powers" and "the brave, kind pious Englishman to whom the benighted natives instinctively and gladly offer worship and sovereignty."[12]

If not for the efforts of his nephew, perhaps the details of Drake's 1572 raid would have remained forever obscure. Drake did not publish an account of the events during his lifetime.[13] His nephew, also named Francis Drake, published the first full account of the raid in 1626, thirty years after the elder Drake's death.[14] The actual crafting of the narrative, though, occurred while Drake was still alive. According to the title page, Philip Nichols, a minister, compiled the narrative proper from the notes of Drake and "Christofer Ceely, Ellis Hixon, and others, who were in the same voyage with him."[15] The narrative was "reviewed also by Sr. Francis Drake himself before his death, & much holpen and enlarged, by divers notes, with his owne hand here and there inserted."[16] More than any other text discussed in this book, *Sir Francis Drake Revived* challenges conventional understandings of authorship by making explicit what can only be implied about the other narratives—authorship is a collaborative process. Here is a text without a central author. At best, Philip Nichols functions as an editor, a compiler of information, of diverse perspectives. Drake functions in the same role with his "owne hand here and there inserted." Drake's nephew was a third editor, who helped shape the narrative by writing a dedicatory epistle addressed to King Charles I, sitting on the throne in 1626, and a second letter to the reader. Both letters express his hope that his uncle's daring deeds might "stirre" up the present age and "advantage future imployments." Then, of course, there are the notes and perspectives from sailors also named on the title page who traveled with Drake and recorded their own versions of events.

Sir Francis Drake Revived registers literally what Roland Barthes understands theoretically about the nature of text as "a multi-dimensional space in which a variety of writings, none of them original, blend and clash."[17] He insists that "the text is a tissue of quotations drawn from the innumerable centres of culture."[18] The author, then, functions as an interlocutor who, according to Barthes, does not create a single meaning but rather compiles—through the act of writing—multiple meanings or discourses in texts. In a sense, all the authors discussed in this book function as compilers, interlocutors who mediate for readers a series of cultural encounters that produce multiple meanings or narratives. The authorial complexities notwithstanding, Drake ultimately takes credit for *Sir Francis Drake Revived*. In an epistolary preface addressed to Queen Elizabeth and signed by Drake in 1592, he calls the narrative "the first fruites" of his pen (sig. A4, verso).[19] Because of this, I assign the narrative's rhetorical design and motives to Drake but with the understanding that Drake's rhetorical imagination has been compromised—that is to say, guided, filtered, and augmented by other perspectives: and not just those explicitly referenced on the title page. As we will see shortly, Drake's interactions with black Africans on the Panama isthmus are intimately linked to Drake's representations of the Spanish and of himself.

Sir Francis Drake Revived is an anti-Spanish tract and propaganda. As such, the text highlights Drake's unique position within the service of the queen and his daring raids on the Spanish Main. In the letter addressed to Queen Elizabeth, Drake reminds her of his faithful service. He is confident that she will find his actions against Spain wholly justified:

> Madam, seeing diuers haue diuersly reported, and written, of these voyages and actions which J haue attempted and made, . . . whereby many vntruthes haue bene published, and the certaine truth concealed: . . . So I haue accounted it my duty, to present this Discourse to your Ma$^{tie.}$ as of right, either for it selfe, being the first fruits of your seruants Pen, or for the matter, being seruice done to your Ma$^{ti.}$ by your poore vassall against your great enemy, at such times, in such places, and after such sorte, as may seeme strange to those, that are not acquainted with the whole cariage thereof: but will be a pleasing remembrance to your Highnesse, who take th'aparent height of th'almighties fauour towards you, by these euents, as truest instruments, humbly submitting my selfe to your Gracious censure, both in writing & presenting. (sig. A4, verso)

Although Drake does not explicitly reference the events at San Juan de Ulúa in this letter, for sure the episode was among the Spanish acts that fueled Drake's deeds against England's "great enemy." In fact, he begins the narrative proper by explaining that the Nombre de Dios raid is retaliation for his "hauing beene greiuosly indamaged at Saint *Iohn de Vllua* in the bay of *Mexico*, with Captaine *Iohn Hawkins,* in the yeares 67. and 68. not onely in the losse of his goods of some value, but also of his kinsmen & friends, and that by the falshood of *Don Martin Henriquez* then the viceroy of *Mexico*" (2). Then, after failing to receive restitution for the losses, Drake says he "vsed such helpes as hee might" by organizing his own retaliatory strikes (2).[20]

Despite what the opening lines of the narrative might suggest, the raid on Nombre de Dios was not simply a personal vendetta. Drake's enmity reflected a national anti-Spanish sentiment. In the second half of the sixteenth century, Queen Elizabeth and Spain's Philip II were involved in a kind of cold war, fueled by religious differences and commercial urgings. England watched Spain warily—and jealously—as Spain's wealth and influence spread across Europe, a growth fueled by New World profits. Among England's fears was that Spain would use its wealth and power to invade northern Europe and re-impose Catholicism. William Maltby articulates the tension:

> Elizabethan England was generally regarded as the natural leader of the reformed camp, while Spain was the natural leader of the Catholics. Though possessing a large Catholic population and Queen who was temperamentally averse to ideologies, England was one of the few European states that possessed both an established non-Roman church and the means with which to resist a revived papacy. Spain, on the other hand, was the greatest military power in the world. It possessed a strong central government and it was overwhelmingly Catholic in policy and popular sympathy.[21]

Queen Elizabeth saw in Drake's early Caribbean escapades an opportunity to attack Spain indirectly and weaken the country financially, thereby reducing the threat of invasion. An added benefit was that Drake's piracy provided a convincing illusion that England could profit from the New World without engaging in the barbarity and cruelty inherent in conquest. As Edmund Campos articulates it, "The virtue of piracy as an ideological alternative to straightforward territorial acquisition and enslavement of native populations was that it constituted a second-hand acquisition that removed the English from the dirty business of labor and exploitation."[22] Queen Elizabeth supported Drake's efforts inconspicuously. She condemned him in public but praised him behind closed doors.[23] All the while England sought to justify its own foray across the Atlantic by propagating the image of Spain as the Black Legend.[24]

Reconstructing the Ethiop

In his efforts to justify his piratical behavior and vilify Spain in his narrative, Drake factors the Cimarrones prominently into the narrative's rhetorical landscape. Mostly, he characterizes them as an auxiliary force. They guide the English through the Panamanian forest; they spy at Nombre de Dios and Panama City. They perform manual labor for Drake and his men. At times, Drake refers to them in possessive terms, as "our Symerons." In short, the Cimarrones are *the help*. A number of historical studies have examined the relationship between Drake and his Cimarrón counterparts. Discussions, however, replicate Drake's perspective of the alliance, assigning him agency as the author of the collaboration and reducing the Cimarrones to servants.[25] This chapter's textual analysis does not take for granted a hierarchical relationship between Drake and the Cimarrones but instead looks beyond Drake's characterization to interrogate how and why the alliance with an English pirate would have benefited the Cimarrones. It is quite possible that they did not see themselves as working *for* Drake but working *with* him. They may have even seen the alliance as one in which Drake was subservient to them. These possibilities manifest themselves when we shift our angle of vision from Drake to the Cimarrones and ask questions (even those that we cannot answer) about their agency. The most important question of all is this: How might the Cimarrones' actions in the material world beyond the text have affected Drake's narrative decisions?

There were approximately three thousand Cimarrones situated into three primary settlements, or *palenques,* on the Panama isthmus. In addition, there were two main Spanish settlements—Panama City on the Pacific side and the much smaller, less populated town of Nombre de Dios facing the Atlantic. The two settlements were separated by a vast jungle, swampland, and scattered mountain ranges that made travel particularly difficult. But travel was necessary as the link between Panama City and Nombre de Dios was one of the most efficient routes, though vulnerable to Cimarrón attacks, for transporting to Spain the gold and silver extracted from mines along the west coast of South America. Sometimes when cargoes started out from Panama City, the mule caravans traveled to the town of Venta de Cruces, about six leagues northwest of Panama City. From there, the cargoes were transferred to boats and carried up the River Chagre to the Caribbean Sea, then sailed northeast to the port at Nombre de Dios. This route, which the Spanish chose mostly for transport of heavy, bulky cargoes, was vulnerable to attacks from French pirates who discovered the route in the 1560s.[26]

By the time Drake arrived on the isthmus in the 1570s, the situation between the Spanish and Cimarrones had already been marked by decades of hostilities that began as early as 1525 when the first enslaved men and women escaped their Spanish masters and hid in the Panama interior. Over the next five decades the Spanish funded expensive military efforts to root out Cimarrón communities and bring the rebellious populations back under Spanish control. Cimarrones actively resisted such efforts, staging their own attacks on Panama City and Nombre de Dios. They raided mule trains and courted or stole away enslaved men and women from Spanish masters. The Cimarrones' activity is recorded quite vividly in the correspondence of Spanish officials living on the isthmus, especially in the second half of the sixteenth century. In 1570, for example, a judge with the Spanish high court, or *Audiencia,* in Panama City complained to the Crown that military strategies for eliminating the Cimarrón threat were ineffective and poorly funded. He beseeched the Crown to increase taxes "on merchandise entering Nombre de Dios," and he predicted that if the Crown did not act soon to secure the isthmus, "the damage will be irreparable, because the multitude of the blacks is increasing, and from everywhere many are joining them, and every day they become bolder" (10). In one particular act of daring in 1570 the Cimarrones constructed a gallows along the road outside Panama City and hung up knives, threatening to behead Spanish military officials.[27]

Although Drake characterizes the Spanish as oppressive and aggressive in their treatment of the Cimarrones, the narrative does implicitly acknowledge the reciprocal nature of the violence. At the beginning of the narrative, Drake and his men are in the Caribbean Sea, sailing north up the coast toward Nombre de Dios. They encounter a group of enslaved black Africans on an island several days east of the town, called the Isle of Pinos [Pines]. According to Drake, those enslaved men, who are "lading planck and timber" onto frigates, explain that Nombre de Dios is expecting the arrival of additional soldiers from Panama to protect them from Cimarrones (8). This is an early indication that the Cimarrones are not a passive presence on the isthmus. Drake dismisses this indication when, in the next line, he explains that the Cimarrones are "a black people which about 80 years past fled from the Spaniards their masters, by reason of their cruelty, and are since grown to a nation, under two kings of their own. The one inhabiteth to the west, the other to the east of the way from Nombre de Dios to Panama" (8). While acknowledging Cimarrón autonomy, the description's pathetic overtone casts Spain as the Black Legend by referencing "their cruelty" and renders the Cimarrones as refugees, who "fled" from their Spanish masters. The Black Legend rhetoric intensifies in Drake's interactions with those enslaved men on the island, who he assumes would become Cimarrones if given the opportunity. After the men inform him of the political situation at Nombre de Dios, Drake commandeers their frigates and sets down the men on the mainland, farther away from Nombre de Dios. He imagines that he has done them a great favor by steering them away from the town, which would allow them to escape their Spanish masters and "perhaps join themselves to their countrymen the Cimarrones and gain their liberty" (8). Here, Drake suggests that he himself is the vehicle to the enslaved men's freedom and their deliverance from Spanish cruelty.

The events that unfold in Nombre de Dios several days later complicate Drake's liberator persona when his predawn breach of the town is made all the more difficult because of the Cimarrones' past activities, which have left the town in a perpetual state of wariness. Despite the early hour, residents are ready to arm themselves as English forces invade the town. According to Drake, the people quickly signal alarms "(being very ready thereto, by reason of their often disquieting by their near neighbours the Symerons) as we perceived, not only by the noise and cries of the people, but by the bell ringing out and drums running up and down the town" (11). The English manage to seize the town but suffer a number of casualties, including a dead trumpeter. They retreat after Drake, shot in the leg, faints. Rather than press forward to raid the town's treasure houses, which Drake insists were full of silver, his men prudently retreat and seek medical attention for Drake.[28] In this opening scene, we see that Drake intends to represent the Cimarrones as oppressed, with himself the avenger. We see just as clearly, however, the struggle inherent in such a rhetorical move because the Spanish and Cimarrones have a contentious history that bears its marks throughout the town, suggesting that the Cimarrones are more than passive victims of an oppressive empire.

In addition to the already volatile political climate on the isthmus, two key figures emerge as especially disruptive in Drake's narrative. The first of these figures is Diego, who is not a Cimarrón but an enslaved man who seeks asylum among the English during that Nombre de Dios raid. As Drake and his men enter the town, they seek out the governor's house, which they find with the help of a captured soldier. They expect to find there a cache of treasure being readied for transport onto the Spanish treasure fleet. Their expectations are confirmed when they see a packed mule ready for travel and a "huge heap of silver" stored in a lower room "being a pile of bars of silver of, as near as we could guess, seventy feet in length, of ten feet in breadth, and twelve feet in height, piled up against the wall" (14). Rather than raiding the house, Drake commands his men "straightly that none of vs should touch a barre of siluer, but stand vpon our weapons" (14). There is a much larger treasure if they keep marching to the "King's Treasure House."[29] At this point, Drake receives word that his pinnaces and the mission are in danger based on information from an enslaved man in the town—Diego. Diego tells the English that the Spanish have 150 soldiers en route to the town, and they will arrive before dawn. In the way of backstory, Drake explains that Diego is one "who in the time of the first conflict came and called to our pinnaces to know whether they were Captain Drake's? And upon answer received continued entreating to be taken aboard, though he had first three or four shot made at him, until at length they fetched him." (15). Drake clearly positions Diego as a refugee. His "continued entreating" suggests a measure of desperation. He is so desperate to escape his Spanish masters, in fact, that he runs toward the English even as they fire "three or four shot made at him."

After Drake and his men retreat from Nombre de Dios—with Diego in tow but none of the town's treasure—they regroup for two days on an island about a league west of Nombre de Dios, the Isle of Bastimientos, or, as Drake and his men call it, the "Isle of Victualles," because of its plentiful resources. Once there, Diego acts more clearly as informant, refugee, and mediator. The English question him regarding the logistics of Spain's transportation of gold and silver from Panama to Nombre de Dios. He suggests Drake's mission would be successful only with the help of the Cimarrones. Diego tells him: "We might have gold and silver enough, if we would by means of the Symerons, whom though he had betrayed divers times (being used thereto by his masters) so that he knew they would kill him if they got him, yet if our Captain would undertake his protection he durst adventure his life, because he knew our Captain's name was most precious and highly honoured of them" (20). Drake again portrays Spain within the discourse of the Black Legend by suggesting that the Spanish "used" Diego to betray the Cimarrones, who now want to kill him for that betrayal. Drake's rescue of Diego, then, is not just a rescue from the Cimarrones but also from the Spanish's poor usage. The moment also establishes Drake's renown with Diego's proclamation that Drake's "name was most precious and highly honoured" on the isthmus. The moment performs pointed rhetorical and discursive work for Drake, but it muddles Diego's character. On the surface, Diego wants Drake to "undertake his protection," but the people from whom he claims he wants protection are the very people he suggests Drake seek out.

This incongruity invites readers to view Drake's portrayal of Diego's actions a little more critically. When we do so, Diego emerges as a much more complicated character. Consider this: Drake casts himself as a liberator in the narrative's opening scene, and Diego plays the part of one needing liberation. Drake entertains notions of self-grandeur, and Diego flatters his ego by proclaiming Drake's name precious and honored. Diego seems to possess a certain savvy, measuring his words to stir Drake's passions and sympathies. Perhaps he dissimulates as one needing refuge, which secures his freedom from Nombre de Dios. Even more interesting is what happens after he joins the English. Diego initiates the English-Cimarrón alliance, which gains him a political advantage. As a cultural mediator, his value increases with the English, and if the Cimarrones really want to kill Diego for past transgressions, then the alliance becomes a peace offering. Through the English and the resources they bring with them, Diego can ingratiate himself to the Cimarrones, an important counterculture on the isthmus that has for decades offered black Africans an alternative to Spanish slavery. It is a win-win situation for Diego, assuming the alliance works. The textual traces of Diego that manifest themselves as incongruity suggest that Diego, more than a rhetorical tool for Drake, pursued his own agenda.[30]

As a textual representation, Diego occupies a rather complex position. He is a primary mediator between cultures, who through his own savvy works situations to his advantage. In African American literature, this kind of representation will eventually become the trickster figure, best represented by Brer Rabbit or the grinning, jovial, overly accommodating slave who behind the grin subverts the will of his master. Diego's representation also evokes seventeenth-century representations of Native Americans. Remember that Drake casts him as a refugee—in need of saving. That, coupled with his role as informant and mediator, renders him a literary progenitor of Native Americans like Squanto and Pocahontas. One of the most popular and enduring New World images of natives from the seventeenth century is of the Massachusetts's seal in which a Native American stands in the center calling out to the English, "Come over and help us."[31] For Drake's purposes, then, Diego is valuable because he embodies Drake and England's role as liberator.

When we read Diego's interactions with Drake against the grain, his character foreshadows the ways in which the Cimarrones at large might dissimulate in their encounters with Drake. The first actual encounter between Drake and the Cimarrones occurs many weeks after Diego initially presents the suggestion. In the weeks leading up to that first meeting, Drake engages in a number of raids, most in the vicinity of Cartagena and other settlements along the coast of present-day Colombia. The raids are difficult to execute as news travels fast in the region. By the time Drake arrives at Cartagena, for example, emissaries from Nombre de Dios are already there. Soldiers patrol the coast, and Drake hears warning bells ringing ominously. He succeeds in capturing several small vessels loaded mostly with foodstuff but fails to capture a large prize.

In late August, he leaves Cartagena and heads back west to find a well-concealed port where he and his men can hide for a while and regain the advantage of surprise. He establishes a hideaway in the Gulf of Uraba, roughly halfway between Cartagena and Nombre de Dios. For fifteen days, the men build a fortified settlement there, dividing their time evenly between hard labor and recreation. In early September, Drake finally takes steps to secure an alliance by sending his brother John Drake with Diego to find the Cimarrones. They head west while Drake takes two pinnaces and heads east again to the Colombian coast in search of treasure and provisions.

The two groups eventually rendezvous at a location Drake calls "Port Plenty," located on the Isle of Pinos. At Port Plenty, Drake receives the news that his brother and Diego succeeded in finding the Cimarrones. He relates the details of that initial English-Cimarrón contact:

> Captaine *Iohn Drake* hauing one of our Pinnaces as was appojnted, went in with the maine, and as he rowed a loofe the shoare· where hee was directed by *Diego* the Negroe aforesaid, which willingly came vnto vs at *Nombre de Dios,* hee espyed certaine of the *Symerons*, with whome he delt so effectually, that in conclusion he left two of our men with their Leader, and brought aboard two of theirs: agreeing that they should meete him againe the next day, at a Riuer midway betweene the *Cabezas* and our Shippes, which they named *Rio Diego*. (33)

Remarkably, Diego approaches the Cimarrones alone, an odd act of courage for one who has previously huddled behind the English, insisting that the Cimarrones want to kill him. By Drake's account, Diego maneuvers a meeting between the two parties. The narrative does not relate the conversation that transpires between Diego and the Cimarrones, but we can guess how the conversation might have unfolded. Might Diego have flattered the Cimarrones (the way he did Drake)? Maybe he tells them that the English have taken him hostage and ordered he do their bidding, or maybe he emphasizes the need for an alliance, convincing them they can exploit English resources. Whatever the conversation the end result is that John Drake "left two of our men with their leader, and brought aboard two of theirs" with plans to meet the next day at the Rio Diego, about twenty miles northwest of Port Plenty.[32] Drake goes on to explain that the two Cimarrón pledges express joy at his arrival: "These two being very sensible men, chosen out by their commander, did with all reverence and respect declare unto our Captain that their nation conceived great joy of his arrival, because they knew him to be an enemy to the Spaniards, not only by his late being in Nombre de Dios, but also by his former voyages; and therefore were ready to assist and fauour his enterprises against his and their enemies to the vttermost" (33). This moment effectively diminishes the Cimarrones, now reduced to a kind of hero worship of Drake. Even the reverential language casts them as inferiors. In addition, we see liberation rhetoric at work; the Cimarrones "conceived great joy" that Drake has arrived to help them against their enemy—the same way Towerson helped residents in the town of Shama and Hawkins rushed to the aid of a Guinea king in Sierra Leone. As a result, the men are "ready to assist and fauour" Drake's "enterprises" as faithful servants. That these two men appear to subordinate themselves to Drake resonates clearly with Diego, who also appears to flatter the Englishman. Given the complex power dynamics at play between the English and Guinean traders in Towerson's and Hawkins's narratives and given the inconsistencies in Diego's representation in this narrative, we should not take for granted the sincerity of Drake's Cimarrón guests. If the Cimarrones believe Drake a demi-god or savior, the terms for their meeting the next day do not suggest it. They swap the same number of pledges, and they agree to meet each other halfway.

If Drake possesses any measure of cynicism about the Cimarrones, the narrative does not display it. He accepts them at face value, an odd naiveté given what he presumably witnessed on Hawkins's third expedition when, according to Hawkins, the Guinea king reneged on his promise to supply slaves. Drake's apparent naiveté might not be naiveté at all. As discussed in chapter 1, Hortop and the Cotton manuscript render the alliance between Hawkins and the Guinea king(s) in Sierra Leone as a fruitful collaboration. If what they say is true, Drake would have seen firsthand the benefits of English-African alliance, not betrayal. Another possibility here is that Drake does not consider at all Hawkins's (failed) alliance. Perhaps, though not likely, he recognizes ethnic and cultural nuance and approaches the Cimarrones without the baggage of those experiences from 1567/68.

Whatever he might have gleaned about black African populations on the African west coast, Drake renders the Cimarrones in Panama in the vein of noble savages. In their meeting that next day at the Rio Diego, the Cimarrones explain that they discard into the river the gold and silver they raid from the Spanish, but they cannot retrieve it presently for the English because the water is too high. Drake then says, "This answer, although it were somewhat unlooked for, yet nothing discontented us, but rather persuaded us farther of their honest and faithful meaning toward us" (36). Drake does not ponder the possibility that maybe the Cimarrones have lied to him, protecting their own stores of wealth.

That the Cimarrones hoard at least some of the gold they raid from the

Spanish is suggested in Drake's interactions with the Cimarrón leader Pedro, the second figure in the narrative who disrupts Drake's rhetorical design. In addition to the episode involving Drake's consumption of the otter meat, discussed in the Introduction, Drake ends his narrative with a final encounter between the two men. That encounter, more so than any other, suggests that the nature of their relationship is a true negotiation between equals. Both the English and the Cimarrones are at port somewhere in a headland of the Cativaas islands, about twenty-five leagues northwest of their old hideaway at Port Plenty. Drake's vessels are finally loaded with treasure after nearly a year of failed attempts to raid storehouses across the Panama isthmus. With the help of the Cimarrones and a French buccaneer named Guillaume Le Testu, they succeed in pillaging a mule train just outside of Nombre de Dios in April 1573. They capture tons of silver and gold, so much they cannot carry it all. What they cannot hold, they bury in crab holes, near rotted trees, and in a shallow river. They come back several days later to retrieve the buried treasure only to discover that the Spanish have recovered most of it—thanks to the tortured confession of a captured Frenchman. Still, Drake and his men walk away with a significant haul.

As he prepares to take his leave of the Cimarrones and the Panama isthmus, Drake performs a final grand gesture. He invites four of the Cimarrón leaders, including Pedro, aboard his ships, to sift through the bounty and take a gift as a token of gratitude. For sure, it is a patronizing gesture, a show of generosity a lord might bestow on a faithful tenant—or more precisely what Queen Elizabeth will do for Drake when he returns home. Pedro, though, refuses the patronizing gesture, turning his attention instead to a French sword Drake had received the month before from Le Testu. The sword had at one point belonged to France's King Henri II. Drake values the sword, which is not part of the bounty from which he invites Pedro to choose. What is more, Pedro requests the sword not as a gift but as a purchase. He offers Drake gold in exchange. Drake hesitates but relinquishes the sword explaining that he

> could have been content to have made no such exchange, but yet desirous to content him that had deserved so well, he gave it him with many good words; who received it with no little joy, affirming that if he should give his wife and children (which he loved dearly) in lieu of it, he could not sufficiently recompense it (for he would present his king with it, who he knew would make him a great man, even for this very gift's sake); yet in gratuity and stead of other requital of this jewel, he

desired our Captain to accept these four pieces of gold, as a token of his thankfulness to him and a pawn of his faithfulness during life. (92)

By focusing on Pedro's profuse gratitude and his vow of "faithfulness during life," Drake diminishes Pedro to the level of servant, one who "deserved so well." Pedro, though, is more than a servant for Drake—as suggested by the four pieces of gold he pays Drake and his expectation that the sword will "make him a great man." Pedro reveals that the gold he offers to Drake is part of a stash he "had hidden, intending to have reserved [it] until another voyage" (91). The Cimarrones apparently do not dump into the river *all* of the gold and silver they plunder from the Spanish. Pedro's apparently calculated moves complicate Drake's rhetorical intentions as the monarchy/subject paradigm Drake attempts to construct by opening up the ships' coffers morphs into a mercantile paradigm. Pedro speaks a commercial English; his actions suggest political ambitions for which he manipulates Drake. Granted, the gold does not impress Drake, given he already has ships full of it. He is locked into this exchange, though, a reluctant peddler who understands he must negotiate; his future relationship with the Cimarrones and further raids on the Spanish are at stake. In a sense, Drake and Pedro's ambitions mirror each other. Drake will present his queen with ships of gold and silver and in return receive acclaim; Pedro will present his king with a fancy French sword and in return will become a great man.

This speculation about Pedro's motives, and by extension those of Diego, gains credence when compared to an incident two years prior on the isthmus involving a Cimarrón named Pedro Mandinga. In March 1571, French pirates planned to raid the trading post of Venta de Cruces on the Chagre River, about five leagues northwest of Panama City. The post served as a way station with warehouses inside which the Spanish stored silver and other valuable goods between the rainy and dry seasons before transporting to Nombre de Dios. To execute their raid, the French relied on the knowledge and scouting ability of one Pedro Mandinga, whom the French had captured and taken back to France in 1569. In 1571, they brought the Cimarrón man back to Panama to lead them to Venta de Cruces. As an incentive for his cooperation, Pedro Mandinga's French master promised him the hand in marriage of an enslaved woman named Marie. Once in the Chagre River, though, Pedro Mandinga abandoned the French. He warned the Spanish, who quickly organized a military force to attack the French pirates. Pedro Mandinga secured his freedom and perhaps a measure of vengeance by leaving the French to wander the Chagre River with the Spanish in angry pursuit.³³ Free of French shackles, Pedro Mandinga headed home—stopping briefly in Panama City to testify before the *Audiencia* about his experiences among the French. It is not clear whether this is the same Cimarrón man who aligned with Drake a year later. Drake offers no information about his ally's surname or ethnic origin, and Pedro was a common name for enslaved men in the Spanish colonies. Regardless, Pedro Mandinga's actions against the French illustrate explicitly what is implied through an against-the-grain reading of Drake's narrative—that Drake's alliance with the Cimarrones was precarious and certainly not inevitable. The Cimarrones apparently were willing and able to manipulate the political climate in Panama to suit their own interests, even if that meant working with, rather than attacking, the Spanish as Pedro Mandinga did in 1571. Perhaps Drake understood the political volatility on the isthmus, ultimately surrendering his fancy French sword to shore up Cimarrón fidelity.

Discursive Fluctuations

In addition to his interactions with specific black African figures, Drake's participation in a Black Legend discourse is complicated by the link between that discourse and transformations in European understandings about human difference. As the transatlantic slave trade grew, creating what Walter Mignolo refers to as a capitalistic "Atlantic economy," so did stereotypes about black Africans. Black African bodies became tropes connoting inferiority, savagery, bestiality.³⁴ About the emergence of racism and its economic impetus, Mignolo argues that "race as racism is a particular configuration that emerged in and during the European Renaissance as an intrinsic part of the consolidation of capitalism in the Atlantic economy and of Western expansion from the sixteenth century until today."³⁵ Mignolo makes current and expands Kim Hall's understanding of race as the consequence of an economic expansion that was also a "linguistic and ultimately an ideological expansion in which writers and travelers grappled with ways of making use of the foreign *materia* 'produced' by colonialism."³⁶ To stabilize an English identity in an ever-expanding world, Hall argues, racial discourse became a useful means for ordering those foreign encounters. That order was achieved through what Hall calls a binary of light and dark, which manifested itself physically as a relationship between fair, English bodies and dark, African bodies.³⁷ Hall maintains it was the "conduit through which the English began to formulate the notions of 'self' and 'other' so well known in Anglo-American racial discourses."³⁸

For Mignolo, unlike Hall, racism was not simply an external, colonial process encoding difference between European metropoles and those exploited peoples in Africa and the Americas. The racial rhetoric turned back toward Europe, according to Mignolo, and became a way for the English in particular to differentiate themselves from the Spanish, who were devalued and darkened through Black Legend rhetoric. In other words, the Black Legend was itself a kind of racial discourse that created a hierarchical system elevating the imperial ambitions of England (and other Protestant nations) above those of Spain. Inside Drake's narrative, then, racial rhetoric appears on two fronts. First, there is the external, colonial front. Through his representations of the Cimarrones, Drake associates blackness with labor and exploitation in the Caribbean. This racial mode echoes Las Casas's insistence in 1516 that the Spanish Crown replace Native American laborers with those from sub-Saharan Africa, which he predicted, "will be a greater service for [the Crown] and more profit, because more gold will be gathered . . . than with double the number of Indians . . . in [the mines]."[39] At the time, Las Casas echoed a common assumption among Europeans that black Africans were built sturdier and could better withstand the harsh work conditions in the tropical climates of the Caribbean. Black Africans for Drake, then, were not only victims of Spanish cruelty. They also were a viable labor source available for transport and sale in the Caribbean (on Hawkins's expeditions) and available for manpower to raid Spanish mule trains. For as much as Drake imagines the Cimarrones in sympathetic terms, rendering them humanely in his narrative, the text also adheres to certain stereotypes about sub-Saharan African bestiality, heathenism, and inhumanity that justified their commodification.

The second front on which racial rhetoric functions in the narrative is intracontinental. Drake's representation of the Spanish centers on what Mignolo terms an "imperial internal difference" designed to denigrate and eliminate a primary European rival to English commercial expansion.[40] In Drake's narrative, Black Legend rhetoric operates as part of a complex racial matrix inside which both Spaniards and black Africans occupy degraded spaces designed to confirm and justify English superiority. Black Africans are pliable in that racial matrix, functioning alternately as victims of a racialized Spain and as racial presences themselves. Ironically, though, that pliable quality in the Cimarrones' representation undermines Drake's efforts to portray Spain as a Black Legend.

An example of the Cimarrones' malleability and the narrative conflict that arises as a result occurs soon after Drake and the Cimarrones meet and agree to collaborate in September 1572. One of the first things Drake does as a result of the new alliance is relocate his camp from Port Plenty at the Isle of Pinos to a location with better natural defenses on an island near the Cativaas, some twenty-five leagues northwest. He names the new camp Fort Diego. They hide out in this location for several months, upon the recommendation of the Cimarrones, who explain that the mule trains travel during the dry season, and if Drake wants to capture them, he must wait until the cargoes begin traveling again. They spend the next several months fortifying the camp and conducting raids, mostly failed, up the Colombian coast.

In January, the Cimarrones finally bring word that the treasure fleet has arrived at Nombre de Dios, which means that mule trains are en route there (or soon will be) from Panama City. The presence of the treasure fleet also means an increase in water traffic as ships loaded with provisions and raw goods are transporting supplies to and from other Spanish colonies in the region. At one point during this time, Drake and his men capture a ship loaded with food provisions heading to Nombre de Dios. Drake takes as hostages thirteen Spaniards, one woman and twelve men. He intends to treat the hostages humanely, which means holding back a band of bloodthirsty Cimarrones. He says:

> [The Spaniards] we used very courteously, keeping them diligently guarded from the deadly hatred of the Symerons, who sought daily by all means they could to get them of our Captain, that they might cut their throats, to revenge their wrongs and injuries which the Spanish nation had done them; but our Captain persuaded them not to touch them or give them ill countenance, while they were in his charge, and took order for their safety, not only in his presence but also in his absence. (52)

Drake's description of the Cimarrones' rage evokes those common stereotypes of black Africans as savage and beastly. They are not the docile, honest, suffering natives Drake portrays elsewhere in the narrative. They stand in opposition to Drake, who treats the Spanish captives "very courteously," civilly. The moment reflects Hall's light/dark binary, rendering the Cimarrones within a blackness discourse. Complicating the representation, though, Drake imagines the moment as an example of Spain's savagery. He explains the Cimarrones' fury as a reaction to the brutality they themselves encountered from the Spanish. In a sense, their savagery is not racial but mimetic, a learned behavior. Both the Cimarrones and the Spanish are blackened at once. Rhetorically, the moment further emphasizes distinctions between Spanish cruelty and English benevolence, a benevolence which extends apparently to protecting even those identified as enemy. The distinction, though, undermines the larger paradigm through which Drake understands the Cimarrones as passive victims and therefore crucial objects of Spanish cruelty. Still recognizing himself as the great liberator, Drake is no longer protecting the Cimarrones. The Spanish occupy the role of (would-be) victims and the Cimarrones are oppressors, an ironic shift that contradicts the narrative's propagandistic intent.

We see this same kind of conflation several scenes later where the discursive function of the Cimarrones becomes more visible—and contentious. With the news that the treasure fleet has arrived at Nombre de Dios and the mule trains, presumably, are on the move down near Panama City, Drake and his Cimarrón allies prepare to march across the isthmus and intercept the treasure on the road between Panama City and Venta de Cruces. With eighteen Englishmen, thirty Cimarrones, and a good supply of shoes, Drake's party sets out on Shrove Tuesday.[41] During the march through dense jungle and across rivers, the Cimarrones perform most of the heavy lifting. They haul supplies, scout, navigate, build shelters. They hunt to feed the forty-eight men, capturing, among other things, the otter Drake initially found so distasteful. Several days into the march, they stop briefly in a Cimarrón town where, Drake notes, the residents "liued very ciuilly and cleanely" (56). The town is organized with well-plotted streets, a dike, and defenses to protect the residents from invaders. They also stop at one point to climb a huge tree, from the top of which Drake can look out and see both the Atlantic and Pacific oceans at once. The sight ignites in him a desire to sail the Pacific.

After two weeks, they approach Panama City. A Cimarrón spy enters the city and learns that a treasure train from Lima is planning to travel that night from Panama City to Venta de Cruces. Drake and the Cimarrones plan an ambush. They wait until nightfall and crouch down in the brush along both sides of the road two leagues outside of Venta de Cruces. The ambush might have succeeded except that one of Drake's men, drunk and overzealous, stands too early and betrays their presence. Those lead mules carrying the bulk of the treasure are able to turn back for Panama City. Drake manages to capture some of the cargo, mostly food and a small amount of silver, nothing of significant value. Rather than retreat quietly through the woods back to Fort Diego, Drake in consultation with Pedro decides to march through Venta de Cruces and "make a way with his Sword through the Enemies" (66). Before proceeding, though, he turns to Pedro and asks "whether hee would giue his hand not to forsake [Drake] (because hee knew that the rest of the *Symerons* would also then stand fast and firme, so faithfull are they to their Captaine.) [Pedro] being very glad of his resolution, gaue our Captaine his hand, and vowed that hee would rather dye at his foote, then leaue him to the Enemies, if hee held this course" (66). Here, the moment turns ironic. If this is the same Cimarrón man who abandoned the French on the Chagre River in 1571, he stands at the threshold of the same town making a similar commitment to another European pirate. The irony is coupled with an uncharacteristic display of paranoia from Drake. For sure, this moment is anomalous in the narrative, a rare display of Drake's vulnerability; it also reminds us of Pedro's agency and influence among the Cimarrones. He has the power, this moment implies, to withdraw from the alliance at will. But what is the source of Drake's fear that Pedro will "forsake" him? Is this the same Pedro Mandinga who proved in 1571 that his only allegiance is to his own self-interest? Drake may have even seen firsthand Pedro Mandinga's cunning. John Cummins speculates that Drake participated in that failed raid of Venta de Cruces back in 1571. If he was involved in that attempt, then his suspicion of Pedro in this moment links to a larger historical, experiential context. That experience invades the text, shrouds the moment in uncertainty.[42] That uncertainty notwithstanding, he accepts Pedro's vow and they march on to Venta de Cruces.

About a mile outside the town gates, they encounter a company of Spanish soldiers traveling with monks. A battle ensues. At first, the Cimarrones hang back as the English and Spanish exchange volleys with their firearms. Once the ammunition is all but spent, the Cimarrones move to the front and engage the Spanish with closer-range weapons. Drake's description of the Cimarrones during this battle is crucial because it is another effort, ironic in its end result, to racialize Spain by showing the monstrosity of the Cimarrones. As they enter the battle, Drake marvels at their valor and war-like energy, which is actually more show than substance: "they all rusht forwards one after another, trauersing the way, with their Arrowes ready in their Bowes, and their manner of Countrey dance or leape, very lustily, singing *Yó pehó, yó pehó*, and so got before vs, where they continued their leape and song, after the manner of their owne Countrey warres" (68). The description, bordering on the exotic, is ethnographic, detailing the Cimarrones' war rituals. There is little information about how the Cimarrones physically engage the Spanish. The threat of violence, their "show" seems to be enough to send the Spanish fleeing into the woods. He does describe one Cimarron who "was runne through with one of their Pikes, whose courage and minde serued him so well notwithstanding, that hee reuenged his owne death ere hee dyed, by killing him that had giuen him that deadly wound" (69). Here, he marvels at the valor. In the next instance, he notes the savagery.

After Spanish troops retreat, Drake and company finally enter Venta de Cruces. The town consists of about fifty houses, which include warehouses, government offices, and a monastery. In the houses, they find three women who have just given birth. "At our first comming into the Towne with Armes so suddenly," Drake explains, "these Gentlewomen were in great feare" (69). They need not worry, though, because Drake has already "giuen strait charge to all the *Symerons* (that while they were in his company, they should neuer hurt any woman, nor man that had not weapon in his hand to doe them hurt, which they ernestly promised, and no lesse faithfully performed)" (69–70). When initially articulating the mothers' fears, Drake does not indicate that those fears are discriminate. Instead, the women are terrified by "our first comming into the Towne with Armes," a semantic formulation that combines the Cimarrones and the English as the source of the women's fears. In that very next line, though, Drake isolates the Cimarrones, linking the women's fears specifically to them. The English men are excluded from Drake's orders on proper conduct. We could assume that at some earlier date, perhaps even before they embarked on the voyage, Drake gave the orders to his men not to attack women and defenseless men. Maybe he does not direct the order to the English because doing so would be superfluous, being as it were a standard code of conduct among Englishmen. Perhaps Drake is asking us to take for granted the civil, humane conduct of the English; what is inherent in the English Drake must instill in the Cimarrones. Rhetorically, the passage above preserves the differentiation between the English and the Cimarrones, who are united in their common enmity for Spain but not in their cultural values.

This is a potentially racializing moment that undermines the narrative's prevailing Black Legend rhetoric, *potentially racializing* because it is not clear what Drake sees as the source of the Cimarrones' presumed capacity for brutish, savage violence. In ordering the Cimarrones to "neuer hurt any woman, nor man that had not weapon in his hand," does Drake believe the Cimarrones are inherently inclined toward savage behavior? Such a belief undercuts his earlier observations about their civility and his portrayal of them as suffering natives. Not only are they not victims of Spain, but they have the capacity to fight back with an indiscriminate brutality. Alternatively, Drake could intend the moment as one last attack of Spain, suggesting that if the Cimarrones have the capacity to slaughter the innocent and defenseless, it is merely mimicry. The above passage is particularly evocative of the numerous examples Las

Casas offers of the violent acts conquistadores inflicted upon men, women, and children in the Americas. In a passage especially relevant to the present discussion, Las Casas describes conquistadores' treatment of pregnant women and babies:

> [The Spanish] hacked them to pieces, slicing open their bellies with their swords as though they were so many sheep herded into a pen.... They grabbed suckling infants by the feet and, ripping them from their mothers' breasts, dashed them headlong against the rocks. Others, laughing and joking all the while, threw them over their shoulders into a river shouting: "Wriggle, you little perisher." They slaughtered anyone and everyone in their path, on occasion running through a mother and her baby with a single thrust of their swords. They spared no one.[43]

The Spanish "spared no one." The English in contrast operate according to what Drake portrays as a more merciful and humane code. He forces his Cimarrón companions to do the same. Drake makes it clear that those Spanish mothers and their infants at Venta de Cruces "had no wrong offered them, nor any thing taken from them, to the *worth of a garter* [emphasis mine]" (70). This moment then is not a simple meditation or observation about the Cimarrones' capacity for violence. It is just as much about the opposition between a barbarous Spain and virtuous England. Even as the moment seemingly bolsters Black Legend rhetoric, though, it undercuts that rhetoric by weakening Drake's portrayal of Cimarrones as victims. Black Legend rhetoric gains its efficacy from the existence of sympathetic victims who can embody the cruelties and savagery of Spanish conduct. Mostly, Cimarrones serve that role in Drake's narrative. Their bloodlust as Drake renders it in this moment, though, creates a representational vacuum as there is no victim to reify Spanish cruelty. Those Spanish women, who would be victims, are saved from such fates, illustrating not Spanish barbarity but English civility. The Cimarrones, as was the case with those thirteen Spanish hostages at Fort Diego a few weeks earlier, once again are (potentially) savage aggressors, not passive, submissive, and long-suffering objects of Spanish cruelty. Because Drake has indulged in racial language throughout the text, this moment does not necessarily reflect Spanish cruelty. It could very well reflect what Drake saw as the innate baseness of black Africans, which disrupts the victim/oppressor paradigm through which he represents the Cimarrones and Spanish elsewhere in the narrative. Ultimately, Cimarrones occupy a problematic, unstable space in Drake's narrative. That instability, resulting from a conflict between Drake's rhetorical ambitions and the material details of his exploits, compromises Drake's narrative, undermining his very project of self-creation and his efforts to condemn Spanish empire.

The Aftermath

After the failed raid attempt outside of Venta de Cruces, the English and Cimarrones made their way back to Fort Diego and waited another three months before finally capturing a treasure train at the end of April 1573. Based on Spanish reports of the raid, Drake and his French allies walked away with between one hundred and two hundred thousand pesos in gold and silver.[44] More than gold, the Cimarrones valued iron for tools and weapons, which they had in abundance after Drake broke down several of his ships and passed along the iron work to the Cimarrones. By all counts, the English-Cimarrón alliance succeeded, and it struck terror in the Spanish living on the isthmus. Leaders in Panama City assessed the situation this way: "This league between the English and the negroes is very detrimental to this kingdom, because, being so thoroughly acquainted with the region and so expert in the bush, the negroes will show them methods and means to accomplish any evil design they may wish to carry out and execute. These startling developments have agitated and alarmed this kingdom. It is indeed most lamentable that the English and negroes should have combined against us, for the blacks are numerous."[45] The English-Cimarron alliance was a "startling" development that "agitated and alarmed" the Spanish because the Cimarrones opened up the Pacific side of Spanish America to the English.[46] Prior to Drake's alliance, English (and French) pirates were limited to raids of Spanish colonies facing the Atlantic Ocean, such as Cartagena, Nombre de Dios, and the numerous Caribbean islands. To access locations like Panama City, the Pearl Islands, and Lima, where large amounts of wealth circulated daily, pirates faced an arduous land crossing that was impossible without a proper guide, which is why the French captured Pedro Mandinga in 1571.[47] Because the land provided a natural barrier, the Spanish left their Pacific settlements lightly guarded. In the 1570s the English attempted to take advantage of this vulnerability with Cimarrón cooperation.

Drake's raid established a (short-lived) precedent. English pirates, some of whom had accompanied Drake, came back to the isthmus in subsequent years looking to replicate Drake's success. The most significant of those was

John Oxenham, who returned to Panama with a seventy-man crew in 1575. Like Drake, Oxenham immediately sought out the Cimarrones who had aided Drake two years before. With the Cimarrones' help, Oxenham crossed the isthmus to the Pacific shore, where he intended to raid ships traveling between Peru and Panama City. He set up base in the Pearl Islands, twenty-five leagues from Panama City. He captured two ships with more than 150,000 pesos in gold and silver, but he failed to escape the isthmus with the prize. Spanish soldiers aggressively pursued and captured Oxenham and his men. A number of Cimarrones and almost all of Oxenham's men were executed, Oxenham in Lima.[48] The expedition failed, according to Oxenham, because his alliance with the Cimarrones fell apart. Tension between the two sides developed after Oxenham decided to release those Spaniards they had captured during their raids on Pearl Island. The released captives quickly informed officials at Panama City about the raids. Spanish soldiers, in the process of pursuing Oxenham and the Cimarrones, destroyed several Cimarrón villages. The Cimarrones scattered; some were killed or captured by the Spanish. The Cimarrones traveling with Oxenham blamed him for the attacks, insisting that he should have killed their captives rather than release them. As a result, the Cimarrones withdrew their help from Oxenham and his men. They refused to feed them, help them find clothes, or supply them with weapons.[49]

Although Oxenham's raid ultimately failed, it made even more urgent Spanish efforts to subdue the Cimarron population. In letters sent to the Crown, Spanish officials living in Panama City and Nombre de Dios repeatedly urged the Crown to increase its military strength on the isthmus by sending galleys to patrol the coastal waters and levying taxes to pay for troops to seek out the Cimarrones and punish them for aiding the English.[50] Military raids, though, experienced only minimal success because the Cimarrones were able to quickly abandon settlements and effectively disappear in the Panama landscape. As one military official noted in 1578, "They do not await the attack; their defence is to flee and to hide in the remotest, most secret fastnesses of the mountains, abandoning their villages, some of which they burned as soon as they knew that our men were approaching" (Wright 211). This official ultimately concludes, "In the conquest of these negroes, experience so far clearly shows how fruitless it is to make war upon them; except it be attempted by firmly establishing settlements among them. Even then, to extirpate them will take a long time and occasion infinite expense to your majesty's royal treasury" (Wright 214).[51] Compromise, not war, eventually resolved conflicts between the Spanish and Cimarrones on the isthmus.

Between 1579 and 1582, the Spanish and the three main palenques of Cimarrones arrived at a series of resolutions that dissuaded those Cimarrones from collaborating with the English and raiding Spanish towns.[52] The resolutions recognized Cimarrón autonomy and granted them land to establish their own settlements but with Spanish oversight. In exchange, the Cimarrones agreed to end raids on Spanish towns. In addition, they agreed to a fugitive slave act that required they return any future runaway slaves to their Spanish masters.[53] These compromises did not immediately and completely end raids, but the Cimarrones ceased to be an obstacle in Spain's efforts to curb English piracy on the isthmus.[54] As for the English, Drake's was the first and last successful collaboration with Cimarrones. He returned to the region three times, in 1577 during his circumnavigation, in 1585, and in 1595, just before his death. To illustrate how quickly and how thoroughly political landscapes can shift, when Drake returned in 1595, Cimarrones actually fought alongside the Spanish to thwart his raid. Despite the short-lived success of Drake's alliance with Cimarrones, the *idea* of such alliances, as illustrated in the next chapter, survived for much longer, well into the next century.

CHAPTER 3

Alliances Real and Imagined
Thomas Gage and Black African Collaboration in New Spain

In 1625, an Englishman named Thomas Gage traveled for twelve years as a Catholic priest through New Spain. In 1648, several years after returning to England and renouncing his Catholic faith, Gage published an extensive narrative of his travels. The text is mostly a scouting report that details the infrastructure and resources of Mexico and Central America (mostly Guatemala), designed to prove the feasibility and necessity of an English invasion of the region. To ensure a successful invasion, Gage proposes that English forces combine with enslaved black Africans and maroons in New Spain. These black Africans, Gage argues, harbor a particularly aggressive enmity toward Spain because of harsh treatment. At one point in his narrative, Gage notes of a band of maroons living in the Guatemalan mountains that they are equipped with "bows and arrows which they use and carry about them, only to defend themselves, if the Spaniards set upon themselves. . . . [They] have often said that the chief cause of their flying to those mountains is to be in readiness to joyne with the English . . . if ever they land in that golfe."[1] This trope of black African/English alliance, epitomized by Drake's Panama exploits, guides but also complicates Gage's representations of black Africans in his narrative.

Gage describes several encounters with black Africans and mulattos, designed to prove black Africans' willingness to ally with England. When we read those encounters against the grain, the black African figures register as more than martial and political pawns in Gage's imperial imagination. Inconsistencies emerge in the moments that suggest alternative narratives and competing interests among Gage and the black Africans with whom he interacts. These counter-narratives matter because, first, they offer clues about the source material from which Gage crafted his own account, highlighting the extent to which the narrative is the product of cross-cultural contact. Second, the counter-narratives—and the disruptions they produce—raise questions about the extent to which black Africans challenged English representational strategies that were key to how they understood national identity and their imperial project. Like Drake, Gage endeavors to render England a more benevolent and pious alternative to Spain in the Americas, and he calls upon Drake's past deeds for inspiration. Unlike Drake, though, Gage does not imagine England simply in opposition to Spain. Instead, he upholds the historic conquests of Spain's own Hernán Cortés as a model of invasion that the English can replicate—albeit in a more humane and godly manner. As material presences, black Africans in Mexico and Guatemala interfere with Gage's imperial formulation by denying England the kind of alliances that allowed Drake to raid Panama and Cortés to invade Mexico. Textually, the interference appears in Gage's narrative in the form of inconsistencies in both characterization and plot as Gage endeavors to represent his interactions with black Africans to mirror Cortés's alliances with Native Americans outside of Mexico City. Importantly, the black African interference that disrupts Gage's narrative correlates with political consequences beyond the text.

Gage publishes his narrative on the eve of Cromwell's Western Design strategy, England's 1655 campaign of invasion in which English forces attempted to seize strategic Spanish colonies in the Caribbean. Gage's counsel and his narrative, reprinted in 1655, were instrumental in shaping Cromwell's policy. Gage traveled along with the expedition. Despite his predictions of an easy conquest that would come with the cooperation of enslaved and marooned black Africans, the campaign failed—partly because black Africans fought against rather than alongside the English. Gage's narrative and the subsequent fallout from England's failed Caribbean invasion bear out what can only be implied in Drake's narrative, that black African cooperation was not inevitable or consistent. This chapter examines the consequences of political and literary rhetoric and the ways in which black African presences in New Spain impeded that rhetoric—and by extension England's imperial agenda.

The Cultural Legacy of Sir Francis Drake

I begin the discussion of Gage's narrative and the Western Design by revisiting Drake and his Caribbean exploits, emphasizing the cultural resonances of his deeds in two texts: Richard Hakluyt's 1584 *Discourse Concerning Western*

Planting and William Davenant's 1659 opera *The History of Sir Francis Drake*. Beginning the discussion here reiterates the political and literary consequences of Drake's Panama raid, providing context for Gage's expectations in his interactions with black Africans and in the counsel he provides to Cromwell to shape the Western Design. As stated in the previous chapter, Drake's Caribbean deeds were central in setting the agenda for English expectations in the Caribbean and imperial expansion. This is evident, for example, in Hakluyt's *Discourse*.[2] In that text, Hakluyt urges Queen Elizabeth to support the colonizing ambitions of statesmen like Sir Walter Ralegh on the grounds that American colonization could strengthen England's trade networks, supply industry for idle men and criminals (who would populate the colony), provide a platform with which the English could contest a growing Spanish empire, and deliver native populations from Spanish cruelty.[3]

Dividing the *Discourse* into twenty-one chapters, Hakluyt presents a rationale for the moral, economic, and political expediency of American colonization. He predicates that expediency, in part, on Drake's past Caribbean experiences noting that "it is knowen" to Drake that "the ilandes there abounde with people and nations that rejecte the proude and bluddy government of the Spaniarde, and that doe mortally hate the Spaniarde."[4] Hakluyt argues that Spain's hold on New Spain is tenuous, made so because they have failed to secure the good will of the region's inhabitants. Consequently, "the Moores, and suche as the Spaniardes have brought thither for the mynes and for slavery, have fled from them into the inlandes, and of them selves maineteine in many places frontier warres against the Spaniarde, and many tymes so prevaile."[5] Drake is valuable, then, because his past interactions with those "Moores and suche" have engendered "greate credite."[6] Hakluyt anticipates that Drake "bringing thither a fewe capitaines and some of our meaner souldiers late trained in the Base Contries, with archers and lighte furniture, &c.," could join "with the Symerons and with those that mayneteyne those frontier warrs" to conquer King Philip.[7] In general, an expectation of collaboration permeates Hakluyt's text, in much the same way such expectations will inform Gage's narrative. In addition to the Cimarrones, Hakluyt anticipates that the Chichimici, a native tribe in northern Mexico, would be ready allies. The Chichimici, he notes, were led by a black African maroon, who "fled from his cruell Spanishe master" and led the Chichimici in a series of successful revolts that forced the Spanish to abandon lucrative silver mines and leave the area.[8] The Chichimici, Hakluyt reports, "are bigg and stronge men and valiaunte archers."⁹ He assures readers that "if wee . . . woulde either joyne with these savages or sende or give them armor . . . wee shoulde trouble the Kinge of Spaine more in those partes . . . and holde him at suche a bay as he was never yet helde at."¹⁰

By utilizing the Cimarrones and the maroon-led Chichimici, Hakluyt predicts, the English would provoke Spain's "greatest feare," which is that the English and native populations would join forces and oust the Spanish from New Spain.¹¹ Hakluyt rehearses those very same fears that pervaded Spanish correspondence in the wake of Drake's Panama raids. Remember that Drake's successful assaults alarmed Spanish officials precisely because they illustrated the efficacy of English–African–Native American alliances, which threatened Spain's wealthiest holdings on the Pacific side of Panama. Unfortunately for Hakluyt—and later Gage—Drake's successful collaboration created a false sense of certainty and continuity as formerly enslaved black Africans especially were decidedly unreliable allies in English quests to usurp Spanish territories in the Americas.

Davenant's opera, though written and performed after the Western Design failed, derives much of its creative energy from the same expectations that motivated Hakluyt (and Gage). What is more, his text offers a bit of irony because at the same time that Davenant presents an opera celebrating Drake's Panama raid and his alliance with Cimarrones, English military forces struggle to maintain possession of Jamaica, which they seized after being repelled from Hispaniola during the Western Design campaign. The struggle in Jamaica is exacerbated by the presence of black African maroons who fight rather than align with the English.¹² Davenant's work offers a dramatic reinterpretation of Drake's deeds in 1572/73. Arranged in six entries, or scenes, the opera re-enacts several moments from Drake's narrative, including his initial meeting with the Cimarrones, his observation of both the Atlantic and Pacific oceans, and his passage through the way station at Venta de Cruces. It ends with the English and Cimarrón attack on Spanish mule trains outside of Panama. The opera magnifies the themes and rhetorical strategies that characterize Drake's narrative. For example, the opera makes reference to Spanish cruelty and casts Drake as a liberating force come to protect Native Americans, who welcome him with enthusiasm. They sing,

> The Lord of the Sea is welcome to Land,
> And here shall command
> All our Wealth, and our Arms;

> For his Name more Alarms
> The Spaniards, then Trumpets or Drums:
> Hark how they cry, Drake comes, Drake comes!¹³

He looms large in the text as a brash, bold sea captain whose reputation precedes him and towers over even that of his fellow English privateer Rouse, with whom Drake aligned briefly in 1572. In the opera, Rouse fawns over Drake, saying, "My fame does lay her Trumpet down, / When yours does publish your renown."¹⁴ Later he proclaims, "What man is that, Lov'd Admirall, / Who does not hasten at your call? / He must be either deaf, or ever lame, / Who followes not your loud and leading fame."¹⁵

Importantly, Davenant emphasizes African-English alliance. He renders the Cimarrones a biddable, accommodating resource for Drake. The Cimarrones welcome Drake to the isthmus with enthusiasm. A Cimarrón leader tells Drake, "Welcom [sic]! And in my Land be free, / And pow'rfull as thou art at Sea."¹⁶ He implores Drake to "Instruct me how my Symerons and I / May help thee to afflict the Enemy."¹⁷ Then, he promises "All other ayds requir'd to thy designe, / Chuse and receive: for all my strengths are thine."¹⁸ Without hesitation, he supplies Drake with his best, most loyal men led by the formerly enslaved man Pedro. In Drake's narrative, an against-the-grain reading of Pedro suggests he was a savvy, opportunistic ally. The opera portrays him in much simpler terms, as a loyal servant, made all the more so by time and experience. The Cimarrón king presents Pedro to Drake:

> Here from my bosom Pedro take,
> And him thy chief Conductor make.
> Who once was an unhappy slave to them;
> But now is free by my deserv'd esteem.
> He is as watchfull as the Eye
> Of Age still wak'd with jealousie:
> And like experience'd Lovers wisely true:
> Who after long suspition find,
> They had no cause to be unkind,
> And then with second vows their loves renew.¹⁹

As was the case in the narrative, through the remainder of the opera the Cimarrones work as guides and as an auxiliary military force for the English. Recognizing the import of the alliance, Davenant ends the opera with this final image, given as stage directions: "The Grand Dance begins, consisting of two Land souldiers, two Sea-men, two symerons, and a Peruvian; intimating, by their several interchange of salutations, their mutual desires of amity."[20] As we will see shortly, the literary fantasy of cooperation, as manifested in Davenant's text, existed alongside the material reality of black African resistance and opportunism. This conflict between fantasy and reality encapsulates Gage's narrative and the imperial policy that narrative helped engender.

Gage's is a hybrid text, part travelogue, part history book, part religious apologia, and part commercial and political brochure in which he argues for a second invasion of the West Indies, one in which the English wrestle control of the region from the Spanish. His text offers one of the earliest accounts of the West Indies from an English perspective. Previously, the English gleaned information about New Spain from Spanish texts, most translated into English. In a prefatory letter to Sir Thomas Fairfax, captain of England's Parliamentary Army, Gage offers up information about New Spain with the hopes that it would be "the subject of . . . future pains, valour, and piety" (unpaginated). To stir national passions in favor of such an invasion, at one point he harkens back to the daring deeds of Drake and Drake's successor John Oxenham in Panama. He describes Drake as a heroic ghost, whose exploits haunt Nombre de Dios many decades later. He writes, "I should wrong my Country if I should not set out to the publike view the worth of her people shewed upon this place [Nombre de Dios], and to this day talked on and admired by the *Spaniards,* who . . . remember Sir *Francis Drake,* & teach their children to dread and fear even his name" (77). Gage praises even more Oxenham, whose attempt on the Panama isthmus was "resolute and wonderfull" (77). He reminds readers that Oxenham, "guided by *Black-mores,*" did the unthinkable by gaining access to the South Sea (or Pacific) and attacking Spain's richest prizes in the Pearl Islands and Peru. "Yet was it such a strange adventure as is not to be forgotten," Gage declares, "in that the like was never by any other attempted, and by the *Spaniards* is to this day with much admiration recorded" (77).

"Nothing . . . More Advantageous" than Alliance

It is no accident that Gage evokes the heroic images of Drake and Oxenham, whose collaborations with black Africans made their exploits possible. Throughout his narrative, Gage discusses the possibility for alliance as key to usurping power. That is to say that among the most valuable resources for an English invasion of New Spain are the people. Drake (and Oxenham) had the

Cimarrones in Panama. In 1648, the English could take advantage of a number of anti-Spanish populations who, Gage assumed, would welcome and work with the English—Native Americans, Spanish creoles, and mulattos and black Africans (those enslaved and marooned). Gage broadens the application of Black Legend rhetoric to include the oppression of Spanish Americans while maintaining England's image as, potentially, a liberating force. He argues about Spanish creoles living in New Spain that they harbor a special resentment toward continental Spaniards. "This hatred is so great," he claims, "that . . . nothing might bee more advantageous then this, to any other Nation that would conquer America. And nothing more easily gained, then the Wils and affections of the Natives [creoles] of the Country, to joyne with any other Nation to free and rescue themselves from that subjection, or kind of slavery, which they suffer under" (9). The suffering to which Gage refers involves class distinctions and political disempowerment. According to Gage, "though there be among [creoles] those that descended of the chief Conquerors; as in Lima and Peru the Pizarros, in Mexico . . . Cortes," continental Spaniards occupy the highest political and religious offices in New Spain, hoarding power and wealth (10). "This is so grievous to the poore Criolio's or Natives," Gage writes, "that my selfe have often heard them say, They would rather bee subject to any other Prince . . . then to the Spaniards" (9).

Even though Gage declares that "nothing might bee more advantageous" than an English-Creole alliance, his representations of Creoles is ambiguous. On several occasions he notes his own tense relationship with this population and suggests their inefficacy as English allies. In the city of Chiapa, for example, he portrays the Creole residents as rustic and uncivilized.[21] Betraying his own elitist leanings, Gage dismisses them as simple farmers who say they are "great in blood and in birth" but are no more than "rich Grasiers" (102). He maintains that they "have most cowardly spirits for warre," and they claim Spanish ancestry but "dare not venture their lives at sea" to see their home country (102). He determines ultimately that "one hundred fighting souldiers would easily . . . gain the whole City" (102).

Gage represents mulattos and black Africans as being especially pugnacious and useful as allies. To illustrate this point, he relates the story of a mulatto man, formerly enslaved to the Spanish, named Lewis. He encounters Lewis in late August 1625 on the island of Guadeloupe, where those aboard the friar's ship stop to restock supplies and water before traveling on to the port at San Juan de Ulúa. Gage's ultimate destination is the Philippines.[22] Guadeloupe, according to him, is a "common Rode and harbor to all Nations that saile to

America," Columbus having first encountered the island in 1493 (17). As they anchor off the shore of Guadeloupe, Gage notes that the island's mostly Carib inhabitants approach them, eager to trade plantains, sugar cane, and tortoises for Spanish wine, iron, knives, and other weapons "which may help them in their Wars" (17). Gage's description of their arrival paints a chaotic but friendly scene in which some European travelers marvel at their first sight of Native Americans, "people naked, with their hair hanging down the middle of their backs, with their faces cut out in severall fashions, or flowers, with thin plates hanging at their Noses, like Hog-rings" (17). The Caribs, Gage writes, fawned "upon us like children, some speaking in their unknown tongue, others using signs for such things as we imagined they desired" (17). The ship transforms itself into an intercultural marketplace and the wine flows freely, so much so that men stumble around "like swine tumbling on the Deck" of the ship (17). He describes the Caribs as peaceful, generous, and kind.

Once they disembark and arrive on the beach, Gage observes for the first time the formerly enslaved man Lewis, who is in conversation with a group of Jesuits arriving on the island from another ship. The entrance of Jesuits on the scene is crucial as Gage is particularly critical and cynical of this religious order, the members of which he describes as ambitious and vain. According to Gage, Jesuits strive to educate the sons of the wealthy to garner favor and power. They also seek the highest religious offices within the church. He insists they are "bold and obstinate in malice and hatred" (5). There is a subtext to Gage's negative description of Jesuits. Gage was born into a devoutly Roman Catholic family that remained so after England separated from the Church in Rome. As a youth, Gage received seminary training in France and then Spain, his father expecting him to become a priest and commit to the Jesuit order. Gage, instead, joined the Dominicans, a decision that so enraged his father that he disinherited Gage (12–13).[23] Adding insult to injury, the Jesuits, according to Gage, harbored a particular animosity toward Dominicans, who antagonized and imprisoned Jesuit founder Ignatius Loyola a century earlier (Gage 5). Gage's description of the Jesuits, then, is much more than disinterested observation.

Gage does not tell readers the content of Lewis's conversation with the Jesuits, but he does provide a short biography for Lewis, who was formerly a Christian and born in Seville, Spain. In Spain, Lewis was enslaved to a particularly brutal master. Through unspecified means, Lewis orchestrated his sale to another master, who was heading to the Americas. As fate would have it, this second master was no less cruel than the first. During a stop at Guadeloupe,

Lewis ran away and hid in the mountains, resolving "to die among the *Indians* ... then evermore to live in slavery under *Spaniards*" (18). Rather than death, he found asylum and freedom with the Caribs. Over the course of twelve years, he was assimilated, adopting the language and dress and disavowing his Christian heritage. He married and had three children. He was assimilated so thoroughly, according to Gage, that it was more by "the Wooll upon his head ... then by his black and tauny skin" or other manners that they knew he was not native to the area (18).[24]

Gage and his Dominican cohort join the conversation between Lewis and the Jesuits. Once the Dominicans learn of Lewis's background, they proselytize to the former Christian, urging him to come back to the church "promising him if hee would goe along with [them], he should bee free from slavery for ever" (18). According to Gage, the proselytizing moves Lewis to tears: "Poore Soule, though hee had lived twelve years without hearing a word of the true God, worshipping stockes and stones with the other Heathens; yet when hee heard again of Christ . . . hee began to weep" (18). Lewis tells the friars that he would gladly go with them "were it not for his Wife and children, whome hee tenderly loved, and could not forsake" (18). The friars assure Lewis that he can bring his family, but as soon as they address one concern, Lewis presents another: "a suddaine fear surprised him, because certain Indians passed by, and noted his long conference with us" (18). Calling Lewis a "poore and timorous Mulatto," Gage explains Lewis's anxiety—if his Carib friends discover his plans to leave with the friars, they will kill Lewis and attack the friars. Gage and the friars tell him "not to feare anything [the Caribs] could doe to us, who had souldiers, gun[s] and Ordnance to secure ours and his life also" (18). Lewis and the friars part ways with the understanding that Lewis will collect his family and meet the friars down by the beach. There a boat would be waiting to transport them to a ship anchored off shore. Reiterating the friars' plan, Lewis requests that the Jesuits specifically come with the boat, and he asks them to dress in black coats, the easier to be seen. Presumably, Lewis invests his and his family's welfare with the Jesuit order rather than the Dominican. Perhaps a bit miffed, Gage notes, "The Jesuits who had begun with this Mulatto were desirous that the happy end and conclusion might bee their glory. So taking their leaves of us, they hastened to the Sea to informe the Admirall of what they had done" and to prepare a boat to transport Lewis and his family (18).

The Dominicans return to their own ship, contenting themselves with their efforts to bring "to the light of Christianity five Soules [Lewis, his wife, and three children] out of the darknesse of Idolatry" (18). After an unspecified length of time, Gage and most of the other Dominicans witness from the deck of their ship a commotion back on the beach. They see Spaniards "running to and fro to save their lives, leaving their clothes, and hasting to the Cock-Boats, filling them so fast and so full, that some sunke with all the people in them" (19). Spanish women run blindly into the sea, facing certain drowning. A barrage of arrows flies from the nearby woods. Gage realizes that the Caribs, who just hours before had been peaceful and accommodating, were now attacking all those Spaniards unlucky enough to be caught on shore, including the party of Jesuits, dressed in black coats standing next to a boat waiting to collect Lewis, his wife, and children. The Caribs kill or wound almost thirty men and women in an attack that begins suddenly and ends quickly, after "not halfe an houre" (19). Ship captains fire several rounds of ordinance in the direction of the beach and dispatch armed soldiers to quell the attack, or "mutiny" as Gage calls it (19).

For anyone who has read about the experiences of Towerson, Hawkins, and Drake, this scene in Gage's narrative looks familiar. It harkens back to the same kind of bait and switch tactics black Africans employed in their dealings with Englishmen in Guinea. This is especially reminiscent of the ambush Towerson and his men experienced at Don Jon's Town. Whatever led the inhabitants on Guadeloupe to attack Europeans on the beach, circumstantial evidence suggests Lewis was somehow involved. Gage notes, "Our Mulatto Lewis came not according to his word; but in his stead a suddaine Army of treacherous Indians" (19). Gage suggests that Lewis might have orchestrated the attack himself after discovering what Gage claims was a Jesuit plot to unmask Lewis as a fugitive and re-enslave him. Or, Gage hedges, Lewis's initial fears were right—the Caribs discovered his plans to leave and therefore killed Lewis (hence his absence on the beach) and attacked the friars. The former explanation renders Lewis a wily, resourceful, trickster figure who has the influence among the Caribs to motivate them to rally toward his protection. The latter explanation, coinciding with Gage's earlier understanding of Lewis as a "poore and timorous Mulatto," renders him a much less agentive figure, his involvement the product of coercion by natives who "made him confesse" his plan to leave (19). Either way, Gage concludes that Lewis's conversation with the friars, the Jesuits specifically, motivated the attack: "Certainly this was the ground of their Mutiny; for whereas L[ewis] before had said, that hee would know the Jesuites by their black Coats, it seems hee had well described them above all the rest unto the Indians, for . . . most of their Arrowes was directed to the black Markes" (19). Five Jesuit priests died or were wounded in the attack.

Lewis is a complex, cross-cultural figure who seemingly exerts some measure of control over events. Note the ways in which Gage's representation of Lewis's actions points to a transformation for the enslaved man. Initially, he is a bilingual maroon who has managed to protect his freedom for twelve years, which suggests a measure of cultural adaptability and social savvy. Then, he transforms himself into a weeping, frightful, lost soul, an object of the friars' mission efforts. By the end of the scene, Gage renders him nebulously—as the chief author or as a coerced agent of the attack on the Spanish. This equivocation on Gage's part seems inexplicable when we consider again Lewis's request that the Jesuits wear black coats. That request comes *during* his conversation with the friars, not at a later date. It might be the case that Caribs on the island discovered the content of Lewis's conversation with the friars. It might be the case that they took offense to the friars' efforts to "steale" away Lewis; they, therefore, turned mutinous (18). But any of this would have come *after* Lewis's request that the Jesuits don the coats. For whatever reason, and Gage only implies that the Jesuits had planned some treachery, it appears that Lewis plots against the Jesuits even as he appears a "poore and timorous" lost Christian. For his part, Gage seems disinterested in Lewis's agentive capacities. He is much more invested in the Jesuits and the outcome of their interactions with Lewis.

In pointing out that the Jesuits suffered heavy losses in the attack, those black coats making them bull's-eyes, and implying it was retribution for a plot to kidnap and enslave Lewis and his family, Gage turns this scene into a cautionary tale. It impresses upon its readers the importance of engaging America's inhabitants with sincerity and integrity. Gage and his fellow Dominicans stand in opposition to the Jesuits. Their goal is not to capture Lewis but to encourage him to "forsake that heathenish life, wherein his soule could never bee saved" (18). Theirs is quintessential mission rhetoric. Remember that, according to Gage, the proselytizing begins only once the Dominicans enter the conversation with Lewis, and they are spared the casualties. Only one Dominican friar is wounded (and dies several days later), which implies that Lewis and the Caribs also recognize a difference between the two orders. In short, the scene at Guadeloupe is crucial to Gage for three reasons. It offers him an occasion to malign Jesuits and by extension condemn what he understands as Spain's treacherous policies in the Americas. It shows the English, through the Dominican example, an alternative model of engagement with America's inhabitants, both those indigenous to the region and those transplanted. And it illustrates the vulnerability of Europeans seeking imperial goals when they lack cooperation from the land's inhabitants.

Evoking a Spanish Past

If Gage's encounter with Lewis is a cautionary tale about the necessity of collaborative relationships, his descriptions of the fall of the Aztec empire epitomize the benefits of such collaborations. From Guadeloupe, Gage continues on to the Spanish Main. His first stop is San Juan de Ulúa, the same port where Hawkins and Drake battled a Spanish fleet nearly sixty years before. From there, he travels by land to Mexico City, all the while describing the surrounding landscape and smaller settlements along the route. He also details the commodities that have sustained those settlements and the richer Mexico City—cloth, chocolate, sugar, and cochineal, among other items.[25] As he enters Mexico City in October 1625, he stops the travel narrative to rehearse with equal measures of awe and condemnation, the history of Cortés's conquest of Montezuma and the Aztecs in 1521. He devotes substantial space to this Spanish history for a number of reasons, one of which is that it reminds readers that Cortés's success was based largely on his ability to take advantage of anti-Aztec sentiment that permeated native communities, like the Tlaxcalteca, at the empire's periphery. Cortés understood, Gage notes, that it was "his best policy to joyne with" those hostile groups "against the Mexicans" (29). An alliance of Spanish and Native American forces descended upon the Aztecs. After "utterly" destroying the city, according to Gage, Cortés "reedified it againe, not onely for the situation and majesty, but also for the name and great fame thereof" (54). Cortés's strategy of collaboration is a model for the kind of takeover Gage imagines the English could stage now a century later. He notes, though, that in rebuilding Mexico City after conquering it, the Spanish decimated the region's Indian populations, with most of them having "beene consumed by the Spaniards hard usage" in performing manual work (55). What is more, he condemns the Spanish as poor stewards of the bounty God supplied in the wake of conquest. By 1625, Gage argues, Mexico City had devolved into a Sodom and Gomorrah. He laments, "How long O Lord God, how long shall the line of the wicked flourish, and the best portion be fallen to Idolaters and to the workers in iniquity?" (61). He predicts that the city's inhabitants will "slip and fall into the power and dominion of some other Prince of this world" (57). Of course, he believes England to be that dominion into which the Spanish will slip and fall.

He advocates what is essentially a second conquest of Mexico City, and an active black African presence in the region is essential for how he believes the English can stage that conquest. Unlike Cortés, who entered Mexico at a time when there was a robust native population of which he could take advantage to form alliances, Gage argues that by 1625, the native population had been drastically reduced. In the immediate aftermath of Cortés's conquest, according to Gage, a hundred thousand houses were built in the vicinity of Mexico City, most to accommodate native inhabitants. By 1625, he writes, the population had been reduced to five thousand inhabitants (55). This vanishing Indian rhetoric pervades his narrative. As to those native populations who managed to survive Spain's tyrannous policies, according to Gage, they have been thoroughly subdued. When describing the plight of Native Americans living in the vicinity of Guatemala, where he settles after leaving Mexico City, Gage argues that Spanish officials living there recognize the danger of Native Americans joining "themselves to any enemy against" the Spanish. The Spanish, therefore, prevent them from carrying weapons or forming armies, not even their "bows and arrows, which their ancestors formerly used" (138). This means generations of natives who are unskilled in the art of battle. He notes the consequences of this Spanish policy:

> And by this it may easily appear how ungrounded they are, who say, it is harder to conquer America now then in Cortez his time, for that there are now both Spaniards and Indians to fight against, and then there were none but bare and naked Indians. This I say is a false ground; for then there were Indians trained up in wars one against another, who knew wel to use their bows and arrows, and darts, and other weapons, and were desperate in their fights and single combats, as may appear out of the histories of them; but now they are cowardized, oppressed, unarmed, soon frighted with the noise of a musket, nay with a sowre and grim look of a Spaniard, so from them there is no fear. (139)

Gage's representation of native communities as oppressed and disempowered here turns ironic. In pointing out how the Spanish neutralize a threat to their own dominance, Gage also points out that those native groups won't be a threat to an English takeover either. The Spanish have made themselves more secure from an internal uprising but less secure against an external invasion. What is more, according to Gage, the Spanish have ignored two other problematic internal threats, their "owne slaves the Black-mores, who doubtlesse to be set at liberty would side against them in any such occasion; and lastly, the Criolians [creoles] who also are sore oppressed by them, would rejoice in such a day, and yield rather to live with freedome and liberty under a forain people, then to be longer oppressed by those of their own blood" (139). For Gage, the greater of those two threats—and therefore the most promising for an English alliance—are black Africans.

Especially in the region of Guatemala, Spanish oppression might have rendered Native Americans as weak and timid, but that oppression seems to have invigorated enslaved black Africans and maroons. Gage often accents his representations of black Africans with adjectives that cast them as valiant, aggressive, task-driven, and efficient. For example, he attributes the strength of Guatemala, as a rich Spanish stronghold, to the work of enslaved black Africans, "a desperate sort of Black-mores" (129). Gage argues that "though they have no weapons but a Machette . . . or lances, to run at the wild Cattel, yet with these they are so desperate, that the City of Guatemala hath often been afraid of them, and the Masters of their owne slaves and servants. Some of them feare not to encounter a Bull though wild and mad, and to grapple in the rivers (which are many there) with Crocodiles, or Lagarto's, as there they call them, till they have overmastered them, and brought them out to land from the water" (129). In this passage, Gage notes the limitless nature of black African valor, which contrasts with Native American populations living in the same area, who are "a people of no courage" (129). Somehow, Spanish masters have managed to corral black African valor, or desperation, toward their own ends. Importantly, though, Gage implies here that the control masters exercise is tenuous, suggested by the fear they have of "their owne slaves and servants."

That fear seems justified as indicated by the bands of Cimarrones who occupy the surrounding mountains and stage attacks against the Spanish at and near Guatemala. Gage provides an extensive description of the Cimarrones, which I quote at length to highlight the crucial rhetorical work the description performs:

> What the Spaniards most feare until they come out of these mountains, are some two or three hundred Black-mores, Simarrones, who for too much hard usage, have fled away from Guatemala and other parts from their Masters unto these woods, and there live and bring up their children and increase daily, so that all the power of Guatemala, nay all the Countrey about (having often attempted it) is not able to bring them under subjection. These often come out to the rode way, and set upon the Requas of Mules, and take of Wine, Iron, clothing and weapons from them as much as they need, without doing any harme unto the people, or slaves that goe with the Mules; but rather these rejoice with

them, being of one colour, and subject to slavery and misery which the others have shaken off: by whose example and encouragement many of these also shake off their misery, and joyne with them to enjoy libertie, though it be but in the woods and mountains. Their weapons are bowes and arrows which they use and carry about them, only to defend themselves, if the Spaniards set upon them; else they use them not against the Spaniards, who travel quietly and give them part of what provision they carry. These have often said that the chief cause of their flying to those mountains is to be in readinesse to joyne with the English or Hollanders, if ever they land in that Golfe; for they know, from them they may injoy that liberty which the Spaniards will never grant unto them. (130)

Gage describes the Cimarrones as a dynamic force, whose numbers grow daily, not only through the process of reproduction but also through a sense of racial unity and common suffering. Their rebellious nature emboldens and beckons the surrounding slave population. And their resistance apparently is effective as "all the power of Guatemala . . . is not able to bring them under subjection." Gage's description evokes the same kind of tense political environment that defined Panama during Drake's and Oxenham's exploits. That evocation is not incidental as Gage has already reminded readers that Drake and Oxenham were able to take advantage of such tensions years ago. Unlike their Native American counterparts, black Africans in and near Guatemala are familiar with weaponry and possess the bellicose nature that makes their military knowledge useful to the English. Referencing again the passage mentioned at the beginning of this chapter, those Cimarrones outside Guatemala are equipped with bows and arrows. They are, according to Gage, a standing army awaiting the arrival of English forces with whom they can align against the Spanish. The English, then, have an invitation and a moral justification for entering New Spain.

Here, Gage points out to readers that the English have an opportunity to replicate Drake's actions, but the outcome Gage imagines is much grander, more imperial, not simply raids to diminish Spanish wealth or effect forms of retribution, which was Drake's primary concern. Gage's more imperial ambitions are illustrated in how he represents the Cimarrones. They are noble savages, who possess a war-like quality that they rein in, only attacking Spanish mule trains to take "wine, Iron, clothing and weapons . . . out of necessity" and only "as much as they need." They employ their weapons in self-defense and only against the Spanish, a restraint that illustrates their humanity and suggests they are tame and manageable. Drake describes the Cimarrones in Panama as nations with their own kings and governance; Gage, though, recognizes no such political autonomy in Guatemala. In fact, the Cimarrones' agency is limited as Gage represents liberty in those final lines as something to be "grant[ed] unto them." In running away from their Spanish masters, then, the Cimarrones do not claim their liberty and self-possession. They are still objects of imperial power; their agency manifests itself in deciding to whom they subject themselves, and according to Gage, they have already made their choice. All the English need do is arrive in the "golfe."

Collaboration and Its Efficacy in the Face of Death

Given Gage's unmitigated belief in the martial utility of black Africans in New Spain, it perhaps comes as no surprise at the end of the narrative when he seeks out the protection of a formerly enslaved black African man he meets outside Guatemala. Through his relationship with this man, Miguel Dalva, Gage is able to provide experiential evidence for the region's collaborative potential about which he can only speculate elsewhere in the narrative. For three years, Gage lives in Guatemala serving as a preacher and a reader, or religious scholar, at a university there. His intense study of religious texts unsettles his prior convictions and convinces him of the "lies, errors, falsities and superstitions of the Church of Rome" (156). He undergoes a crisis of faith that he believes will make him vulnerable to the Inquisition.[26] To avoid that fate, he resolves to leave the church and New Spain and return to his home in England. Church and governmental officials in Guatemala deny his request for a license to leave, demanding he serve out the remainder of his ten-year commitment in New Spain. He determines then to travel to Native American communities outside of Guatemala to learn the languages and preach. In doing so, he hopes to earn the money he will need to provide his passage back to England at the end of his tenure. After a short stint in Petapa, a town in the valley outside Guatemala, he spends the next five years preaching to the Pokoman-speaking descendants of the Mayas in the neighboring towns of Mixco and Pinala, where he encounters a number of "dangers and deliverances" (166).

As the primary religious authority in Mixco and Pinala, Gage observes that inhabitants there only outwardly profess Christianity but inwardly "are given to witchcraft and idolatry" (166). Initially, he understands this hypocrisy as evidence of the "cruelty of the Spaniards," who do not concern themselves with

Native Americans' salvation or their general welfare. He preaches a series of sermons condemning Spaniards' treatment of natives, and he offers his living quarters as an asylum for those natives seeking spiritual or physical refuge. As an advocate for the native inhabitants, Gage quickly falls out of favor with one Spaniard in particular, who has a reputation for treating his servants especially cruelly. Gage's sermons so enrage this Spanish master that he threatens to kill Gage, one day brandishing a sword in Gage's front yard. At that point, Gage thinks it prudent to seek protection. He "called for a Blackmore Miguel Dalva a . . . lusty fellow who lived" near Gage (167). As a bodyguard of sorts, Dalva accompanies Gage as he moves about the two towns.

Dalva protects Gage not only from the threat of Spaniards but also from hostile Native Americans. Gage is rather zealous in attempting to root out the idolatry he sees plaguing the area. In his sermons he condemns such practices, denouncing native women as witches and destroying idols and temples. Dalva is his main ally in those efforts. In Mixco he encounters a rich and powerful native family of idol worshippers, the Fuentes, who overtly with "very faire tongue[s]" preach the Christian gospel and give freely to the church. Covertly, according to Gage, the family members undermine Gage's teachings. He discovers this duplicity after a feast when a family member publicly complains that the town is "deluded, and brought to worship a false God" because of the teachings of the Spanish. The man, drunk from overindulging at the feast, urges his fellow inhabitants to ignore Gage's teachings and "follow the old ways of their Forefathers, who worshipped their Gods aright" (171). Through word of mouth, Gage discovers that some Native Americans have been conducting idol worship secretly in a cave in the nearby mountains. Accompanied by Dalva and several others, Gage finds the cave and confiscates the idol, a black, wooden figure in the shape of a man's head and shoulders. He observes that the idol is reminiscent of those images of saints worshipped in the Catholic Church, which he also argues is guilty of idolatry (174).[27] The next Sunday he displays the idol during worship service and delivers a sermon about the evils of idolatry, with Dalva standing "neer the Pulpit" (174).

After the sermon, he then chops the idol into pieces with an ax and burns it before the congregation. This public desecration of a sacred object provokes outrage among members of his congregation, the Fuentes family in particular. "Afterwards," Gage says, "they acted most spightfully against me, and conspired day and night to get me at some advantage, and to kill me" (175). He accuses members of the Fuentes family of breaking into his home at night to attack him, after which he again seeks the aid of Dalva, who is "able to fight alone with any halfe dozen of Indians" (176). The next time a break-in occurs at Gage's home, Dalva is there. Upon hearing the intruders, Gage says, "the Black-more . . . tooke in his hand a couple of brick-bats of many which lay under the table for a worke which I had in hand, and as he opened the dore made a little noise, which was to them an item to flie down the stairs, and to run (as they thought) for their lives" (176). Dalva's valor is reminiscent of Gage's characterization of those machete-wielding slaves and those Cimarrones in Guatemala. While Dalva's presence in Gage's home does stop the late night break-ins, though, it does not prevent Gage from being assaulted. A month later, while Dalva is engaged elsewhere, members of the Fuentes family lure Gage to a house where they attack him with a stick and a knife. They stab him in his hand and break several of his teeth. He leaves Mixco and Pinala shortly afterward but not before ensuring his attackers face justice, with some of them imprisoned at Guatemala and others banished from the town. Rhetorically, Gage relates his experiences in Mixco and Pinala to illustrate the limits of his missionary efforts. He argues that Native Americans in Mixco "mutiny" against him because the Church sends a contradictory message by requiring them to worship saints but also condemning other forms of idol worship. He leaves the towns, he says, feeling "pity and commiseration" toward the inhabitants. "Certainly they are of a good and flexible nature," he argues, "and (were those Idols of Saints statues removed from their eyes) might be brought easily to worship one onely God" (178). Gage finds his efforts greatly compromised by the very entity on whose behalf he works.

The anecdote is also crucial because it illustrates a vital relationship between Gage and his *blackamoor* bodyguard, without whose efforts Gage might not have survived his stint in Mixco and Pinala. He calls Dalva a "true and trusty" friend (181). Sentimentality underscores his understanding of their relationship. As he prepares to leave New Spain for good, he withholds that information from Dalva, "lest the good old Black-more should grieve thinking never more to see me, and for the love he bare me . . . seek to stop me" (181). Given the close bond Gage says he forged with Dalva there is surprisingly little information he provides about the man. Unlike Lewis, for whom Gage provided a biography that covered his birth to the present, Dalva comes with no such personal context. He functions as a deus ex machina device, an agent of God that magically appears when Gage needs protection. Does he have a family? Under what circumstances does he arrive in the Guatemalan valley? How did he learn the use of weaponry and garner a reputation for valor and martial skills? Why does he help Gage? What are his personal motivations and ambitions? These questions are crucial because they emphasize the absence of particularity. His name notwithstanding, Dalva could represent any one of those Cimarrones or enslaved black Africans Gage references elsewhere in the narrative who he insists would readily ally with the English against the Spanish. In fact, Gage represents Dalva in the same vein; he is dependable, aggressive, effective with a weapon, loyal, valiant. In other words, divorced from a personal history, Dalva is a generic figure. Presumably, New Spain teems with Miguel Dalvas, ready and willing to serve. His character perpetuates an illusion by providing that illusion with a face and name. While Lewis illustrates the need for alliances, Dalva illustrates the viability of those alliances.

Anti-Allies: Countering the Imperial Narrative

Gage ends his narrative with a final encounter that actually undermines his claims for the plausibility of English–black African collaboration. Once he resolves to leave New Spain in 1637—after twelve years of traveling, reading, preaching, and observing—Gage travels from the Guatemala valley through Nicaragua and Granada to the settlement of Carthago, in present-day Costa Rica. From there, he boards a frigate heading to Portobello and Cartagena, Spanish port cities facing the Caribbean Sea. While en route, the frigate comes under attack by pirates flying a Dutch flag. Gage, understanding they do not have the means to resist, bemoans the fact that he soon will lose all the wealth he had accumulated while working in and near Guatemala, a sum in money and valuables he estimates at nine thousand pieces of eight (or Spanish dollars). Bracing themselves for brutality and robbery, those aboard Gage's ship are "somewhat comforted" when they see that the captain for the Dutch pirates is a mulatto born and raised in Havana (188). The passengers assume that the Spanish connection will translate into mercy. According to Gage, this mulatto pirate has a particular animosity for his birth nation resulting from "some wrongs which had been offered unto him from some commanding Spaniards in the Havana." Gage explains the manner in which the mulatto came to be in the service of the Dutch. Some years before, he fled Havana in a boat "out onto the Sea, where were some Holland Ships waiting for a prize" (189). The mulatto refugee threw himself on the mercy of the Dutch pirates, "which hee esteemed farre better then that of his own Countrymen" (189). According to Gage, the mulatto promised the Dutch to work with them against the Spanish, "which had most injuriously and wrongfully abused, yea and . . . whipped him in the Havana" (189). Gage's backstory does not make explicit whether the mulatto was enslaved or free when he fled.

When the mulatto pirate boards the frigate carrying Gage, he and his men confiscate nearly all the passengers' valuables, the majority of which come from the friar. Gage notes that the mulatto "had found little worth his labour, had it not been for the Indians offerings which I carried with mee" (189). Gage lost that day the equivalent of seven thousand pieces of eight in money, pearls, and precious stones. The booty was so substantial, according to Gage, that the pirates "loathe the rest of our grosse provisions of Bacon, Meale and Fowles, and our money tasted sweeter unto them, then the Hony which our Frigat also afforded them" (189). The captain does extend a measure of mercy to Gage, because he is a friar, by leaving him his sleeping pallet, books and a few other trinkets. In addition, Gage manages to keep hidden a small sum of money. Surprisingly, even as the mulatto pirate robs Gage of nearly all his wealth, he does so apologetically. According to Gage, the pirate implores him to "bee patient, saying that hee could doe no otherwise then he did with my mony and Pearles, and using that common Proverbe at Sea . . . to day fortune hath been for mee, tomorrow it may bee for thee: or to day I have got what tomorrow I may lose again" (189). The apology and the mercy are noble gestures. Gage also interprets the robbery as God's judgment, punishment for him having accumulated the wealth by perpetuating a ministry that encouraged the "superstitious and idolatrous masses" in New Spain (189).

He resigns himself to Divine will, but the resignation is short-lived. After robbing the passengers, the mulatto pirate prepares a formal dinner aboard ship to which he invites Gage. After the meal, Gage appeals to the captain to restore his valuables on the grounds that he is "no *Spaniard*, but an *English* man born" (emphasis in original 189). He assumes that the fact he is not "of an enemy nation to the Hollanders" will make the captain more amenable to his request (190). The captain, though, disregards the national distinction, telling Gage that he "must suffer with those, amongst whom [he] was found" (190). Next, Gage asks the captain to take him along to Holland. From there he could secure the short passage to England. Again, the mulatto pirate denies his request. He tells Gage that he has several other destinations planned before returning to Holland, and he expects to engage Spanish ships along the way, conditions that would compromise the friar's safety. The friar, then, returns to his former state of resignation, commending himself "again to Gods providence and protection" (190). After a day spent transferring their boon from one ship to another, the pirates leave, granting the passengers just enough provisions to get to the nearest port.

Gage's discussion of this pirate attack is yet another occasion to justify anti-Spanish sentiment. The mulatto's actions are retribution for past slights, not the deeds of a rogue, depraved pirate. Gage renders the mulatto sympathetically. In a particularly sentimental moment during dinner, the pirate asks Gage to seek out his mother if Gage is ever in Havana and tell her "how that for her sake hee had used [Gage] well and courteously in what hee could" (189). To further mitigate the pirate's rogue behavior, Gage diminishes the autonomy and power that we would associate with a captain by explaining that the mulatto was working under the authority of another, more renowned pirate, Pie de Palo (or Wooden Leg). The mulatto, then, could "doe no otherwise" than to take Gage's money and valuables. As he takes his leave, the pirate thanks Gage and the other passengers for "their good entertainment" of him while aboard their ship (190).

Gage interacts with the pirate based on certain assumptions that prevent him from at least considering the possibility that the pirate is not the noble victim he imagines, this despite the fact that the pirate challenges those assumptions with excuses that preserve his self-interest all while charming the friar. Note the reverential treatment the pirate affords Gage. He allows him to keep some few items; he *invites* him to dinner. In the end, he does not sink or confiscate their ship, which he says is in deference to Gage. Even his refusal to take Gage to Holland is presented as a concern for the friar's welfare rather than his own self-interest. Gage does not acknowledge that he and the pirate operate on different registers. For Gage, nationality matters. Initially, he believes that the mulatto pirate robs him because he associates him with Spain. Divesting the pirate of this false notion, though, does not improve his situation. Rather, it reveals that the pirate possesses no sense of allegiance or alliance with Gage—even if they presumably share a common foe. In fact, the pirate elides national distinctions in his insistence that Gage, even as an Englishman, must suffer the same fate as the Spaniards by virtue of being on the same ship. The moment reminds readers of what Sir Francis Drake must have known if not in 1573 then certainly by 1595 when Cimarrones turned against him in Panama—that English–black African alliances in the Americas were circumstantial, not inevitable.

This mulatto pirate, Miguel Dalva, and Lewis all occupy crucial space in Gage's narrative and in his conception of an English invasion of New Spain. He imagines that England can replicate Cortés's sixteenth-century invasion of Mexico. Importantly, just as Cortés benefited from alliances with Native American communities hostile toward the Aztecs, Gage argues that black Africans could be a resource for the English to overthrow the Spanish. In this way, Gage establishes a parallel rather than opposition between England and Spain. His approach to empire harkens back to Richard Eden and his 1555 *Decades of the Newe Worlde or West India,* discussed in chapter 1. Eden, in heralding the overseas achievements of Spain, urges the English to mimic Spain's deeds, which are a "good example to all Chrystian nations to folowe."[28] He encourages "al other to theyr poure to attempte the lyke vyages."[29] Other scholars have already noted England's paradoxical desire to imitate and condemn Spanish empire.[30] I note the appearance of this paradox in Gage's narrative to emphasize the ways in which black Africans posed representational problems for English writers attempting to articulate England's imperial design.

As mediated presences in Gage's narrative, black Africans impede Gage's efforts to articulate England as a second imperial coming to the Americas. Reading their representations against the grain suggests that Gage's black African counterparts, Lewis and the mulatto pirate in particular, are motivated by interests that conflict with Gage's and England's. They undermine Gage's portrayal elsewhere in the narrative of black Africans as the equivalent of Cortés's Native American allies, malleable and ready to work on behalf of English empire. Despite what the mediated presences of black Africans suggest, Gage remained committed to the idea that the English could take advantage of anti-Spanish sentiment, and he saw himself as an English spy. He addresses the narrative to the military commander Thomas Fairfax and embraces his role as informant, thanking God, who "hath made use of mee as a Joseph to discover the treasures of Egypt, or as the spies to search into the land of Canaan" (212).

The Consequences of Political Rhetoric and Failed Alliances

Gage publishes his narrative amid the turmoil of the English Civil War, a conflict that spanned nearly ten years, ending in 1651. The war, largely a power struggle between Parliament and the Crown, resulted in the execution of King Charles I, the exile of his son, and the dissolution of the monarchy. England became a Commonwealth under the leadership of Oliver Cromwell, its lord protector. During this nearly decade-long period, known as the Interregnum because the monarchy was restored in 1660, Cromwell turned his attentions toward England's long-standing rival Spain. He endorsed foreign policies designed to mitigate Spain's power both on the continent and abroad.³¹ In 1654 he began devising a strategy, in secret, to subdue Spain by way of the Americas. Using sea and land forces, Cromwell planned a series of invasions of Spanish colonies in the Caribbean.³² That strategy, or Western Design, echoed the observations Hakluyt made back in 1584 in his *Discourse Concerning Western Planting* that "if you touche [King Philip II] in the Indies, you touche the apple of his eye; for take away his treasure . . . which he hath almoste oute of his West Indies, his olde bandes of souldiers will soone be dissolved, his purposes defeated, his power and strengthe diminished, his pride abated, and his tyranie utterly suppressed."³³ The Western Design was, according to Carla Gardina Pestana, "a first step toward the complete ouster of Spain from the Western Hemisphere."³⁴

Gage was instrumental in shaping Cromwell's plan. In addition to the information he presents in his travel narrative, which was republished in 1655, he writes a letter to Cromwell in 1654 in which he reiterates some of the observations from the travel narrative, including his expectations for English–black African alliances.³⁵ He provides Cromwell six reasons that "this is not a worke so hard and difficult as is by some apprehended."³⁶ Among those reasons he points out that many of the richest cities in the region are poorly defended, lacking manpower, as well as weapons and other defensive structures. In addition, the Spaniards who live there cannot stage a defense because they are "lazy sinfull people, feeding like beasts upon their lusts, and upon the fat of the land, and never trained up to warres."³⁷ Just in case the English fear attacks from maroons and enslaved black Africans, Gage assures Cromwell that as far as "Mulattos and Negros opposing, there is no feare, for if any armes were committed to them, soone mighte the masters feare to bee overpowered by their slaves and servants."³⁸ As he does in the narrative, here Gage suggests that the English should supply black Africans with weapons, again representing them as pugnacious. He also reiterates the tense sociopolitical climate that he noted in his travel narrative was characteristic of New Spain:

> "Because there are many strivings and factions among them, as Criolians, or thereborne Spaniards, against such as come from Spaine, Mestizos, Mulattos, and Negros against both, and all against the poore Indians; so that the factions which were amongst the Indians of Tlaxcala and Mexico were Cortez . . . his best advantage to conquer that land with 500 or 600 men; so no doubt but their present factions may bee any other nation's advantage to conquer them againe. And if at

the first arrival any nation shall proclaime liberty to Mullatos, Negros and Indians, for such a liberty they would joyne with them against the Spaniards, as I have often heard them say, when there I lived.[39]

Gage makes more explicit what he implies in the narrative. Just as Cortés took advantage of internal strife in and near Mexico that allowed him to conquer the Aztecs with minimal manpower, the English can do the same by exploiting tensions among the racial and ethnic groups in New Spain. The final lines of the above passage evoke those conversations Gage says he had with Cimarrones in the Guatemalan mountains who, with bows and arrows at the ready, were awaiting the arrival of the English (or Dutch) to liberate them. It is a reminder of the moral and ethical contours of this proposed invasion.

With Gage sailing along as a chaplain, an English military fleet departed England in December of 1654, under the joint command of General Robert Venables (in charge of soldiers) and Admiral William Penn (in charge of seamen). Cromwell's orders to these commanders did not specify a first target in the Caribbean, allowing Venables and Penn to decide which colony to strike first. Cromwell and his advisers, however, did offer a number of suggestions, among them the islands of Hispaniola, Cuba, and Puerto Rico, and Cartagena on the mainland. Venables and Penn chose Hispaniola, an island that Cromwell predicted "may probably be possest without much difficulty."[40] Cromwell's prediction echoes Gage's. In his letter to Cromwell the previous year, Gage noted that defenses at Hispaniola were minimal and insisted that a conquest there would provide the English a symbolic victory that would lead to the fall of other colonies. Although possession of the island would not provide the English with vast resources and stores of wealth, "Hispaniola was the Spaniards first plantation," he writes to Cromwell, "and therefore would bee to them a bad omen to beginne to loose [sic] that, which they first enjoyed"[41] Aside from the symbolism, Gage insisted the island would be an easy conquest because it was sparsely populated. That he expected they would benefit from alliances with the non-Spanish inhabitants goes without saying.

With some eight thousand land soldiers and another thousand sailors, an English military fleet arrived at Hispaniola in April 1655. By sea, they attempted a siege of the capital city, Santo Domingo, and they disembarked the land force to march on the city. Despite Cromwell and Gage's assessments of the island's weak defensive system, the siege proved ineffective, as did the land march. The Spanish had strengthened the island's defenses some years before. Venables's soldiers suffered the most. After disembarking forty miles from their intended target, they trekked four days across rough terrain with no guide and little water and food. Initially, it seemed that Venables and his men would benefit from the kind of alliance Gage predicted. On their third day of marching, they arrived at a plantation and, according to one soldier, "there came in a negro to us, who had civill entertainment and the Generall's protection; he gave us hopes of more negroes coming in, which succeeded not."[42] In the three weeks they attempted to conquer the island, the English found little succor from black Africans, enslaved or marooned. In fact, black Africans were among the most aggressive of the island's inhabitants to resist English occupation. They staged a number of ambushes along the road to Santo Domingo. Their resistance combined with that of another group of inhabitants called "cow killers," which English sailor Henry Whistler describes as "vagabonds that are saved from the gallows in Spaine."[43] They were sent to Hispaniola, according to Whistler, specifically to slaughter wild cattle and harvest the hides. In consequence, they were especially adept with weapons. Whistler notes, "If it were not for theas Cowkillers and the Negors the spaniyards ware not abell to hould up his hand against any ennemie."[44]

The resistance struck terror in the hearts of Venables's soldiers. Poorly disciplined, poorly trained, and poorly equipped with weapons, many fled instead of fought. One English soldier provides the following anecdote to illustrate the chaos that ensued from the fear that permeated the English camp. When 1,500 English soldiers stopped at a bay for water, the soldier writes, "there came downe to them 2 of our owne negroes to drink likewise, which some of them spying cried 'the enemy,' upon which all immediately threw away their armes, and ran for it, some for feare leapt into the river, whereof 3 were drowned, soe much were we cow'd and daunted."[45] To dissuade the fear—or more precisely channel it in another direction—Venables eventually issued the order "against runaways, that his next fellow should kill him, or be tried for his own life."[46] In the wake of Gage's prediction that English forces could easily rout "lazy, sinful" Spaniards and align with eagerly awaiting black Africans, Venables's land forces suffered a thousand fatalities (the result of enemy attacks, dehydration, and sickness) compared to forty from Hispaniola.[47]

Needless to say, the invasion failed, and it did so for a number of reasons. There were issues related to logistics and execution: the expedition's co-commanders distrusted each other; they communicated poorly with each other and with their troops; the forces were poorly supplied with food and water, which made them vulnerable to illness; and without adequate weaponry, they were ill-prepared for Spanish resistance, especially that posed by the island's black African inhabitants. In addition to those issues, some of Venables's contemporaries understood the failure as a Divine judgment, believing that Cromwell, in Pestana's words, had somehow "sinfully called down the wrath of the Lord."[48] Still others believed the failure resulted from the defective English character of those sailors and soldiers who manned the expedition.[49] Remember Venables's complaints about his troops' cowardice and poor discipline.[50] Venables and Penn needed to save face and salvage something of the expedition that might mollify Cromwell's anticipated outrage. They did not immediately inform Cromwell of their failure. "Narratives of triumph," as Nicole Greenspan points out, "were preferable to those of defeat."[51] So the commanders withheld information while channeling their imperial energies toward a new target, Jamaica, "hoping that Jamaica would" provide "reports of military victory."[52]

Jamaica was at the time a minor Spanish outpost, lightly guarded. The English were able to occupy the island, admittedly a "smaller success," despite violent clashes with the inhabitants.[53] The most aggressive resistance again came from maroons and enslaved black Africans, many of whom the Spanish freed just before fleeing the island in the wake of English arrival. The Spanish employed the same strategy—the promise of freedom—that Gage had predicted would make black Africans amenable to the English cause. What is more, the Spanish forged alliances with those black Africans to stage raids against the English. As at Hispaniola, in Jamaica black Africans succeeded in propagating fear among English soldiers. The Spanish captain Julián de Castilla notes of one black African ally that "he was a fine marksman, and did not waste a shot; whenever he fired, he indicated his mark, saying to his comrades: 'That Englishman drops now.'"[54] As part of English occupation of Jamaica, Venables spread his troops across the island with instructions to establish living quarters in the newly abandoned farms and plantations. They planted crops and built defensive structures. When a joint force of thirty Spanish soldiers and maroons attacked English forces quartered at one outlying ranch, the "encounter struck such terror to the rest in those parts and on those farms, that they afterwards retired in all haste, abandoning what they had planted, and their blockhouse, which they had erected to protect themselves."[55]

Cimarrones who had allied with the Spanish or who were working on their own behalf in Jamaica frustrated English efforts toward conquest, so much so that, as Castilla notes, "the English entertain a marked aversion to the negroes, because they have been unable to reduce them to their following."[56] Venables and Penn failed to achieve the kind of strike that would in fact "touche the apple of [Spain's] eye." They returned, disgraced, to England, Penn in June and Venables in July. Cromwell temporarily imprisoned both in the Tower of London, accusing them of abandoning their posts and his Western Design. Gage stayed on in Jamaica, dying there a year later from illness that decimated the troops.[57] In those months leading up to his death, he must have experienced some measure of cognitive dissonance as he watched Spain take advantage of the kinds of alliances he had thought were reserved for the English. For five years, English troops struggled to quell the guerilla attacks of hostile Spanish and African forces. They finally succeeded, ironically, when a Cimarrón leader named Juan Lubolo and his followers defected to the English side. As it turns out, English-African alliances did make the difference. With his defection, Lubolo deprived the Spanish of much-needed food and manpower, which Lubolo had been supplying the Spanish. Once aligned with the English, Lubolo provided valuable intelligence about Spanish hiding places and war strategy. "This was a staggering blow," as S. A. G. Taylor notes, "and it was to prove the death-knell of the Spanish cause."[58] With black African assistance, the English were finally able to claim conquest of Jamaica and establish civil government in 1660.[59]

To some extent, Gage's narrative was a valuable tool for emphasizing the importance of alliances as key to European occupation of American territories. In addition, his narrative illustrates England's struggle to condemn Spain's colonial enterprise while at the same time admiring the deeds of its earliest conquistadors. Gage articulates England's own imperial potential within the context of Spanish history and of a black African population that was actively engaging the social and political landscape in Mexico and Central America. As a disruptive energy coursing through Gage's narrative, the mediated presences of black Africans matter in his text because they underscore the central importance of collaboration—and its precarious nature—as a primary tenet of England's imperial design in Spanish America.

Venables and Penn's failures in the Caribbean suggest that Gage overestimated the ease with which England could establish alliances with black Africans and imitate Cortés's American invasion. England's failed efforts to conquer Hispaniola and the protracted resistance mainly from black Africans they encountered in Jamaica illustrate that discourse and fantasy did not align with the material realities. Gage wrote a narrative and then encouraged

Cromwell to craft foreign policy that derived its imaginative energy from a combination of fact and fantasy, all the while failing to account for the agentive potential of black Africans. Gage was not alone in underestimating black African autonomy and agency in the Americas as England sought to expand its overseas reaches in the mid-seventeenth century. Richard Ligon, who traveled to Barbados to manage a sugar plantation at the same time Gage published his narrative, embellished his account of Barbados with a few imperial fantasies of his own.

CHAPTER 4

Consuming Beauty
Richard Ligon, Black African Women, and a Reciprocity of Power

Despite Venables and Penn's failed efforts in the Caribbean, Cromwell and his advisers did not immediately declare the Western Design a failure. For several years they debated ways to modify the strategy to shore up an English presence in the region. Several months after England took Jamaica in 1655, Cromwell issued a proclamation encouraging English men and women to move to the island. He promised them certain allotments of land, including twenty acres for every male over twelve years of age, military protection, tax and rent abatements for a set number of years, and a share of the profits gained from exploitation of the island's natural resources, including game and mineral mines.[1] While Cromwell worked to make Jamaica more appealing for the English, Richard Ligon pursued a similar agenda in Barbados with publication in 1657 of his *True and Exact History of the Island of Barbadoes*.

Ligon traveled through the Caribbean in 1647 to pursue business in Barbados. In the travel narrative he published a decade later, Ligon painstakingly describes the island. In addition to vivid descriptions of flora, fauna, and climate, he describes the people, culture, and religions. He explains the island economy, driven by sugar and slavery. He even includes maps and financial charts to illustrate land values and profits. His narrative recounts the quotidian. Despite the outcome of events in 1655, Ligon's text offered hope that English expansion in the West Indies was still a possibility.

Given the narrative's painstaking and methodical attention to detail, it is no surprise when, barely ten pages into the text, Ligon patiently explores his encounter with a beautiful black enslaved woman on the Cape Verde island of Santiago. Like so many English voyages to Guinea and the Caribbean, including those of Hawkins and Drake, Ligon's ship stopped in the Cape Verde islands for food and fresh water. In Santiago, still controlled by the Portuguese in the mid-seventeenth century, Ligon and several of the crew dine one evening with the island's governor in a set-up reminiscent of a European royal court. Ligon notes the culture that surrounds him—the table setting, food, wine, servants, musical entertainment. He also describes the governor's mistress, who is a "Negro of the greatest beautie and majestie together: that ever [he] saw in one woman" (12).[2]

Even more meticulously than he renders the governor's house, Ligon describes the mistress, draped in silks, satins, laces, and fine jewels, which are various shades of blue, purple, and orange. A green turban and thin veil cover her head. He notes her tall, stately posture and graceful demeanor, and she has a pair of exotic eyes, which he describes as the "richest Jewells: for they were the largest, and most oriental" that he had ever seen (12). At one point the woman lifts her veil as if offering him full access to gaze upon her. This ethnographic moment reduces the woman to the cultural landscape. Like the food, entertainment, and accommodations, she represents the governor's opulence. When Ligon can observe no more, he then speaks to the woman, praising her beauty and majesty. He pays suit, lavishing her with gifts of gold and silver fabrics. She accepts the gifts and implores Ligon to think of some way she might be able to reciprocate his favor. Ligon leaves this sexual innuendo unexplored. He ends the encounter, saying, "Other addresses were not to be made, without the dislike of the [governor], for they are there as jealous of their Mistresses, as the *Italians* of their wives" (13).

Ligon prolongs the courtly energy of his narrative by constructing another, parallel, scene. Soon after he takes his leave of the governor's mistress, he encounters two black African maidens drinking water at a well. Their beauty is just as remarkable as that of the mistress. They are "wanton, as the soyle that bred them, sweet as the fruites they fed on" (16). Again, once the observation ends, Ligon offers the girls gifts and praise, hoping in exchange for some measure of returned affection. The girls accept his gifts but do not speak to him. They turn their faces and whisper to each other. Ligon's love goes unrequited. He ends the moment with a lyrical soliloquy about beauty and passion.

On the face of it, these two moments in Ligon's narrative appear as exotic—and typical—ethnographic moments of travel writing. The women are part of the Atlantic landscape that Ligon has rendered for a reading audience back in England. They are novelties similar to the birds, climate, fruit, and so forth that Ligon will describe later in the Caribbean. As typical as the moments are, however, they are also atypical, as evident in the very fact that

Ligon seems to undergo a transformation through the course of the scenes. He begins as a detached observer invested with an imperial gaze designed to control, to conquer everything in its sight.[3] Once he showers the women with gifts and compliments, he turns into a love-struck suitor interacting with the women through a discourse of courtship. Here I rely on Catherine Bates's understanding of courtship as a process in which a suitor modifies his "behaviour and utterance with a view to attracting favour and winning from the object of his devotion some longed-for token of esteem."[4] The narrative also undergoes a formal transformation. Prior to his descriptions of the women, and afterward, Ligon relates details objectively, as matters of fact. The writing is almost scientific, mechanical in its specificity. In those moments when he mentions the black African women, though, wonder infuses the writing; the language turns toward passion and love. The travel and commercial narrative becomes—just for a moment—a courtly romance.

This generic disruption in and of itself might not be remarkable. Ligon, for sure, was not the first European male traveler to imagine himself the subject of an American romance.[5] Rather, the disruption is remarkable because it is driven, in part, by the actions of the women he observes. Ligon decides to court the women after his observations alone fail to satisfy his curiosity. The women themselves to some extent limit Ligon's observations by raising and lowering veils or covering portions of their faces with their hands. The women become objects of desire, to be pursued, conquered, and exploited. They are available for imperial consumption much like the flora and fauna Ligon describes elsewhere in the narrative.[6] However, by turning himself into a courtier, Ligon inevitably positions the women into a paradigm that centers on the concept of reciprocity. The reaction of the courted is equally important as the actions of the courter. Without that reciprocal action, a suitor cannot complete the ritual of courtly love. In other words, once Ligon dons the role of courtier, he opens a narrative space for the women to act, to become something more than objects of desire, consumable goods. Only the mistress reciprocates the courting by accepting Ligon's gifts and offering him a brief conversation. The two maidens refuse to act out the ritual. They leave Ligon standing in silence at the well.

In this chapter, I examine the manner in which Ligon articulates his encounters with black African women in Santiago to cohere with an imperial discourse that renders the Caribbean a bounteous space available for European, English in particular, use. The narrative disruptions that characterize the representations, though, suggest that the women's material presences impede

Ligon's efforts. They dictate how Ligon negotiates his roles as observer, participant, and ultimately, as writer, compromising the narrative's imperial ambitions. Elsewhere in the text, Ligon describes enslaved black African women as monstrous bodies hunched over in sugar fields with babies strapped to their backs that they nurse even while they work. The women Ligon encounters in Santiago, though, are not fertile bodies valuable for both their labor and reproductive capabilities; in fact, only one of the women is actually enslaved, and her labor does not produce tangible, material goods. These women consume more than they produce. Through flirtation, they procure goods from Ligon, which they add to existing stashes or use immediately, pulling him into modes of interaction that disrupt the reproducer/producer paradigm that would have rendered the women commodities. The representations of these women point to Ligon's limitations as an individual and as a colonial agent promoting colonization. What is more, they challenge English understandings of the Caribbean as a passive landscape and black African women as objects of that landscape, available for productive and reproductive purposes.

Ligon—Historian, Advertiser, Ethnographer

In early modern England, travel narratives were, to use Howard Marchitello's terminology, narratives of possession. "This writing," Marchitello argues, "offers the implicit formulation of its own nature as essentially descriptive: explorers voyage into the unknown lands of the New World and return to write their supposedly objective descriptions of them. Yet we know that this promise of theoretical objectivity in fact breaks down almost immediately and the writing that emerges from its ruins is a more or less explicit narrative of possession."[7] The objectivity "breaks down," Marchitello argues, because the descriptive mode gives way to the narrative mode, in which the person or object being described suddenly becomes secondary to a larger rhetorical purpose—be it commercial, political, cultural, etcetera. The description becomes imbued with meaning, intent. In this regard, Marchitello echoes Kim Hall, who argues about the nature of description in travel writing that it "becomes in such texts not a neutral term of observation but an act connoting ownership and control."[8]

The descriptive mode in travel writing gains its power, its efficacy, through its unassuming veneer. Because the writer appears objective, he also appears accurate and credible, which gives him the power through writing to create whatever he wants—and whomever he wants. This dynamic informs Ligon's use of description when writing anecdotes about beautiful black African women. However, something happens that prompts him to abandon the travel writing mode in favor of one more fanciful, romantic. The interruption is all the more striking given the economic and political design of Ligon's narrative.

A *True and Exact History* promised a financial recovery for Ligon and urged further English settlement and investment in the Caribbean. His purposes for writing the narrative are manifested in the preface, where he explains that he returned to England in debt. He wrote the narrative in 1653 while in debtor's prison. The preface consists of an epistolary exchange between Ligon and the lord bishop of Salisbury, Brian Duppa. Ligon also includes a laudatory poem by George Walshe. Apparently, the bishop, with whom Ligon had had previous conversations about his time spent in Barbados, suggested he write a detailed account. The bishop urges him to find "some Noble person, that may with more advantage, take you and your Book into the same Cock-boat with him, and keep you this Winter both from cold and hunger" (unpaginated).

Likely, Duppa and Ligon believed a book about Barbados would be financially viable because of its potential to promote English settlement in the Caribbean, including England's newly acquired Jamaica. Karen Kupperman, in her recent edited edition of Ligon's narrative, argues that Ligon structures his narrative, adding charts, diagrams for sugar works, and other information, to serve as a "prospectus for investment in the Jamaica project."[9] As for Barbados, it had always factored prominently into Gage's and Cromwell's ideas for an English invasion. Gage insisted that Barbados could supply the expedition with ten thousand fighting men.[10] Cromwell, in his instructions to Venables and Penn, ordered the commanders to stop first in Barbados to secure additional men, supplies, and counsel, assuming that English officials stationed there would have valuable knowledge to help craft a plan of attack.[11] In addition, Thomas Modyford, a Barbados planter who would become governor of Jamaica, understood Barbados as a crucial way station. In 1654 he wrote to Cromwell, "Upon any design out of England upon the Spaniards in the West Indies, it seemeth to be most adviseable, that the general should land in Barbados with 2000 men in November, if he can, where he shall be sure to double his number."[12] Modyford deemed Barbados "the magazine of all necessaries."[13]

Venables's *Narrative,* an apologia explaining the failure of the general's mission, best illustrates the importance of Barbados in the execution of the Western Design. Among his litany of excuses, Venables writes, "After a most Merciful and good hand of God towards us at Sea, the twentyninth last we came to Anchor at Carlisle Bay. The next day we landed and fell about our work: but presently of our selves, and by friends privately, were assured (which we find true) that all the Inhabitants were against our design, as destructive to them, and that they would not really and cordially assist us."[14] Venables complains that men, quality weapons, and cooperation were in short supply in Barbados. The point here is that Barbados was central in Cromwell's desires to plant the English in the West Indies to establish England's "economic prowess, military dominance, and a vastly increased empire in the Americas," as Carla Pestana articulates it.[15]

To establish himself as a credible source of information about the commercial viability of the region, Ligon relies heavily on descriptive writing. He represents himself as the consummate observer, one who can see with an unusual acuity, a gift he developed in his younger years as a student of art and music. He reveals in the preface that he had some experience with painting, and he designs the narrative as a visual experience, not just a textual one. As he explains to the lord bishop, "Being cast into Prison, I was deprived both of light and lonelinesse, two main helpers in that Art; and so being disabled to discern or judge of Colours, I was compelled to express my designes in Black and White: So that now you will finde exposed to your view, a piece of wild *Grotesco*, or loose extravagant *Drolorie*, rather than a Regular piece of Story or Landscape. Rough drawn, and unproportionably stell'd, though it be, I here present it" (unpaginated).[16] The bishop dismisses Ligon's self-consciousness, responding, "You say, that in your younger time, you acquainted your selfe with Musick and Painting; and had you not said so, the reading of this Book would have made me say it for you; for, it is so Musically made up, and all the descriptions so Drawn to the life, that I know no Painting beyond it." The bishop's letter, even more so than Ligon's own words, asserts Ligon's credibility as an observer. Duppa proclaims, "I know none that hath written of this Argument before; and next, I am perswaded, that having read this Description of yours, none that come after will venture upon it." Ligon's text is the final word. But his text is not the only word. His narrative of Barbados joined a collection of accounts of the island, of the West Indies, that were popular because of their commercial usefulness.[17]

When the English arrived in Barbados in 1625, they found it abandoned, although there was evidence of a Native American presence at some earlier date. The English quickly claimed the land and planted tobacco, expecting the crop to provide the same kind of financial bounty it provided for the Virginia colony. They soon discovered, though, that the soil could not sustain a viable tobacco crop.[18] In the 1640s, planters turned their attention to sugar cultivation, for which the landscape was much better suited. Because sugar was a labor-intensive crop and required massive plots of land, the plantation landscape shifted from small farms to huge plantation systems.[19] This meant fewer investment opportunities for newcomers, who struggled to find land. In 1651 one traveler to the island discouraged others from settling there. After declaring that "this island flourisheth so much, that it hath more people and commerce then all the islands of the Indies," the writer warns off further plantation, saying, "In regard the sellers are well matched by the buyers, I conceive it the worst plantation to go to either to live or make a voyage and returne. For what is here is as well in the rest of the islands, and much more conveniency to plant, for here they have too many people, and in them there is too few, and in most of them ground enough."[20]

Unlike migrants to portions of the North American mainland, many of whom were prompted by religious or political dissent, most Englishmen who traveled to Barbados saw it as a financial investment. For those writing about the island then, their narratives became scouting reports. Two years after the arrival of the English, John Smith described Barbados as possessing "good ground; abounding with an infinite number of Swine, some turtles, and many sorts of excellent fish; many great ponds wherein is duck and mallard; excellent clay for pots, wood and stone for building."[21] Another observer declared Barbados one of the most suitable for plantation.[22] Cromwell's imperial design for the West Indies attests to the political import of narratives such as Ligon's. The narrative's overall emphasis on Barbados's commercial viability renders all the more striking Ligon's digression with the mistress and virgins at the well, especially because those encounters occur on an island that is economically unviable and irrelevant to Cromwell's plans.

Santiago, under control of what was by the mid-seventeenth century a relatively weaker Portuguese empire, was the first of the islands in the Cape Verde archipelago to be occupied by the Portuguese in 1462. Initially, it was a bustling center of trade for the empire, producing rum, cotton, and cattle. Those goods were traded for slaves along the West African coast. Hawkins stopped there on his Guinea/West Indies voyages in the 1560s.[23] When Ligon arrived in 1647, however, the island had lost its vitality, having been plagued over the years by severe droughts and famines that ruined food and trade supplies. Attacks from French, Dutch, and English pirates further exacerbated the island's decline. Sir Francis Drake raided its capital city, Ribeira Grande, in 1585.[24] The island Ligon observes is void of vegetation, livestock, any real commercial usefulness. He explains that the commodities on the island are "few, and inconsiderable; Sugar, Sweet-meats, and Coco-nuts, being the greatest trade they had" (18). The moments detailing his encounters with beautiful black women, then, appear a bit self-indulgent, an opportunity to ponder aesthetic rather than commercial and political concerns.

Ligon acknowledges the moments' incongruity. After describing the women, he writes, "But you will think it strange, that a man of my age and gravity, should have so much to do with Beauty and Love" (17). He responds to prospective critics by saying, among other things, that there was not much else to focus on in Santiago. From his perspective, the island is not commercially viable, but it is rich in one thing—beauty. Ligon's explanation might perhaps justify the length of his digression and even the tonal and rhythmic shifts, but it does not account for the generic disruption the moments produce. The anecdotes are romantic, courtly musings nestled into a narrative largely designed to encourage Englishmen to invest in the Caribbean. For sure, Ligon's narrative sojourn in Santiago, though odd, is not wholly extraneous material. It serves a larger commercial purpose by emphasizing through opposition the vast richness and culture of Barbados. Though relevant, Ligon's musings maintain a disruptive quality in his text resulting from his encounters with black women, which makes those musings rich sites for contemplating the impact of black women's material presences on English conceptions of their imperial project and on colonial contact narratives.

The Problem of Black African Femininity

Much like the other writers discussed so far, Ligon relies on racial myths and assumptions to articulate his travels through the Caribbean and motivate English investors. He does this primarily through his representations of black African women not in Santiago but in Barbados. His descriptions center mostly on the women's breasts, through which he naturalizes the link between somatic features and labor. He writes, "The young Maids have ordinarily very large breasts, which stand strutting out so hard and firm, as no leaping, jumping, or stirring, will cause them to shake any more, than the brawns of their arms. But when they come to be old, and have had five or six Children, their breasts hang down below their Navels, so that when they stoop at their common work of weeding, they hang almost down to the ground, that at a distance, you would think they had six legs" (103). Here Ligon evokes rhetorical strategies from his predecessors of representing black African women in monstrous terms.[25] Remember Towerson's descriptions of black women's breasts along the Melegueta Coast.[26] Both as those of maidens and those of mothers, black women's breasts carry the weight of their perceived abnormalities, their inhumanity. Importantly, those breasts, central to the process of reproduction, also signal that the abnormalities are innate and reproducible.

Ligon goes on to explain that the children (themselves future workers) of these women "when they are first born, have the palms of their hands and the soles of their feet, of a whitish color, and the sight of their eyes of a blueish color, not unlike the eyes of a young Kitling; but, as they grow older, they become black" (103). The monstrosity self-perpetuates. So does the labor. These kinds of representations, Jennifer Morgan notes, "indicated that [black enslaved women] did not descend from Eve. . . . Such imaginary women suggested an immutable difference between Africans and Europeans, a difference ultimately codified as race."[27] Morgan argues that black women signified and, through procreation, were seen to perpetuate racial differences, differences that rendered black Africans as subhuman and therefore fit for slavery. The women appear a robust and fertile human resource of which Barbados planters could take advantage. The problem for Ligon, though, is that the black women he meets in Santiago do not confirm his prior racial conceptions. When he first encounters the governor's mistress, after he recovers from the shock of her beauty, Ligon wants to see her teeth to find if they are "yellow and foul," which, he says, is a general feature of the teeth of black Africans. When finally she smiles, she reveals "rowes of pearls, so clean, white" (12). These three women do not fit conventional modes of representation. They are not grotesque or crude and savage in their mannerisms or monstrous in their anatomy. In Ligon's mind, the women are a more refined, elevated form of blackness. His reaction to them registers an intersection between race and social class. That is to say, Ligon's observations delineate two categories of black women, only one of which he marks as suitable for the back-breaking labor of sugar plantations. The other category of women he locates within a court setting as the objects of courtly romance.[28]

Like race, gender complicates Ligon's descriptions of the three black African women. As a social marker, gender in early modern Europe worked similarly to race—a system of social practices (or experiences) that gained credence from the observable biological differences in women's and men's bodies. And like race, gender codes, as Susan Dwyer Amussen points out, were essential to maintaining an ordered society in the early modern period, a society in which men and women interacted in complementary roles.[29] Those roles dictated that men and women exhibit "essential" and visible forms of masculinity and femininity in their dress and comportment. Anthony Fletcher argues, "While sex was still unstable and indeterminate it was the more important to ensure that gender provided a respected foundational structure which could make sense of each person's identity and enable society to function without disorder."[30] According to Fletcher, masculinity demanded men conduct themselves with discretion, good judgment, benevolence, and patriotism.[31] Femininity on the other hand, dictated that women appear modest and virtuous.

In early modern England, white women specifically embodied this brand of femininity. Africans, both men and women, stood in opposition. Therefore, to be a "black" woman was itself a social conflict. As Kim Hall points out in her examination of the relationship between gender and race, "'Black' in Renaissance discourses is opposed not to 'white' but to 'beauty' or 'fairness,' and these terms most often refer to the appearance or moral states of women."[32] According to Hall, black men and white women formed a binary that allowed Englishmen to first of all, "project onto the bodies of white women the anxieties of an evolving monarchial nation-state in which women are the repository of the symbolic boundaries of the nation."[33] Not only did white women represent an essential Englishness, in opposition to an African foreignness, but, Hall also argues, white women form the boundaries of whiteness and masculinity. "When white women," Hall maintains, "bear the symbolic weight of the culture in this way, attention is deflected from the equally vulnerable bodies of white men and the potentially threatening bodies of black women."[34]

Black women posed such a threat, as Lynda Boose notes, because they challenged patriarchal power. While Boose attributes the rise of what she terms "white racism" to several factors in this era, she privileges the influence of gender, focusing on that aspect of gender that deemed men the sole progenitors of the next generation. Theories about reproduction marked women as merely receptacles, or incubators, housing the offspring; they had no influence over the bodily features of that offspring. These theories were especially appealing to men because they positioned them as the dominant sex and assured them "perfect self-replication," according to Boose, the promise that they could produce children that would perpetuate their image.[35] White women did not disturb these ideas because the children produced by the union of a white man and white woman would have, presumably, exhibited no external signs of a maternal genetic influence. Likewise, the union between a black man and a white woman did not challenge reproduction theories because the offspring would likely assume the darker hue of the black father. The union between a white man and a black woman, though, was unique and especially egregious because the offspring not only bore the racial mark of "blackness" but also existed as physical proof of woman's active contribution in the reproduction process. Boose argues of this particular type of union that it forced a white male culture to concede that "not only was black more powerful than white and capable of absorbing and coloring it, but that in this all-important arena of reproductive authority, black women controlled the power to resignify all offspring as the property of the mother."[36] Consequently, when black women appear in the literature, Boose argues, their reproductive "power" is muted, repressed.

This repression is exhibited in Ligon's representation of the slave mistress and the two maidens. When Ligon transforms them into courted women, their race becomes less central to the encounter; the same is true of their sexuality and reproductive capabilities, because the main point of the courtship ritual was not marriage or even a sexual liaison. The rhetoric of courtship provided male courtiers "a rich and varied means of exploring relations with their sovereign, allowing them to rehearse alternative and competing experiences: success and failure, domination and subordination, obedience and subversion."[37] In other words, courtiers used courtship to fantasize about various models of empowerment. Courtship was an exercise in control that Elizabethan men, in particular, employed to assuage their anxieties about living under the rule of a female Crown. Just as courtiers did not pursue the queen for her sexual or reproductive power, Ligon sixty years later does not pursue the mistress and the virgins at the well to satisfy physical passions. Rather, he attempts to ritualize the encounters to understand them, to control them. As I will argue shortly, the pursuit is both the means and the end.

The three women, however, exist in a nebulous space that presents a quandary for Ligon. They are black Africans who do not fit conventional representations. They are women who reside outside the gendered norms of an "ordered English society" because of their race. What is more, the power that Ligon can claim over these women is limited, restricted to the text. Physically, he cannot own them. The mistress is already possessed by another, and the virgins at the well are freeborn. The problem is compounded by the fact that Ligon displaces them rhetorically. He places them into a court setting, wooing them similarly to the manner in which English women would have been pursued at court. At stake is the social order that Amussen and Hall argue was so imperative to English culture and imperial expansion in the seventeenth century. For all of Queen Elizabeth's efforts to purge her nation-state in 1601 of "blackamoors," Ligon in 1657 situates three black African women right into the heart of that nation-state.[38]

Black African Beauty and an Imperial Blind Spot

When Ligon first beholds the governor's African mistress, his gaze becomes a camera lens providing a close-up. To return to the description referenced at the beginning of this chapter, Ligon notes of her physical appearance that she was

> a Negro of the greatest beautie and majestie together: that ever I saw in one woman. Her stature large, and excellently shap't, well favour'd, full eye'd, & admirably grac't; she wore on her head a roll of green taffatie, strip't with white and Philiamort, made up in manner of a Turban; and over that a sleight vayle, which she tooke off at pleasure. On her bodie next her linen, a Peticoate of Orange Tawny and Skye Colour; not done with Straite stripes, but wav'd; and upon that· a mantle of purple silke, ingrayld with straw Colour. This Mantle was large, and tyed with a knot of verie broad black Ribbon, with a rich Jewell on her right shoulder, which came under her left arme, and so hung loose and carelesly, almost to the ground. On her Legs, she wore buskins of wetched Silke, deckt with Silver lace, and Fringe; Her shooes, of white Leather, lac't with skie colour; and pinkt between those laces. In her eares, she wore Large Pendants, about her neck; and on her armes, fayre Pearles. But her eyes were her richest jewells: for they were the largest, and most orientall, that I have ever seene. (12)

Ligon experiences a kind of wonder, a reaction common in New World travelers. I evoke here Stephen Greenblatt's understanding of colonial encounter. He argues that Europeans traveling in the early Americas "experienced something like the 'startle reflex' one can observe in infants: eyes widened, arms outstretched, breathing stilled, the whole body momentarily convulsed."[39] Ligon's "startle reflex" appears in the extreme language with which he describes the mistress's beauty. She is the most beautiful *woman* he has *ever* seen, exceptional beyond race, space, and time. Immediately, she disarms any prior conceptions Ligon might hold, and he readily concedes she is an anomaly that exists beyond the limits of his imperial gaze. The mistress is the equivalent of Sir John Mandeville's one-footed African or the people with no heads that Sir Walter Ralegh claimed existed in South America.[40] The mistress is an equally incredible vision that, in Greenblatt's words, "arouses wonder . . . so new that for a moment at least it is alone, unsystematized, an utterly detached object of rapt attention."[41] The mistress does indeed command Ligon's full attention. The narrative action halts as he describes the image in front of him.

Even as the wondrous sight arrests Ligon, though, he attempts to control the vision. As Greenblatt argues, the early travel writer's sense of wonder, an internal response, exists alongside an external object, in this case the mistress, "that can, after the initial moments of astonishment have passed, be touched, cataloged, inventoried, possessed" by the traveler.[42] So Ligon's vivid physical description is an effort to catalog, to interpret, what his eyes have seen. The details appear structured and systematic, the language quasi-romantic, reminiscent of courtship manuals that provide men instruction in the art of eloquent speech. Such manuals offer step-by-step guidelines for how men should approach women. The manuals teach men how to present gifts, write love letters, express affection and give compliments. The manuals also offer examples of eloquent descriptions of beauty, illustrating ways that a suitor can speak appropriately about a woman's various body parts, including her eyes, mouth, arms, thighs, hair, hands, feet—even her womb. One manual, for example, instructs men to compliment a woman's lips as ". . . roses over-washt with dew, doe by her breath their beauties still renew."[43] The same manual describes a woman's knees as "these knots of joy and gems of love" that "with motion makes all graces move." For an all-encompassing beauty, like that of the enslaved mistress, the suitor can proclaim "every part impartes a grace, and beauty dwels in every place."[44]

Ligon employs romantic, courtship language in his description of the mistress which is designed to visually possess all of her. Note the manner in which his gaze begins with a focus on the woman's physical stature. He offers general descriptions about her body size. Then he moves from the general to the specific when he recounts in detail her clothing. He describes what she wears atop her head, then moves down her body to her legs and feet. No inch of her escapes his perusal—her arms and hands, her ears. If he can see the parts, make sense of them, then perhaps they will cohere into an intelligible whole.

His ability to possess her visually, however, has its limitations because she does not stand passively under Ligon's gaze. Remember that when he describes the veil she wore, he also reveals that "she tooke [it] off at *pleasure*." This is a reminder that the only way Ligon has access to such an involved description is because the mistress allows herself to be seen, and she can control the extent to which he "sees" her. Only because she lifts her veil at her *pleasure*, in fact, does Ligon gain access to her "oriental" eyes. This is striking because it denotes the limit of Ligon's knowledge. His gaze alone can produce only a quasi-conquest of this woman. There is a point beyond which he is denied access. So long as he remains a detached observer, the mistress will maintain a wondrous quality, an inaccessibility.

To fully understand this vision, then, and eliminate the wonder, Ligon renegotiates his relationship to the mistress. He devises a plan to engage her in conversation. Desirous to hear her speak, he writes: "Seing all these perfections in her onely at passage, but not yet heard her Speake; I was resolv'd after dinner, to make an Essay what a present of rich silver silke and gold Ribbon would doe, to perswade her to open her lips" (12). Hearing her speak would allow Ligon to achieve two goals. First, it would position the mistress within a normalizing racial discourse. He explains that getting her to *open her lips* is born "partly out of a Curiositie, to see whether her teeth were exactly white, and cleane, as I hop'd they were; for 'tis a generall opinion, that all *Negroes* have white teeth; but that is a Common error, for the black and white, being so neere together, they set off on another with the greater advantage. But looke neerer to them, and you shall find those teeth, which at a distance appear'd rarely white, are yellow and foul" (12). Her teeth would provide Ligon proof to confirm what he already believes about black Africans. She would be the exception that proves the rule. The second reason speech is so important, and Ligon claims this is primary, is that hearing her speak—if indeed her speech is graceful—would "unite and confirme a perfection in all the rest" of her he has seen. Her speech, then, offers yet another form of validation of an imperial gaze that has already deemed the woman as exceptional, a marvel. By choosing to interact with her, not merely watch her, Ligon transforms himself from a detached observer to a participant in the scene. In this role, he believes, he can more fully manipulate the mistress's actions to demystify her presence and more clearly locate her within a blackness discourse. It is a way for him to gain control of a viewing subject who, by piquing Ligon's curiosity, is quickly taking control of him.

Here the writing turns ambivalent. Ligon relies on the familiar by looking for a grotesque quality in the woman's physical features. He deals with the wonder, attempts to control it, by reverting to a racial discourse. At the same time, though, he hopes the mistress does not fit the convention. He actually wants her teeth to be white and her speech to be *graceful,* he says, "to set her off in [his] opinion, the rarest black swanne that [he] had ever seen." Ligon wants her to retain a measure of wonder, but it is not the same kind of unsystematic wonder that Ligon himself experienced when first seeing her. This wonder is fabricated, manufactured by Ligon himself, a wonder he situates in the combination of her race, beauty, and graceful speech and then presents to readers.

Ligon's rhetorical maneuver is problematic because it depends on his ability to manipulate the mistress. What is more, he relies on a ritual of English courtship to affect that manipulation, "to make an Essay what a present of rich silver silke and gold Ribbon would doe, to perswade her to open her lips." In doing so, he places himself at the mercy of the mistress, who can decide for herself whether she wants to smile and/or speak to Ligon. Bates argues about the ritual of courtship: "As a game, role, or way of behaving, courtship is often seen to be a highly codified system, a series of signs aimed at reassuring the prince or mistress of the suitor's unquestioning and dutiful service. And these signs must be interpreted and decoded correctly in order to manipulate the prince or beloved into making the desired gesture of return. But a courtier could never guarantee the hoped-for response, of course, and, however circumspect, judicious, rhetorically aware, he could be cruelly spurned, his suit rejected or ignored."[45] Quite suddenly, the scene between Ligon and this mistress becomes a collaboration that relies not merely on Ligon's observation but on the interaction of two self-possessed subjects.

Rhetorically, Ligon begins the courtly ritual with yet another observation that relocates the mistress from the space of the governor's mansion to the English royal court. Just before he approaches her to "make an essay," he watches her movement, noting that it is "with far greater majesty, and gracefulness, then I have seen Queen *Anne,* descend from the Chaire of State, to dance the Measures with a Baron of England, at a Maske in the Banquetting house" (13). Suddenly, we are in England watching the queen enjoy entertainment in the great hall. Ligon has associated his foreign experience with the familiar, located the mistress in relationship to a recognizable model of femininity—Queen Anne. And to evoke that measure of wonder in the reader, he maintains an extreme rhetoric by elevating the mistress above the queen. He even goes so far as to assign her a royal court, "attendants on such a state and beautie" (13). Ligon's placement of the mistress into this royal context achieves two ends. First, it helps to justify his decision to interact with this woman within a discourse that had at one time been reserved for royalty. Second, it is a kind of mental foreplay for Ligon and a foreshadowing for the reader of the wooing that soon follows. He ends the observation with a mock humility, saying he would have "made a stop, and gone no farther" in his quest to court her. But then he remembers "she was but the Padres Mistres, & therefore the more accessible" (13). The display of humility, then, is not about the mistress at all but Ligon's recognition of what would have been considered impertinent if the mistress were indeed English royalty rather than merely "the Padres mistres."

And so the game begins. Ligon explains: "I made my addresses to her, by my interpreter; & told her, I had some Trifles made by the people of *England*, which for their value were not worthy her acceptance, yet for their Novelty, they might be of some esteem, such having bin worn by the great Queens of *Europe*, & intreated her to vouchsafe to receive them" (13). Interestingly, he provides a summary of his address to the mistress rather than the specific dialogue, perhaps because that address is being mediated through a translator? Given the nature of his physical description of the mistress and his choice to court her, perhaps Ligon took a page from the courtship manual *Mysteries of Love,* which instructs the suitor to flatter his mistress with lines such as "*Apollo* hath given you his orient Brightness; *Venus* her curious Shape; *Jupiter* his high and stately Forehead; the God of Eloquence his flowing Speech: and all the Female Deities have show'd their Bounties and Beauties on your Face."[46] Perhaps Ligon took the manual's advice and told the slave mistress that her eyes, which he previously referred to as jewels, were specifically "diamonds set in foils of polisht Ivory."[47]

Because Ligon does not relate his exact words, however, we have to assume that the dialogue is secondary. The gifts of silver silk and gold ribbon, which he has wrapped in paper, are the most important aspect of his pursuit. Those gifts take on a special significance when we consider the relationship between clothing and status in early modern English culture. There were specific sumptuary laws that governed which classes of people could wear certain colors and types of fabric. For example, women in lower classes were forbidden from wearing "any cloth of gold, tissue, nor fur of sables: except duchesses, marquises, and countesses in their gowns, kirtles, partlets, and sleeves; cloth of gold, silver, tinseled satin, silk, or cloth mixed or embroidered with gold or silver or pearl, saving silk mixed with gold or silver in linings of cowls, partlets, and sleeves."[48]

Such statutes had been part of English culture—all of Europe—for centuries, and although they were not strictly enforced and repealed at the turn of the seventeenth century, they illustrate the efforts made in English society to differentiate categories of people based on external cues. As Susan Vincent notes, the anxieties out of which English sumptuary laws arose did not disappear with the repeal of those laws in 1604. The laws "acknowledged and addressed widespread underlying anxieties, that ranged from moral degradation to social and financial chaos" that would be concerns throughout the early modern period.[49] Here, Ligon encourages a kind of cross-dressing. He presents high-end fabrics to a black African mistress who is already garbed in fabrics and jewels fit for royalty. What is more she acts like royalty with the graceful demeanor and walk. If they were in English society, the woman's dress might threaten the social order, and Ligon's presentation of the fabrics might be a social class transgression. However, in the space of the governor's mansion, where, if we remember, the woman is "but the Padres mistres," there is no danger of conflating the woman's royal-like dress and demeanor with high breeding or royal status. Her black skin does what her dress cannot; it visibly orders her socially within the governor's mansion and within the minds of Ligon's readers, who all know that no amount of elaborate, expensive fabric can "wash an Ethiop white."[50] At this point, the courtship takes on a carnivalesque quality with Ligon's assurances to the mistress that the fabrics will make her European royalty, given that they are the same kinds "worn by the great queens of Europe." Ligon appeals to—perhaps even mocks—the mistress's assumed vanity even as he presses his courtly suit. He amuses himself at the mistress's expense.

What happens next illustrates the collaborative nature of the courtship. He hands over the gifts, noting that the mistress "with much gravity, and reserv'dness, opened the paper; but when she lookt on them, the Colours pleased her so, as she put her gravity into the loveliest smile that I have ever seen. And then shewed her rowes of pearls, so clean, white, Orient, and well shaped, as *Neptunes* Court was never pav'd with such as these" (13).[51] On the surface of it, the woman seems to succumb to Ligon's courtly spell. He has succeeded in accomplishing his first goal. She has smiled at him, revealing a set of perfect teeth, confirming his original assessment of her beauty as exceptional. The extent to which Ligon has manipulated that smile is evident in the fact that she initially looks at the paper-clad favors with "gravity and reserv'dness" but then her countenance changes.

That change, though, is a key moment because it suggests something about the mistress's own ambitions. Here, I argue, Ligon overestimates his own power and dismisses the agency shown by the mistress. Remember that the presentation of the gifts is preceded by Ligon's soliloquy. For all his efforts to playfully signify the gifts, the woman does not respond warmly. Ligon's speech act does not elicit the desired response of smiling; nor does his act of giving the gifts. She knows what is wrapped in the paper even as she opens her hands to receive them because Ligon told her, just as he explained the gifts' value beforehand. His words leave her cautious or cynical, maybe, as she receives the gifts with gravity and reservation, not excitement. Her stern countenance melts only *after* she actually sees the fabrics, the colors of which "pleased her so." Her smile is not a result of the clothes being English-made or novelties worn by European queens. She imbues the fabrics, rather, with her own system of value, one located in the fabrics' materiality, the visual qualities.

We cannot access or assess the specifics regarding how or why the mistress finds value in the fabrics. The moment is especially intriguing, however, when we consider how black African women manipulated and flouted certain apparel laws in colonial America to express themselves. For example, in the later eighteenth century, Louisiana's governor passed what became known as the tignon laws, which mandated that all slave and Creole women wear headdresses when in public to differentiate them from white women. The laws targeted those quadroon and octoroon women whose skin color and hair texture showed no visible evidence of their black African ancestry. These women, adhering to the laws, began making elaborate, ostentatious headwear that showed off their creativity and wealth. They used the headgear as a status symbol that allowed them to both accommodate the law and resist it. For sure, the elaborate garb of the slave mistress in Santiago symbolizes the governor's wealth. This scene in Ligon's narrative, though, reveals her as more than an object. We do not know exactly how the mistress will use the clothes or why exactly the fabrics' colors matter. We do not even know whether she truly finds value in the cloths at all. This moment, though, suggests that Ligon's courtly manipulation alone does not prompt her reaction. We are left to wonder how she, like those black African women flouting tignon laws in New Orleans, will incorporate the fabrics into a personal expression.[52]

As the scene progresses, Ligon continues to credit his manipulation. After the mistress looks at the gifts and smiles, she then looks up at Ligon in a manner he interprets as desire. He writes:

> [She] gave me such a look, as was a sufficient return for a far greater present, and withall wisht, I would think of somewhat wherein she might pleasure me, and I should finde her both ready and willing. And so with a gracefull bow of her neck, she took her way towards her own house; which was not above a stones cast from the *Padres*. Other addresses were not to be made, without the dislike of the *Padre*, for they are there as jealous of their Mistrisses, as the *Italians* of their wives. (13)

Here the ritual seems complete, a quintessential moment of courtship. He bestows the mistress with favors; she bestows him with gratitude and esteem. Compare this moment to a scenario from the courtship manual *The Academy of Complements*. In the manual, the writer illustrates the proper etiquette for presenting and receiving gifts: a suitor should offer the following words when presenting a lady with a gift, "Pardon mee, if I, moved thereunto by the zealous affection which I beare you, doe here express it in the dumbe language of a small present, unworthy your acceptance; yet I pray weare it for my sake, it may draw down your eye to think on me, who now am wounded by the powerfull beames of your beauty."[53] Notice how the suitor's humility governs the scenario, the same kind of humility Ligon displays when he presents the clothes to the mistress and tells her that the gifts are but "trifles" and "not worthy her acceptance." According to the manual, a lady's proper response should be, "it would shew a scornefull mind in me not to accept your love tendered unto mee in such a visible manner; yet I am sorry you should bee at so great and needless charges: for wherein can I serve you to make requital?"[54] Gratitude marks the response, the same kind of gratitude the slave mistress displays in her insistence that Ligon should "think of somewhat wherein she might pleasure [him], and [he] should finde her both ready and willing."

On the surface, this appears a clear moment of conquest for Ligon as a suitor. Not only has he gotten the mistress to smile but also to speak. Again, he does not share the specific dialogue, which presumably he receives from the interpreter. Her words, though, are less important than the actual act, a product of his manipulation, evidence of his control. To his mind, he ends the encounter on his terms, suggesting that he does not press his suit further to avoid potential conflict with a jealous governor.

Important to note, this ending allows Ligon to racialize the woman in a way he had been unable to achieve previously by indulging in—just for a moment—a sexual fantasy, which moves beyond the intent of a courtship ritual. He suggests that the mistress warmly receives his advances. According to Ligon, she offers to pleasure him—however he sees fit—and then turns toward her house, which "was not above a stones cast from the *Padres*." Is this an invitation for Ligon to follow her? As Barbara Bush points out, stereotypes about enslaved women as promiscuous abounded. Unlike enslaved men, who were valuable almost exclusively for their labor, enslaved women were expected to perform sexual duties, as we see with the governor's mistress. Such demands, Bush argues, have "coloured and influenced both contemporary and modern attitudes to the black woman, not only in her sexual sphere, but also as a worker, mother and wife."[55] European misconceptions about enslaved black African women included images of those women as promiscuous, unfaithful, and lacking maternal feeling, qualities antithetical to those European notions of femininity mentioned earlier. As a result of misconceptions, black women became a means for European men to indulge certain sexual fantasies. They "came to represent the delights of forbidden sex," as Bush notes, and their "sexual attributes were highly and often sensationally exaggerated."[56] The governor's mistress seems to serve such a function for Ligon.

The fact that Ligon has successfully coaxed specific actions from the mistress suggests that he has succeeded in controlling her representation. And yet, one tiny moment in the final lines of the exchange challenges Ligon's rendering of the entire episode. Throughout the scene, Ligon assumes the power to observe. He does, after all, possess that imperial gaze, not to mention the pen. Consider the instance, though, when Ligon says the mistress "gave me such a look" after receiving the fabrics and offering a smile. The mistress reciprocates a gaze of which she has been the object. Just as Ligon can assess her physicality, the moment reminds us that she maintains a similar prerogative to gaze back upon him, not an imperial gaze but a gaze nonetheless. What does she see when looking at Ligon? Now, there is another perspective from which to consider the encounter.

Presumably the woman's knowledge of English culture was limited given her inability to speak English. Does she recognize Ligon's particular re-enactment of a courtship ritual? Does she sense the mockery that accompanies the gifts? Perhaps she does experience a sexual attraction and invites Ligon back to her home. On the other hand, maybe she understands Ligon as a love-struck Englishman falling at her feet. Her acceptance of the gifts, her flawless smile, her sexual *invitation* very well could be patronizing gestures not unlike the niceties Queen Elizabeth would have directed at her own liege of courtiers. His explanation of the clothes probably impresses the mistress about as much as Pedro's offering of gold pieces impressed Drake, who already had two shiploads of valuables. The mistress is already attired in the finest, most elaborate and exotic of garbs. If the timing of her smile is any indication, she finds much more use in the colors of the fabrics than in the fabrics themselves. That the woman merely patronizes Ligon is also suggested by the graceful bow she offers him just before turning her back and walking away to her own home. She ends the interaction, not Ligon—a gracious dismissal, perhaps, rather than an invitation?

Myra Jehlen reads this exchange between Ligon and the mistress as an illustration of Ligon's complex views regarding slavery. Specifically, she understands the moment as empathic, one in which Ligon is "brought to feel warmth, generosity, empathy, and in short the whole panoply of humane feeling."[57] If he is "brought" to this "panoply of humane feeling," what or *who* causes it? For Jehlen, it appears to be Ligon and his own sense of ethics. She argues that he recognizes the "basic laws of human relations."[58] Jehlen stops short of conceding any agency on the part of the mistress in helping to provoke that reaction in Ligon. If Ligon's politics appear "complex" or contradictory, I would argue that the mistress helps bring it about. Reading against the grain reveals the moment's ambiguities. We do not know for sure why the mistress chooses to interact with Ligon, and therein lies her power—her inaccessibility. This in turn reminds us of the limitations of Ligon's own rendering of this woman. He does not recognize her engagement in the moment. He ingests her gaze, her dialogue, all her actions into his own system of meaning. He attempts to fill in the gaps with his own speculation but still cannot create an encounter devoid of questions, ambivalence—some measure of uncontrolled wonder.

Two African Maidens and an Expanded Blind Spot

Ligon's encounter with the governor's mistress provides him a model for his descriptions of a couple of maidens whose beauty again overwhelms him. He attempts to map onto them that same rhetoric of courtly love, a process that ends this time in unequivocal rejection. Several days after his encounter with the black mistress, Ligon, still in Santiago, stands at a well gathering water. He notices a group of young black women, to whom he refers as nymphs, cavorting near the well. Soon two of the girls break away from the group and come over to the well to fill containers. He describes them as "creatures, of such shapes, as would have puzzelld *Albert Durer,* the great Mr of Proportion, but to have imitated; and *Tition,* or *Andrea de Sarta,* for softnes of muscles, and Curiositie of Colouring, though with a studied diligence; and a love both to the partie and the worke" (15). Ligon's encounter with the mistress has emboldened him as a courtier. The diction becomes even more poetic, more romantic—more courtly.[59]

In this description, Ligon does not begin with a close-up portrait of the girls, as he did with the mistress. Rather than controlling the scene by cataloging the girls' features, he immediately infuses them with a quality of wonder.

He declares their beauty so striking that it escapes characterization. He writes, "To expresse all the perfections of Nature, and Parts, these Virgins were owners of, would aske a more skillfull pen, or pencill then mine; Sure I am, though all were excellent, their motions were the highest, and that is a beautie no painter can expresse, and therefore my pen may well be silent"(15). This insistence on his inadequacy to articulate the vision is rhetorical posturing; in the very next instance he does precisely what he claims he cannot do adequately—he describes the girls. Just as with the mistress, he contextualizes their wonder within a racial discourse. They, too, contradict the conventional black African characteristics, but rather than deeming them exceptional the way he does the mistress, Ligon creates a new category of blackness for these girls.

They do not resemble the women of "high *Africa*; as of Morocco, Guinny, Binny . . . Angola, Aethiopia, and *Mauritania*, or those that dwell nere the *River* of *Gambia,* who are thick lipt, short nosed, and commonly low foreheads" (15). These virgins, instead, are unique in coloring, fluid and graceful in motion, and elegant and ornate in fashion. They are bejeweled in pearls, other beads, and ribbons. They are garbed in elaborate fabrics of silk, linen, and taffeta. Indeed, they are "compos'd of such features, as would marre the judgment of the best Paynters, to undertake to mend" (16). While he acknowledges their misfit in terms of one normalizing context, Ligon creates a new normalizing paradigm in which these two girls are not anomalies—remember all the references to the mistress's exceptionalism, which is absent in Ligon's descriptions here—but rather portraits of the young beauty that exists on the island of Santiago. The girls are two of the "many pretty young Negro virgins" Ligon initially notices near the well (15). He strips them of their individuality, portraying them as images of the beauty English travelers can expect to find in exotic places. They are meek, modest, prudent, shy *portraits* of the typical customs and manners of island women.[60]

After remarking on their beauty, Ligon then pays suit to the girls. His strategy for wooing them largely follows that aimed at the mistress, and he seeks a similar goal. "Seing their beauties so fresh and youthfull," he says, "withall the perfections I have named, I thought good to trie, whether the uttering of their language, would be as sweet and harmonious, as their other partes were comely" (16). Again through a translator, he addresses the girls with a barrage of flattering statements about their beauty and demeanor, which we get as summary. In reaction, according to Ligon, "they appeard a little disturb'd; and whispered to one another, but had not the Confidence to speake aloud" (16). Already, we see how Ligon interprets their actions from his presumed position of dominance. He assumes their disturbance, the whispering, is related to uncertainty, intimidation brought on by his presence. He does not acknowledge the irony of the moment—the girls speak, just not to him. Also worth noting, they whisper to exclude the interpreter, not Ligon, who could not decipher their speech even if he could hear it. In this instance, the girls limit access. They choose to shut themselves off. Ligon's words once again fail to bring about his desired response.

To coax them out of what he interprets as intimidation, Ligon moves into the next phase of the courtship. He explains, "I had in my hat, a piece of silver and silke Ribbon, which I perceiv'd their well shap't eyes, often to dart at; but their modesties would not give them Confidence to aske. I tooke it out, and divided it between them, which they accepted with much alacritie" (16). The favors are loaded with presumption. He reads desire into the girls' eyes and believes he can manipulate that desire to make the courtship successful. It appears he has read their desire properly because they accept the gifts with "alacrity." This moment is also fascinating because it suggests a certain amount of communicative savvy on the part of the virgins. They convey signals to Ligon—the darting of their eyes toward the fabrics—that in turn manipulate him. And they do this while withholding the one thing Ligon wants—conversation.

The girls appear rather active in deciding the extent to which they will interact with Ligon. He explains that in gratitude for the fabrics he presents them, the girls drink from the well. He determines that this act is in deference to him, perceiving it "by their wanton smiles, and jesticulations, and casting their eyes towards me: when they thought they had exprest enough they would take in their Countenances, and put themselves in the modestest postures that could be" (16). The girls appear a bit coquettish. They play into the courtship, with one exception. They are quickly becoming the manipulators. Once again, they grant Ligon limited access, this time hiding behind a "countenance" of modesty, which only intensifies Ligon's courtship efforts, leading him to present them yet another favor.

This time it is a drink he takes from a special English brew, which the girls accept, but Ligon says in despair, "All this would not give them the Confidence to speake, but, in mute language, and extream prety motions" (17). Ligon fails to converse with the girls, who "shewed, they wanted neither wit nor discretion, to make an answer" (17). They simply choose not to speak to him. The girls' silence does not make sense until he resorts to that normalizing racial discourse, blaming the failure on the fact that "it was not the fashion there, for young Maides to speak to strangers, in so publick a place" (17). Ligon does not reveal how he learned of this social more that dictates the girls' silence. It is nonetheless an effort to understand and therefore control the girls' actions. However, it does not overwrite the agency they employ in the encounter. If indeed it is a social custom for maidens not to talk to strangers, then the girls, not Ligon, set the terms of engagement. The English courtship ritual Ligon intends gets usurped by the virgins, who drag him into their cultural system of silence.

To deal with this failed courtship, Ligon retreats into the imaginary. He creates in his mind a quandary—having to choose between two equally beautiful maidens. He marvels:

> For, so equall were there Beauties, and my Love, as it was not, nor could be, particular to either. I have heard it a question disputed, whether if a Horse, being plac'd at an equall distance, between two bottles of hey, equally good; and his appetite being equally fix'd upon either: Whether that Horse must not necessarily starve. For, if he feed on either, it must argue, that his appetite was more fixt on that; or else, that bottle was better than the other. Otherwise, what should move him to chose one before the other? In this posture was I, with my two Mistresses; or rather, my two halves of one Mistresse: for, had they been conjoyned, and so made one, the poynt of my Love had met there; but, being divided, and my affection not forked, it was impossible to fix, but in one Centre. (17)

Ligon's articulation of his dilemma echoes poetic lines found in *The Mysteries of Love,* in which the writer presents a series of verses and compliments for use by potential suitors. One verse in particular reads: "Black, or fair, or tall, or low / I alike with all can sport; / The bold sprightly *Thais* woe, /or the frozen Vestal Court: / Every Beauty takes my mind, / Ty'd to all, to none confin'd."[61] The subject of this verse and Ligon are trapped in the same paradoxical state—captive to multiple mistresses and yet committed to none. Ligon shows himself the consummate courtier beleaguered by his love for two women. Note that by the end of his contemplative passage, the two virgins previously described as modest, demure, innocent, and fresh have now been transformed into—not just mistresses—but *Ligon's* mistresses. The transformation, let us remember, occurs solely in Ligon's mind.

After Ligon contemplates his love for the two equally beautiful maidens, he then minimizes the entire episode. Perhaps he senses that his musings on African beauty are excessive. He justifies his digression by proffering three reasons for the relevance of the anecdotes. First of all, he reminds readers, he is a painter at heart; he observed these African women as one studying his craft. His next reason slightly contradicts the first; his gaze was slightly off-kilter by the fact that he had "been long at Sea, without setting foot on any land and that hath a property to make all land-objects beautifull" (17). His last reason for the long digression on love and beauty was that he had nothing else on which to focus his attention. "For the Iland, a place of very little or no traffick," he writes, "could not afford much of discourse. Cattle they have very good, and large, which they sell at very easy rates; and likewise Horses, of excellent shapes and mettle" (17–18). This last reason—more than the previous two—recontextualizes the black African virgins and mistress, who have now become substitutes, stand-ins for the kind of resources on which Ligon would have commented had they been present on the island. In addition, the women correlate with the bounty Ligon describes once he arrives in the Caribbean.

Beautiful and Monstrous

Ligon's affective musings about the women in Santiago anticipate an "emotive and romantic stylisation of nature," a consumptive process that Mimi Sheller argues would come to characterize eighteenth-century English narratives about the Caribbean.[62] Specifically, Sheller argues that early European Caribbean narratives often depicted the region in terms of picturesque scenery that was alternately "cultivated" or "wild and sublime," depictions that encouraged European exploitation.[63] Sheller understands consumption very broadly in symbolic and material terms as "ingestion, invasion, incorporation, infection, appropriation, sacrifice, and exhibition, as well as various processes of possessing, destroying, using up, and wasting away."[64] My understanding of consumption and its relationship to the black women Ligon encounters is narrower, involving specifically possession and use. In this way, Ligon's portrayal of the women reflects the general tendency of early English literature about the Caribbean to articulate the region as a bountiful space with use value. "In the age of 'discovery,'" as Sheller argues, "interest in the New World was largely acquisitive and depictions conveyed the utility" of the landscape and offered "information on how to cultivate" that landscape.[65] In other words, they render the Caribbean as a space that can be, like the governor's mistress and virgins at the well, cataloged, controlled, possessed—and ultimately used. The women maintain a disruptive quality in Ligon's narrative, though, because they deny Ligon the use-value associated with consumption. They are not merely objects of the landscape and therefore consumable. If we read Ligon's text against the grain, accounting for the material realities of Ligon's encounters, those women actually consume Ligon by manipulating his curiosity for their own gain. Ligon, ironically, becomes an object of desire—because of his access to tangible items. This disruption matters because it challenges the narrative's representational schema that renders the Caribbean a passive and bountiful landscape available for easy English exploitation. Like the other examples of black Africans in this book, these women destabilize the notions of self, nation, and empire that were central to the rhetorical aims of English colonial contact narratives.

Although we cannot know with certainty the material details of Ligon's interactions with the women, the impact of those encounters manifests itself structurally in Ligon's narrative, illustrating the collaborative nature of the black African women's mediated presences. Through his encounters, Ligon transforms himself from an imperial agent into a courtier, ensnared by the intrigues of black women in Santiago. He does not offer any other black African figure, man or woman, the kind of representational space or imaginative energy he devotes to these women. In fact, once he arrives in Barbados, Ligon situates his observations within conventional racially gendered and imperial discourses. The most obvious example of this is his monstrous description of enslaved women working in Barbados sugar fields, discussed earlier.

In her work, Morgan argues that Ligon spends so much time explaining his encounters with beautiful black women in Santiago in the opening pages of the narrative to magnify through opposition the monstrous descriptions of enslaved women as chattel hunched over in Barbados sugar fields. She imagines that the opposing descriptions exist in a coherent narrative flow, a bait-and-switch tactic. I argue the opposite, that the monstrous description does not subsume the earlier descriptions of black African beauty. Rather, Ligon's descriptions of African beauty interfere with his efforts to participate in a normalizing blackness discourse that would reduce enslaved women to monstrous presences. If we compare how the descriptions are written, his encounters with beautiful women are much more imaginative, excessive—even overpowering in their totality. A passion, a creativity, a playfulness infuse the writing which are absent later in the text. The description of women with sagging breasts displays none of that same imagination. The monstrous description, in fact, occupies only a few lines taken from conventional discourse.

As Morgan herself points out, black African women often appeared in early modern texts as grotesque or monstrous, undesirable. The moment in Ligon's text, then, reads as almost obligatory, catering to English readers' expectations. In a sense he fulfills a rhetorical duty. Confirmation that he saw the same kind of images that other English travelers, like Towerson, saw before him lends credence to Ligon's imperial gaze—and ironically provides credibility for the more incredible visions of beauty he witnessed in Santiago.

Ligon must present the familiar if he wants English readers to accept his narrative's authenticity. He has the added responsibility of ensuring that his text buttresses an English social order that was, as Amussen argues, very much dependent on racial and gender distinctions. If such distinctions, though, are designed to establish order out of chaos, as Kim Hall maintains, the slave mistress of the governor of Santiago and the virgins at the well do the opposite for Ligon's narrative. They create more chaos because Ligon does not encounter them within typical normalizing discourses. The mistress, especially, reflects English civilization and femininity. She—as a foreigner—is the exemplar of that femininity. Ligon's portrayal of these black African women in his narrative is not a solo project. The women have their own agendas that register in the narrative and circumscribe Ligon's rhetorical choices. They maintain a complex relationship to the systems of production/consumption in the early Atlantic world as they are not producers (and reproducers) but consumers of material goods. In a text designed to herald Barbados's commercial viability and the consumptive possibilities for the English, black African women in Santiago show us that the potential for profit in the Atlantic world was not the sole province of Europeans.

CHAPTER 5

Locating Africa in the Americas
George Best, Sir Walter Ralegh, and the Quandaries of Racial Representation

S tudies of race in the early modern era almost always chart a course through George Best's 1578 travel narrative, *A True Discourse of the Late Discoveries . . . of Martin Frobisher,* which relates Frobisher's quest for a northwest passage to China. In the narrative, Best deems black skin an infection of blood, a curse passed down from God to the descendants of Noah's son Ham. For some scholars, his text is an early example of the cultural attitudes that fueled modern-day racism. Others argue the opposite, that Best's narrative points to a different understanding of human classification, one rooted in cultural differences, not the scientific discourses that would come to define race and racism post-Enlightenment.[1] For as prevalent as Best's text is in such discussions about race, Sir Walter Ralegh's 1596 *Discovery of the Large, Rich, and Beautiful Empire of Guiana* is never mentioned. His text does not engage racial issues in the same overt fashion as does Best's narrative. He does, however, write about cultural differences, comparing Native Americans to black Africans or meditating on those groups' tawny skin color. Neither text relates specific interactions between the writer-travelers and black Africans, but images of black Africans (and of sub-Saharan Africa) circulate through the texts like ideological currents.

As scholars continue to debate the origins of our modern understanding of race, I examine Best's narrative in conjunction with Ralegh's to explore the ways in which English ideas about sub-Saharan Africa informed the imaginations of the earliest English travelers to the Americas. Both Best and Ralegh employ black African imagery as an essential, if problematic, mediating tool to contemplate cultural differences, more clearly delineate Englishness against a rhetoric of monstrosity, and reconcile various moments of cognitive dissonance in which their expectations do not align with their experiences.[2] Their narratives grapple with cosmographical quandaries, not the least of which is how and where American indigenous groups fit into a larger world order. They also are heavily invested in advancing England's overseas interests, responding to Spanish empire. Best saw England's future in the arctic northwest, still largely untapped by Europeans; Ralegh turned his attentions southward, insisting that Guiana could be a base from which to usurp control of the Caribbean from Spain. In their texts, issues of natural history, empire, religion, and national identity all collide. I offer a discussion of how and why Best and Ralegh mediate these issues in terms of race, and I emphasize the consequences they encounter in doing so. Textual analysis of both narratives reveals the manner in which previous English encounters with sub-Saharan Africa both guide and undermine the narratives' larger cosmographical and imperial rhetoric, resulting in narrative dissonance. Black Africans function as a disruptive *absence* in the texts, illuminating the important role sub-Saharan Africa occupied in England's understanding of its imperial enterprise in America, even shaping English conceptions of the region's native inhabitants.

Best, the Curse of Ham, and Inuit in the Balance

Although George Best's narrative is largely about the Arctic and Frobisher's exploits there, two often-cited passages from the text center on references to Africa, which appear in prefatory material preceding his discussion of Frobisher's travels. Both passages help Best make larger claims about the achievements of Frobisher's voyages, which he sees not in the sighting of new lands or acquisition of material resources but in the production of knowledge. Frobisher's voyages were remarkable, according to Best, because they produced a new understanding about climate and its effect (or lack thereof) on human bodies. Based on his observations of people living in the Arctic and his experiences traveling in the region's extremely cold temperatures, Best concluded that climate had little effect on human physiognomies, contradicting centuries of scientific wisdom that linked the somatic variances among human populations to differences in climate. To bolster his claims, Best turned to prior English knowledge about sub-Saharan Africa.

In the first of these two passages, Best deems black Africans' skin color an infection of blood rather than a consequence of extreme heat:

I my selfe have seene an Ethiopian as blacke as a cole brought into Englande, who taking a faire Englishe woman to wife, begatte a sonne in all respects as blacke as the father was, although England were his native country and an English woman his mother: whereby it seemeth this blacknesse proceedeth rather of some natural infection of that man, which was so strong, that neyther the nature of the clime neyther the good complexion of the mother concurring coulde any thing alter, and therefore we can not impute it to the nature of the clime. (54)[3]

In the second passage, Best suggests that we can "impute" African blackness to a curse that befell Noah's son Ham because of a sexual transgression he committed while aboard the Ark. As Best explains, Noah "straightly commanded his sonnes . . . that during the time of the floud, while they remained in the arke, they should use continence and absteine from carnall copulation with their wives" (55). Ham violated this command, driven by sexual passion and a desire to produce the first heir who would populate the post-Diluvian world. As punishment, according to Best: "God would a sonne shuld be born whose name was Chus, who not only itself, but all his posteritie after him, should be so black and loathsome that it might remaine a spectacle of disobedience to all the world. And of this blacke and cursed Chus came all these black Moores which are in Africa" (55–56). Best's understanding of blackness as a hereditary rather than climatic phenomenon illustrates the shift that Mary Floyd-Wilson notes occurred at the end of the sixteenth century when theories of human difference moved away from explanations centered on climate.[4] Earlier, ethnic (or proto-racial) differences had been attributed to properties of climate that interacted with fluids, or humors, inside the body, which produced variety in skin tones, temperaments, even intelligence and morality. The dark skin of black Africans was explained as an overabundance of black bile created by the extreme heat near the equator. Bodily features—and the ethnic/racial classifications they produced—were mutable and intimately tied to place. Such ideas contributed to the anxieties English travelers experienced about moving beyond their climate region. Best challenges this relationship between race and place, or what Floyd-Wilson calls geohumoralism, by locating black African difference not at the nexus of climate, space, and bodily humors but in a biblical curse inherited through blood.

Scholars often extract the above passages from the larger narrative, examining what they can tell us about English attitudes toward black Africans in the early modern era. Alden and Virginia Mason Vaughan, for example, argue that Best's understanding of dark skin as infectious and cursed, reveals his "blatant chromatic bias."[5] Imtiaz H. Habib argues that Best's representation of blackness illustrates English fears of a growing black African population in Renaissance England. According to Habib, Best attempts to extract black Africans from an English body politic by casting "blackness as an aberrant physiological condition."[6] The above passages from Best's narrative have become the sixteenth-century equivalent of sound bites. Unfortunately, such reading in isolation reiterates the overly simplified African/European binary with which we often frame discussions of race in the early modern era. If we only examine these passages from Best's narrative for what they reveal (or do not reveal) about racial attitudes toward black Africans, we overlook their context and the ways in which he attaches ideas about blackness to those Inuit populations he encountered during his travels through the arctic northwest.[7]

Best attempts to understand indigenous peoples' somatic and cultural features through the story of Ham. He suggests that the nature of Inuit difference, like that of black Africans, is bodily rather than climatic—which means that the American environment is harmless to would-be English explorers. Best, however, leaves unanswered this question: If the source of black African difference lies in a biblical curse passed down from God, what is the source of Inuit difference? How do they fit into a cosmos cultivated by a higher power and populated by the seed of Noah? These questions haunt Best's narrative and his racial theory, which destabilizes the very bodies it is intended to stabilize—not those of black Africans but of Inuit.

The Three Voyages and Their Personnel

Frobisher's voyages to the Arctic began in 1576 as a mission to find a northwest trade route to the rich settlements of Asia. Rather than undertaking arduous land voyages or traveling southern sea routes that Portugal and Spain mostly controlled, the English sought a more direct, and autonomous, path. Englishmen had been lobbying the Crown to pursue an expedition to the northwest throughout the sixteenth century, and in 1576 Sir Humphrey Gilbert published a treatise arguing for the existence of such a passage and the feasibility of its navigation by English ships.[8] Two years before the publication of Gilbert's treatise, Martin Frobisher was planning his own northwest voyage. By 1574, Frobisher had garnered a reputation as a competent though perhaps shifty seaman. Over a forty-year career, he planned, participated in, or led a number of expeditions, some of which may have been piratic in nature, to parts of

Africa, the West Indies, and, of course, the Arctic.[9] In 1588, he was among the English naval leadership, which included Hawkins and Drake, that repelled the Spanish Armada.

In the second half of the sixteenth century, the Arctic was one of several regions to which the English turned to expand trading networks and exploration, partly in response to the growth of Spanish imperialism in the Americas. In fact, Frobisher did not conduct his expeditions in an Arctic vacuum. As Thomas Symons and David Quinn remind us, the same political expediency that fueled Frobisher's quest also fueled Drake's activities in the Caribbean and his circumnavigation in 1577. Symons argues, "Frobisher's search for the Northwest Passage was a companion piece to Drake's exploration of the western shores of North America via the Southwest Passage of the Straits of Magellan."[10] Quinn argues similarly of Drake's exploration of the California coast, where he met the Miwoks discussed in chapter 2, that his mission was "not only to penetrate the Spanish dominated Pacific but also to find, if he could, the Pacific opening of the Northwest Passage and to map out a land base for future English domination of Northwestern America."[11] Essentially, English activity to the north unfolded in tandem with campaigns and raids in the Caribbean and on the Spanish Main.

The English, as discussed in chapter 1, also looked to West Africa to expand their trade reaches. Frobisher actually began his sea career, in his late teen years, as a fledgling merchant on Thomas Wyndham's 1553 Guinea voyage. He was among the forty survivors who limped back to England. Then on John Lok's 1554 voyage, Frobisher offered himself as a pledge in trade negotiations with town leaders at Shama. Negotiations went awry, and Frobisher was kept as a hostage. Perhaps to shore up trade alliances with their neighbors at El Mina, Shama leaders passed Frobisher to the Portuguese. For two years, Frobisher remained in Portuguese custody, transferred from Guinea after nine months to a jail in Lisbon.[12] He may have been ransomed by a relative, the London merchant and investor Sir John York, in whose home Frobisher spent his early teen years.[13]

Those early voyages to Guinea resonated years later in Frobisher's Arctic enterprise. In Richard Willes's 1577 expanded reprint of Eden's *Decades*, he writes that Frobisher began conceiving of a northwest voyage as a consequence of imprisonment at El Mina and Lisbon. According to Willes, Frobisher learned of the existence of a northwest passage from a fellow prisoner, a Portuguese man.[14] So, when Frobisher approached John Lok's youngest brother, Michael, in 1574 about planning an expedition to the Arctic, West

Africa lurked in the backdrop of the enterprise's conceptual framework and Best's narrative.[15] As we will see, Best links those early Guinea voyages to Frobisher's Arctic expeditions to illustrate the diversity and success of English mercantile and navigational efforts.

The first Frobisher voyage left England in June 1576 with three ships (two barks and a pinnace) and thirty-five men. Though the crew departed to some fanfare and a send-off from the queen, they quickly encountered misfortunes. Early in the voyage, one of the barks turned back for England and the pinnace, carrying several men, was destroyed in a storm. Frobisher ploughed ahead with the one remaining ship. He entered what he believed to be a channel, dubbed Frobisher's Strait, to the Northwest Passage but did not pursue the course because of bad weather. On this first voyage, Frobisher also encountered the native residents of Baffin Island, or Meta Incognita, as Queen Elizabeth would name the region. As a consequence of that cultural encounter, Frobisher lost five men he assumed were kidnapped by the Inuit. He, then, captured an Inuk man. The man died soon after arriving in London. In addition to one captive, Frobisher's men brought back from the voyage certain material objects, one of which was a mysterious black rock. Three assayers deemed the rock worthless, but a fourth found trace amounts of gold. Despite skepticism from some, including several members of the queen's Privy Council, Frobisher and Lok found enough investors to plot a second voyage—among them the queen and Humphrey Gilbert, whose 1576 treatise initially lent credence to the enterprise.

That second voyage in 1577 had mining as its primary goal, and Frobisher's ships would be loaded with some two hundred tons of ore. Finding the Northwest Passage became secondary. Frobisher also tried but failed to find the five Englishmen he thought kidnapped the year before. He and his crew encountered more settlements of Inuit; those encounters grew increasingly violent. As a result of two skirmishes, he brought back to England three Inuit captives—a man, a woman, and a nursing baby. All three died within months of their arrival from injuries sustained during the capture or from exposure to European disease.[16]

The Queen and other investors pushed Frobisher to undertake a third voyage even before the ore from that second voyage could be processed to extract any gold. Despite the promise of huge financial gains, the venture experienced financial strain from the start. Lok struggled to find the funds to pay salaries and other costs related to the second voyage, and debt mounted as Lok and Frobisher relied on credit and investor capital to fund the final trip. The primary mission of the 1578 voyage was again mining, and Frobisher's fleet grew to fifteen ships. Among secondary objectives was the establishment of a colony of one hundred men on Baffin Island who could scout the terrain and continue mining through the year. To aid in that effort, equipment included parts of a prefabricated cabin to house the colonists.

Frobisher's efforts to navigate fifteen ships through the icy waters of the Arctic proved an ordeal. A ship carrying parts of the prefabricated cabin sank after hitting an iceberg. Frobisher and his advisers abandoned the plan for a colony. Instead, they built a smaller stone house at Countess of Warwick Island, with plans to return that next year. Inside the house they left behind objects, such as bells and knives, intending the objects as gifts for those Inuit curious enough to explore the dwelling. From this voyage, Frobisher's crew brought back to England more than 1,200 tons of ore, which they discovered soon after to be iron pyrite, fool's gold. The venture, then, left massive debts, the majority of which fell on Lok's shoulders.[17] He faced suits from creditors for decades and never recovered financially.

Best, absent on that first voyage in 1576, served as a lieutenant for the second and captain of one of the ships for the third. His father worked as an interpreter for the Muscovy Company, which would have exposed Best early on to discourses about lands to the northeast prior to Frobisher's expeditions. He found himself part of Frobisher's crew not because of his seafaring knowledge but, presumably, because of his connections to a high-ranking member of Queen Elizabeth I's entourage—Christopher Hatton. Best served as an aide to Hatton, who was a member of the Queen's Privy Council and vice chamberlain of her household. He invested in Frobisher's second voyage. Best served as Hatton's eyes and ears, safeguarding Hatton's (and the Queen's) investment. Best dedicates the narrative to Hatton and assures him in the dedicatory epistle that the narrative presents "the plain truth, and ful discourse of the whole service" (17).[18]

Understanding the Arctic by way of Africa

Best's narrative chronicled all three voyages, offering a comprehensive understanding of Frobisher's Arctic efforts. *A True Discourse* appeared very soon after Best's return from that third voyage in 1578—and before they discovered the ore worthless. He intended it as both an official record and an apologia against "sundry untruths" that had "spred abroad, to the gret slaunder of this so honest and honorable an action" (17). Best was responding to those who criticized

Frobisher's leadership on the voyages. In a document published shortly after Frobisher's return from that final voyage, Frobisher's critics listed twenty-three "abuses" he allegedly committed that threatened the Arctic enterprise, which did not find a northwest passage and struggled to reach financial solvency, despite anticipation of huge profits from ore. Among the allegations were that Frobisher misallocated resources (in particular food and money), overpaid sailors, navigated ships poorly, and "did refuse [the] conference and counsel" of his crew (361).[19] Lok was among Frobisher's most vocal critics, describing Frobisher as violent and arrogant. Frobisher leveled his own criticisms at Lok, accusing his partner/investor of mishandling funds and withholding sailors' pay.[20] Best declares Frobisher an able captain and portrays the Arctic voyages as successful. He does this by arguing that the voyages are most valuable because they produced knowledge, not about a northwest passage but about climate and its effects. In the dedication to Hatton, Best writes that "the passage to Cataya were not found out, neither yet the golde ore prove good, wher of both the hope is good and gret" (20). Promises of gold notwithstanding, Best lauds the venture as "most notable and famous . . . both for the worthinesse of the attempt, for the good and quiet government, for the greate and marvelous daungers, for the straunge and unknown accidents of the unknown corners of the world" (18).

The design of the text reflects Best's central aim. Three separate narratives recount each of the voyages. While the second and third narratives provide detailed information about the corresponding expeditions, the first narrative offers little information about the actual particulars of that first voyage; it is instead heavily polemical and theoretical. Best begins by listing twelve conclusions or points of "instruction" readers can take away from the text, among them that it is "pleasaunt and profitable . . . to attempt new discoveries, either for the sundry sights and shapes of straunge beastes and fishes . . . and the infinite treasure of pearle, gold and silver" (15). From the very outset, Best portrays the voyages as exemplary. He characterizes England's travels to the Arctic northwest as equally significant as Portuguese and Spanish travels in the mid- and south Atlantic. He describes the decades culminating in Frobisher's voyages as England's "flourishing age," a time of great advancements in the sciences and particularly in navigation. He declares "no nation comparable unto us in taking in hande long travels and voyages by lande" (41).

After positioning England as a key player in uncovering knowledge about the globe, Best turns to the cosmographical theory of inhabitable and uninhabitable zones that had prevailed before the sixteenth century and could be summarized in three central propositions: (1) that the known world is comprised of only three land masses, Asia, Africa, and Europe, (2) that those land masses fall into one of five zones and that three of those zones are uninhabitable, two being frigid and one hot, or torrid, and (3) that the nature of a place dictates the cultural and somatic features of the life forms that reside in it. According to this theory, the Arctic should have been uninhabitable for human beings or, at best, populated by monstrous races. Frobisher's voyages, however, showed that prediction to be incorrect.[21]

Best describes six, not three, land masses and credits the English alone with discovering one of them—Terra Septentrionalis, a reference to Frobisher's discoveries in the Arctic. He imagines the newly encountered lands as room for the English to spread out: "Men need no more contentiously to strive for roome to build an house on, or for a little turffe of ground, of one acre or two, when great countreys, and whole worlds, offer and reache out themselves, to them that will first voutsafe to possesse, inhabite, and till them" (38). By declaring the world largely inhabitable, Best repeats what was quickly becoming an accepted fact among geographers and cartographers, as represented in Mercator's 1569 world map and Abraham Ortelius's 1570 world atlas. Importantly, he provides eyewitness, experiential proof. He declares that the Arctic is inhabitable and not occupied by monstrous races, but this is more than a neutral fact. Evidence that physiology is not determined by climate could, as David Whitford articulates it, assuage fears that "one's skin might turn a different colour or that one might take on the emotional characteristics of a different region."[22] If the cultural and physical features of the Inuit are not climate-based but innate, by extension so are those of the English. Best introduces Africa and Africans into his Arctic narrative in order to help him make this case.

Best's references to sub-Saharan Africa and Africans almost all appear in the theoretical and polemical material that frames the 1576 voyage. These references extend his argument against the theory of zones. The example referenced at the start of this chapter—of an African man, his English wife, and their black son—serves as evidence. The olive hue of those Inuit Frobisher had kidnapped and brought back to London in 1577 provides Best with a second example:

> And for a more fresh example our people of Meta Incognita (of whome and for whome thys discourse is taken in hande) that were brought this last yeare into Englande, were all generallie of the same coloure that

many nations be lying in the middest of the middle zone. And this their coloure was not only in the face, whiche was subjecte to sunne and ayre, but also in their bodies, which were still covered with garments as oures are, yea the verye sucking childe of twelve moneths age hadde his skinne of the very same coloure that most have under the equinoctial; which thing can not proceed by reason of the clime, for that they are at least tenne degrees more towards the north than we in Englande are; no, the sunne never commeth neere their zenith by 40 degrees, for in effect they are within three or four degrees of that which they call the frosen zone, whereby it followeth that there is some other cause than the climate, or the sunnes perpendicular reflection, that shoulde cause the Ethiopians great blacknesse. (54)

The Inuit's slightly tinted skin color, rather than the African's blackness, takes center stage. Best emphasizes this example of human difference, calling it "fresh" and suggesting that it is an even more valid illustration of his overall point. Yet, Best treats Inuit somatic features differently than those of black Africans. He characterizes the black African's color as a freak of nature, an "infection." The color of the Inuit lacks that aberrant quality. In fact, there is an element of the familiar as he links them to those people living in "the middest of the middle zone" with similar coloring. The similarity he notes, though, disappears in those final lines when Best realigns the Inuit with much stranger, more anomalous black Africans, concluding that Inuit physical features and proximity to the frozen zone prove something about the essential qualities of Ethiopian blackness. Ironically, the passage presents a series of premises about Inuit that lead to a conclusion about the nature of black Africans. Whitford argues that Best's representations of the Inuit "make America and Americans a less dramatic and scary 'other' and at the same time ameliorate fears of the 'other' by locating a more cursed and loathsome 'other' in a place that England had little or no interest in during the sixteenth century—Africa."[23] I agree with Whitford that representations of Inuit and Africans combine to mediate a larger conversation about otherness, but Best makes this rhetorical move precisely *because* of English interest in and prior understanding of Africa. Given that interest, Best's choice to insert a discussion about cosmography and the nature of blackness into a text about the Arctic is not an odd, obscure reference to a region that was incidental to the intellectual and imperial imagination of England.

Best explicitly references those early voyages to Africa in illustrating the expansiveness of English Atlantic exploration: "The Englishmen have made sundrye voyages to Guinea and Binny . . . whereby appeareth, that the English nation, by their long and dangerous navigations, have diligently and paynefullie searched out by sea the temperature of all the zones, whether they were burning, frozen, hot, colde, or indifferent, even from the pole Artike to the equinoctiall" (41). In this way, the English surpassed the Spanish and Portuguese, who could not claim successful travel to or experiential knowledge of the Arctic. What is more, the very figurehead for the Arctic venture, Frobisher, embodied the superiority of English exploration. His experiences literally stretched from "the pole Artike to the equinoctiall." We can only speculate about the kinds of conversations Frobisher and Best might have had about Africa and the Arctic while Best served alongside Frobisher in the flagship on that second voyage and then as captain of his own ship on the third.[24] It is certain, though, that Best knew about those Guinea voyages. It appears that he relied on knowledge the English gathered there to articulate the features of the Arctic.

After comparing the climates and somatic features of people in the two regions, Best proceeds to his discussion of the Hamitic curse. In that passage, referenced at the beginning of this chapter, he evokes a discursive tradition from the medieval period when the curse served to explain hierarchies of power.[25] Medieval exegetes determined that Ham suffered two punishments; he was marked on the skin, and his offspring were doomed to lives of perpetual servitude, mimicking Ham's own figurative enslavement to earthly passions. Best interprets the marked skin as black but does not mention the sentence of enslavement; his project is not to re-create in England power differentials between black Africans and the English. Rather, the Hamitic curse is a rhetorical tool he employs to define and fix the identities of those Inuit who populate the Arctic northwest. To explain human difference, Best exchanges environmental rationales with hereditary ones, which, in turn, recasts the northwest landscape as nonthreatening to English identity. As Benjamin Braude argues: "The Curse of Ham not only created African identity; it was also essential to the fixing of white identity. Just as Africans made it possible for Europeans to master and tame the wild reaches of the lands beyond the Western ocean, so a theory of African origins allowed Europeans to tame the fear that they themselves might become as wild as the lands they sought to conquer."[26]

The Hamitic curse, though, even as it fixes English and African identities, muddles more than it clarifies the nature of the Inuit. Best ends his explanation of the curse by rehearsing the widely accepted belief that the three sons of Noah spread throughout the known world and repopulated it: "After the water was vanished from off the face of the earth and that the land was drie, Sem chose that part of the land to inhabit in which now is called Asia, and Japhet had that which now is called Europa wherein we dwell, and Africa remained for Cham and his blacke sonne Chus" (56). Here, Best reverts back to the very same cosmology he had just a few pages before dismantled when he declared the Earth comprised of six land masses, not three. He adds an element of the familiar to the otherwise unfamiliar, presenting a racial theory that is not completely foreign—and therefore unbelievable—to his readers. As William H. Sherman notes about the delicate balancing act of early English travel writing, it "was marked by complex rhetorical strategies. Its authors had to balance the known and the unknown."[27] Best's effort to accommodate readers' prior knowledge writes the Inuit out of his previously established world design. In his understanding of how Noah's sons populated the known world, there is no mention of the Arctic and no clear relationship between the Inuit and Noah's offspring. Without a clear story of origin for the Inuit, Best's readers are left to wonder whether the Inuit are, in fact, human or whether they are the monstrous product of the Arctic's extreme cold.

(De-)Humanizing the Inuit

Best offers few encounters with or stories of monstrous races, a rhetorical move that emphasizes the humanity of the Inuit. Unlike his predecessors and contemporaries (Mandeville, Eden, Towerson, Ralegh), Best does not regale readers with stories of quasi-humans. In at least one instance, he all but dismisses the presumed monstrosity of a would-be Inuk captive. On the second voyage the crew captured an older woman, along with a younger woman and her nursing baby, after a clash between Frobisher's men and a small group of Inuit near Yorkes Sound. The latter two were kept as hostages, but the older woman was released. Dionyse Settle, a passenger on that second voyage, explains in his account of the voyage that the woman was released because Frobisher's men feared she was a devil or witch, based on what they perceived as physical abnormalities that in turn suggested further, unseen deformities. The men "plucked off her buskins, to see, if she were cloven footed, and for her ougly hewe and deformitie, we let her goe."[28] Best writes simply that the men feared she was "a divell or some witch," because she was "old and ougly" and "therefore let her go" (142–43). He acknowledges the crew's fear without linking it explicitly to speculation about the woman's physical abnormalities, grounding their fears in the natural process of aging (because the woman was "old and ougly") rather than in the corruption of a body affected by extreme climate.

This is not to say that Best's narrative does not engage the monstrous. Best does not abandon monstrosity rhetoric; he modifies it by relocating monstrosity from the body to the flora and fauna of the Arctic. Then he imbues those monstrosities with elements of wonder. In other words, he rearticulates the monstrous as sources of fascination, marvels to behold and possess, proof of the Arctic's bounty. He describes "monstrous fishe and strange fouls" (124) and "monstrous lies of ice" that are "marvellous to behold" (126). At one point he lingers on a description of a huge fish, perhaps a whale:

> Upon another small iland here was also founde a great deade fishe, which, as it should seeme, had bin embayed with ise, and was in proportion rounde like to a porpose . . . havying a horne of two yards long growing out of the snoute or nostrels. This horne is wreathed and strayet, like in fashion to a taper made of waxe, and maybe truly be thought to be the sea Unicorne. This horne is to be seen and reserved as a jewel, by the Queens majesties commandement in hir wardrop of robes. (134)

Best articulates the fish's strangeness in terms of the familiar image of a porpoise. Its oddest feature—the wreathed, straight horn—assumes a religious significance when he compares it specifically to a taper, a kind of ceremonial candle used in devotionals. By the end of the passage, the horn becomes an object of wealth. The fish is not simply a monstrous creature, proof of the dangers that lurk in the Arctic. Best transforms the animal's grotesque, dead body into a marvel, endowing it with an aesthetic value and consumptive possibility as a luxury item. His rhetoric here evokes the same kind of cognitive process Ligon experienced when encountering the governor's mistress in Santiago. Best's momentary shock gives way to a more systematic observation, again what Greenblatt refers to as cataloging and possessing.[29] When Best proceeds to give his vivid physical description of the fish, he is attempting to control, and thereby possess, the Arctic's perceived bounty.[30] His description of the fish creates a kind of natural anomaly that is not to be feared as the monstrous product of an extreme climate. Instead, it becomes at once a source of wonder and a commodity.[31]

Best fills the landscape with marvelous sights, paralleling previous English accounts of exotic regions and perhaps satisfying readers' expectations that anomalies exist in faraway lands. Remember Eden's extensive descriptions of the marvels that comprise the West African landscape. Best is free, then, to contemplate the more human qualities of the Inuit. His first description of the Inuit comes at the end of the 1576 voyage when Frobisher enters Frobisher's Bay. According to Best, Frobisher looked out on the water at what he initially thought were "porposes or seals, or some kind of strange fishe" but turned out to be "men in small boates" (73). Best explicitly clarifies that what initially appeared monstrous was actually human. Certainly, Best employs the denigrating language typical of European descriptions of other, especially non-Christian, cultures. Shortly after recognizing the Inuit as men, he calls them "subtile traytours" when they take five of Frobisher's men hostage. The Inuk man Frobisher captures in response would be taken back to England as "a sufficient witness of the captaines farre and tedious travel towards the unknown parts of the world, as did well appear by this strange Infidel, whose like was never seen, [read], nor [heard] of before, and whose language was neyther knowne nor understood of anye" (74). No longer human, this man becomes objective proof of Frobisher's exploration, like the ore, grass, and flowers other sailors brought back from the voyage. This denigrating language, though, does not characterize him as monstrous; Best writes the man into an Old World context by labeling him an infidel.

The label of infidel might appear an odd rhetorical choice, one that links the Inuit to those Muslim and other non-Christian cultures who were Christendom's primary adversaries during (and after) the medieval Crusades. By calling the man an infidel, Best evokes legal discourse that perhaps helps to justify Frobisher's foray into the Arctic and the travelers' treatment of the Inuit. As Robert A. Williams points out in his study of western legal thought and American colonization, long before Columbus entered the Caribbean in 1492, legal rationales existed to legitimize the land dispossession and conquest of people deemed heathen or infidel.[32] Williams argues that European countries on the eve of New World exploration operated according to a "Law of Nations," an idea originating in the Middle Ages that dictated "Christian Europe's subjugation of all peoples whose radical divergence from European-derived norms of right conduct [i.e. Christianity] signified their need for conquest."[33] In the Americas, according to Williams, the image of a crusading "Christian warrior knight" conquering pagan lands became an "iconography of the Christian merchant-adventurer" whose mission was the conversion of heathens through the combination of commerce and religion.[34] When Best calls this captive man an infidel, he gestures toward the legal, and therefore moral, validity of Frobisher's treatment of the Arctic's original inhabitants.

His representation of the Inuit's presumed heathenism, though, is more complex. While he describes one man as an infidel, he describes others as possessing more civil, humane virtues. This is most apparent in his account of the captives taken on that second voyage. In addition to the mother and child captured near Yorkes Bay, a man was captured near Mount Warwick, on Hall's Island. The man and woman were strangers to each other, but once they were brought aboard the same ship, Frobisher's crew expected them to immediately bond, perhaps even form a sexual relationship. Best writes that "having now got a woman captive for the comfort of our man, we brought them both together, and every man with silence desired to behold the manner of their meeting and entertainment, the whiche was more worth the beholding than can be well expressed by writing" (144). Frobisher's crew, however, saw the two captives interacting with extreme modesty. Initially, the woman turned her back on the man and sang "as if she minded another matter," according to Best. Eventually, the man initiated communication, telling the woman "a long solemne tale . . . whereunto she gave good hearing, and interrupted him nothing till he had finished" (144). Best describes the woman's demeanor as demure. He does not—perhaps because he cannot—relate the man's specific words. What matters most, though, is the easy companionship they created after the speech, the woman especially assuming the kind of gendered role that would have been prevalent in England—and presumably among Arctic populations. According to Best, she "spared not to do all necessarie things that apperteyned to a good huswife . . . for when he was seasick, she would make him cleane, she would kill and flea the dogges for their eating and dress his meate" (145). She was indeed the model "huswife" in every aspect but one. The two remained chaste. Best marvels at their degree of modesty: "I thinke it worth the noting the continencie of them both . . . and they both were most shamefast least anye of their privie parts should be discovered, eyther of themselves or any other body" (145). The woman reflected an unparalleled feminine virtue. This anecdote suggests that not only were the Inuit not monsters, they also were not irredeemable savages.

Best ends his narratives of the three voyages with an addendum in which he offers a more specific, detailed ethnographic discussion of the Inuit: "A General Briefe Description of the Countrey, and Condition of the People, which are Found in 'Meta Incognita.'" At times, the addendum's ethnographic discussion appears to embrace the predictions of zone theory—that the cold climate of the Arctic would, in fact, produce quasi-humans—by representing the Inuit as, at least, behaviorally monstrous. He describes the men as exceptional hunters with nimble, athletic bodies. The women paint their faces with blue ink and wear their black hair long. They live in caves. They dress in animal furs to keep warm during frigid winters and sometimes go naked during extreme summers. Descriptions of the people are juxtaposed with descriptions of the extreme climate, which Best notes was "far more excessive in both qualities [hot and cold], than the reason of the climate shoulde yeelde" (282). He theorizes that this climate anomaly may be a function of local conditions: "Meta Incognita is much frequented and vexed with eastern and northeastern windes, whiche from the sea and ice bringeth often an intollerable cold ayre" (282). These details, according to Best, offer the reader a picture of the "nature of this country called Meta Incognita, and the condition of the savage people there inhabiting" (280–81). Here, the Inuit are "savages," who eat their meat raw, attack their foes with an animal-like ferocity, and "hunte for their dinners or praye, even as the beare or other wilde beastes do" (283).

At other times in the addendum, Best's descriptions of Inuit social interaction, cultural mores, and somatic features refute zone theory and complicate his notions of race. He returns to the encounter between the male and female captives taken on the 1577 voyage and their behavior, so strikingly demonstrating what he deemed civil virtues. In the addendum, the man and woman are no longer simply the subjects of a fascinating anecdote. Now, they *exemplify* general modes of social interaction among the Inuit. On the basis of the two captives' interaction, Best determines that the Inuit "are exceedingly friendly and kinde harted, one to the other. . . . They are very shamefast in betraying the secretes of nature, and verye chaste in the maner of their living" (284). The woman's unparalleled virtue was not, as it turns out, unparalleled but rather typical—or so Best claimed.

In the addendum, Best implicitly locates the Inuit within the lineage of Noah, by proposing a kinship with the descendants of Sem in Asia: "These [Inuit] I judge to be a kinde of Tartar, or rather a kind of Samowey[sic] . . . eaters of themselves, and so the Russians their borderers doe name them. . . . I finde, that in all their maner of living, those people of the northeast [Samoyeds] and these of the northwest are like" (281–82). Even as the passage suggests the Inuit's monstrosity by linking them to cannibalism, it situates the Inuit within a biblical—and therefore human—tradition.[35] As added irony, the comparison of the Inuit to Tartars—both populations living along the same latitude and sharing cultural traits—evokes the very same zone theory Best has discredited throughout the narrative.

Importantly, the comparison of the Inuit to Tartars does not confirm any essential truths about the nature of the Inuit. Best notes that the Inuit are like the Samoyed Tartars of Asia only in "maner of living," not in their somatic features. Instead, the Inuit are "of the coloure of a ripe olive," he muses, "which how it may come to passe, being borne in so cold a climate, I referre to the judgement of others, for they are naturally born children of the same couloure and complexion as all the Americans are, which dwell under the equinoctial line" (282). As Best points out here, the Inuit escape geohumoral explanations. Their color also escapes biblical logic. Best notes that all people on the earth "must needs come of the off-spring eyther of Sem, Cham, or Japhet, as the onely sonnes of Noe, who all three being white and their wives also, by course of nature should have begotten and brought forth white children" (55). The Curse of Ham explains why black Ethiopians seem to defy this "course of nature." If the Inuit are Sem's offspring, as Best implies by linking them to the Samoyeds, the Inuit do not fall under that skin-darkening curse, their physical and cultural differences, then, inexplicable.

Beyond Best's Theory

Best's rhetorical decision to render the Arctic within the context of Africa becomes all the more striking when we consider the other developing discourses through which the English were beginning to understand the nature of America's indigenous populations and rationalize their own fledgling imperial ambitions. Regarding the nature or origins of American Indians, one theory deemed them to be descendants of the Ten Lost Tribes of Israel. This theory was based loosely on biblical scripture and referred to the eighth-century conquest of Israel by Assyrians. As a result of that conquest, ten tribes of the nation of Israel either assimilated into Assyrian culture or were exiled, wandering east toward Asia, then crossing a strip of land that connected Asia and America.[36]

Other English discourses centered on Native Americans discussed them not in terms of their origins but in terms of England's relationship to America and its inhabitants. Aware of the moral and ethical consequences of their encounters with the Americas, the English sought ways to justify their foray into the region. Theodor de Bry's 1590 edition of Thomas Harriot and John

White's *Brief and true reporte,* recording their observations of what is modern-day North Carolina, suggested one way to rationalize the prospect of an American empire: by understanding Native Americans' apparently more primitive existence as being analogous to that of the Picts, conceived of as the wild, uncivilized ancestors of the English. This analogy created a link between the English and the Romans, whose imperial presence in early Britain tamed the Picts. If the Romans cultivated the ancient Picts, the English rationalized that they could do the same for Native Americans. According to Gordon Sayre, this theory allowed the English to see themselves as "repeating the imperial project that had brought civilization to the British Isles."[37]

An even more pervasive theory for justifying an English American empire centered on Spain's infamy as the Black Legend, discussed at length in this book's Introduction and chapter 2. While Best does not invoke Spanish cruelty directly, other documents relating to Frobisher's enterprise suggest that the English were self-conscious about their treatment of the Inuit. Among the instructions for the second voyage was the order that Frobisher and his men should take only a few captives and "have great care how you doe take them for avoidying of offence towards them and the contrie."[38] Even as the English were forming new understandings about Native Americans, Best constructed his own theory that relied in part on English knowledge of Africa for its authority. In doing so, he complicated emerging discourses about Native Americans, race, and empire. His text suggests that preconceptions about sub-Saharan Africa had broader consequences in shaping the terms of English encounters in regions thousands of miles away from Guinea. Perhaps the text's longest-lasting contribution remains the racial theory—centered on the Hamitic curse and informed by previous English encounters with West Africa—that both energizes and strains his larger rhetorical aims. Even as Best employs black Africans as a mediatory tool to locate human difference in the body rather than in the landscape, his racial theory obscures the nature of the very population he must define in order to *prove* the Arctic to be inhabitable—the Inuit. They remain a nebulous, undertheorized presence in the foreground of his narrative.

Ralegh's Quest for Gold: Guiana, Guinea, and the Mirror Effect

While Best's meditation on human difference drives his text, racial language and imagery work more subtly in Ralegh's. The only overt mention of a specific black African figure occurs in a scene where Ralegh and a small contingent of his men explore the Lagartos River, a tributary of the Orinoco, while in search of Guiana's capital city, Manoa, or El Dorado. The journey is arduous. Food and water are scarce; the heat is unbearable. The river is dangerously narrow; its banks are overcrowded with shrubbery and trees, the branches of which Ralegh and his men chop away with their swords. Suddenly, the landscape changes, opens onto an Edenic scene. On either side of the river, the vegetation turns into lush, green plains sprinkled with groves of trees. The land and river brim with a variety of fish and birds and deer that "came downe feeding by the waters side, as if they had beene vsed to a keepers call" (113).[39] This is "the most beautifull countrie that euer [Ralegh's] eyes behld"—with one exception (113). The river teems with lagartos, or crocodiles, from which the river takes its name. Ralegh describes them as "ugly serpents" that interrupt a fruitful and serene Eden. To illustrate their beastliness, he relates the demise of one of his sailors, a "Negro" and "very proper yoong fellow," who inexplicably "leaps" out of the ship "to swim in the mouth of this riuer" (113). He is "deuoured with one of those Lagartos" (113).

The moment offers a dramatic account of the sailor leaping over the side of the ship; the description of him as "a very proper yoong fellow" mocks his unwise decision to swim in crocodile-infested waters. Neil Whitehead calls this moment "spurious" given that Ralegh does not note in ship registers black African sailors among his crew.[40] Rather, the moment "is there to validate Ralegh's experience in Orinoco as truly exotic."[41] Whitehead echoes V. S. Naipaul's very pointed suggestion that Ralegh adapted this anecdote from one presented in an account of John Hawkins's second voyage to Guinea and the West Indies in 1564.[42] A sailor traveling with Hawkins related an incident in a river in the West Indies:

> We saw many *Crocodile* of sundry bignesses, but some as bigge as a boate, with 4. feete, a long broad mouth, and a long taile whose skinne is so hard, that a sword wil not pierce it. His nature is to liue out of the water as a fregge both, but he is a great deuourer, and spareth neither fish, which is his common food, nor beastes, nor men, if hee take them, as the proofe thereof was knowen by a *Negro*, who a[s] hee was filling water in the Riuer was by one of them caried cleane away, and neuer seene after.[43]

The sailor noted that they found the same kind of monstrous reptiles "in the time of our being in the Rivers Guinie" in West Africa.[44]

Ralegh's credibility in this moment notwithstanding, the scene allows him to articulate American exoticism in terms of beasts and black bodies. This articulation matters in terms of the narrative's larger rhetorical strategies because it offers a commentary about the region's imperial viability. The lagarto's physical consumption mirrors Ralegh's anticipation of England's figurative consumption of Guiana, a region Ralegh insists is there for the taking, a passive virgin "that hath yet her Maydenhead" (211). Just as the sailor all but offers up his body to crocodiles—by leaping into the river—Guiana offers itself to England. Ralegh participates in what Mary Fuller describes as a colonial romance, a way of representing the region's natural environment that emphasizes "not wildness [and] lack of discipline" but "an unoccupied place of enjoyment and exploitation."[45] The sailor's death, though, complicates the romance. This space is not simply available for "enjoyment and exploitation." The gruesome death illustrates that the landscape—or more precisely the life forms that occupy that landscape—has the potential to be consumed *or* to consume. Ralegh mutes this potential reciprocity by marking the sailor's racial identity, rendering him foreign, which casts the moment as a phenomenon, an anomalous episode that does not typify the fate of Englishmen, who presumably make more prudent, rational choices. After all, only the leaping, swimming Negro sailor gets consumed. The sailor's death, though, belies Ralegh's presentation of Guiana as an easy conquest by suggesting the region's potential for danger. The union of lagarto and Negro sailor functions as a microcosm for the larger community of monsters and dark bodies—associated with Africa—that lurk in the shadows of Guiana and simultaneously define and disrupt Ralegh's narrative drive toward empire and gold.

Like Best, Ralegh's narrative is plagued with contradictions stemming from his use of racial imagery that destabilizes his imperial vision for Guiana. Before offering a textual analysis of those contradictions, I discuss the imperial and personal energies that shape the narrative. Eclectic passions defined Ralegh's life. He was interested in poetry, science and warfare, travel and sea navigation. He was a politician and courtier, one of the favorites of Queen Elizabeth. He organized and funded a number of early English voyages to the Americas and led efforts beginning in 1585 to establish a permanent English colony at Roanoke on the coast of present-day North Carolina. The colony failed but Ralegh maintained his commitment to American exploration. In the 1590s he turned his attentions to the northeast corner of South America, concerning which he had heard rumors about a golden empire. In 1595, he himself led an expedition to explore the region that consists of portions of present-day Venezuela, Guyana, and northern Brazil. From the voyage Ralegh brought back grandiose claims but very little material proof about massive stores of gold in a city the region's inhabitants called Manoa, which was said to be the capital of a powerful and rich empire called Guiana. The next year, he published his claims in a narrative, *The Discoverie of the Large, Rich and Bewtiful Empyre of Guiana*. Ralegh's contemporaries viewed his claims with skepticism, mostly because he lacked concrete evidence.[46] He returned from the expedition with a tiny sample of gold. In a note to readers preceding his narrative, Ralegh explained that he had neither tools nor manpower nor the time to extract significant amounts of gold from the mines. In addition, his was not a mission for profit but for information and confirmation of El Dorado. He writes, "It became not the former fortune in which I once lived, to goe journeys of picorie, and it had sorted ill with the offices of Honor, which by her Majesties grace, I hold this day in England, to run from Cape to Cape, & from place to place, for the pillage of ordinarie prizes" (6). In other words, the expedition was not designed to make his own fortune—an endeavor that would have been beneath his social and political dignity—but to make the fortune of England.

The Discoverie is both a scouting report and a record of Ralegh's heroic deeds. In publishing his account, Ralegh had two goals. As Joyce Lorimer articulates it, "The first was to assemble sufficient support for the conquest of the golden civilization. . . . The second . . . was to achieve, by the act of offering to the Queen the possibility of such a conquest, re-entry into her court and into the El Dorado of her favour that he had once won and now lost."[47] Ralegh lost the queen's favor in 1592 after she discovered that he and one of her ladies-in-waiting had secretly married.[48] The Queen imprisoned Ralegh and his wife in the Tower of London for several months. After his release, the Queen continued to deny him the benefit of her company at court. The tone of Ralegh's narrative, then, is both imperial and ingratiating.

The narrative begins with his arrival in Trinidad; the island lies just off the coast of the South American mainland. There, he attacks the Spanish city of St. Joseph and takes as hostage the island's governor, Antonio de Berrío. In the opening pages of the narrative he also provides a historical overview of Guiana that links the region to Peru. According to Ralegh, during the Spanish invasion of Peru in 1533, a younger brother of the slain Inca ruler Atahualpa fled east, taking with him a number of followers and caches of gold.[49] They settled in Guiana, where they built a new empire, the capital of which was the city of Manoa, which, according to Ralegh, "for the greatnes, for the riches, and for the excellent seate ... farre exceedeth any of the world" (37). By giving Guiana a past, and assuaging readers' doubts about "how this Empire of Guiana is become so populous, and adorned with so manie greate ... treasures," Ralegh confirms its present state (35). He derives credibility by linking the unfamiliar with the familiar.

As part of the region's historical overview, he recounts Spanish efforts to locate Manoa. Since the 1540s conquistadores had tried and failed to find this imagined golden city. Ralegh interprets their chronic failure as a divine mandate for the English. He concludes, "It seemeth to me that this Empire is reserved for her Majestie and the English nation, by reason of the hard successe which all these ... Spaniards found in attempting the same" (51). He attaches that presumed divine mandate to a moral imperative to liberate the region's natives from the oppressive yoke of the Spanish. According to Ralegh, natives complain of numerous acts of Spanish cruelty. He describes in particular Berrío's alleged cruelties in Trinidad:

> Every night there came some [natives] with most lamentable complaints of his cruelty, how he had devided the iland & given to every soldier a part, that he made the ancient Casiqui which were Lordes of the country to be their slaves, that he kept them in chains, & dropped their naked bodies with burning bacon, & such other torments, which I found afterwards to be true: for in the city after I entred the same, there were 5. of the Lords or litle kings ... in one chaine almost dead of famine, and wasted with torments" (29).[50]

Explicitly donning a liberator persona, Ralegh tells the inhabitants of Trinidad that Queen Elizabeth has sent him specifically to "free them ... and with al to defend the country of Guiana from their [Spanish] invasion and conquest" (31). This speech follows his attack on St. Joseph, casting the assault as an act of liberation. As was the case with the narratives discussed in previous chapters, Ralegh's text propagates anti-Spanish rhetoric to justify English imperial aims.

After providing a historical overview of Guiana and defaming the Spanish presence in Trinidad, Ralegh moves on to the mainland, to a location north of the Orinoco Delta. Traveling south toward the Orinoco River, he encounters members of a native group who call themselves Orenoqueponi. According to Ralegh, the Orenoqueponi are from Guiana but name themselves in accordance with their proximity to "the great river of Orenoque" (141). The Orenoqueponi provide Ralegh crucial eyewitness testimony about Manoa.

Similar to the alliance between Drake and the Cimarrones in Panama, Ralegh's alignment with the Orenoqueponi promises them protection from the Spanish in exchange for knowledge. Importantly, the Orenoqueponi serve as a stable, constant center against which Ralegh outlines a rather chaotic periphery of dangerous, hostile nations of Indians and monsters. To order the chaos, Ralegh describes those nations along a continuum of human difference from the ideal human, most like the English but for the tawny skin, to the monstrous, represented by headless men and cannibals. Not surprisingly, for those nations that resemble most closely the English, Ralegh can provide visual proof through firsthand encounters. In other words, they are closest to the center, interacting with Ralegh and the Orenoqueponi. The periphery is populated with those not-quite-human and monstrous races that Ralegh learns of only as secondhand information. The periphery is also where a gold-rich Manoa lies, which Ralegh also learns of only through secondhand accounts. He never physically sees this golden city. Scott Oldenburg has noted the relationship between distance and difference in Ralegh's narrative where Manoa and monsters "stand not only at the edge of blank spots on [Ralegh's] map . . . but at the border of natural categories."[51] I am most interested in the association between that border region and Africa and the ways in which that association destabilizes the narrative.

In her meticulous examination of the development of Ralegh's text from manuscript to publication, Lorimer names three strategies Ralegh employs to prove the abundance of gold in Guiana. He relies on a combination of Spanish gold fever (El Dorado must be there because the Spanish have been searching the same region for decades), native word of mouth (especially the Orenoqueponi), and history (Guiana and its people are descendants of those Inca who fled, taking their gold with them, after the fall of Peru).[52] My discussion argues for a fourth strategy—the coupling of Guiana with Guinea. Before illustrating how Ralegh evokes images of Africa and its effect on the narrative, I offer one hypothesis for why he does so. The same way that Best writes against certain cosmographical theories, Ralegh appears to be drawing from scientific traditions that begin with Aristotle's theory of mineral formation, discussed in this book's first chapter. To recap, Aristotle proposed that rare metals were created through a process of exhalation where the sun's extreme heat interacted with minerals beneath the earth. So, the Torrid Zone produced not only monsters but also gold. In his *History of the World*, Ralegh echoes Aristotle's understanding of gold formation, saying, "Yea, it is believed, and it is very probable, that the gold which is daily found in mines and rockes underground, was created together with the earth."⁵³ Long before the Spanish invaded the Aztec and Inca empires in the Americas, West Africa was a prominent symbol of golden abundance fueled by European beliefs in the relationship between extreme heat and valuable minerals. Likely, it was more than coincidence that Eden preceded his narrative of English voyages to Guinea with a scientific treatise about the origins and formations of metals, including gold. The treatise, which is a translation from Latin of Vannuccio Biringuccio's *De La Pirotechnia*, notes that the "greatest plentie of this metal [gold], is founde in Scithia, in those provinces which we commonly caule the East partes, where the sonne extendeth his chiefe force and vigour."⁵⁴ With an emphasis on the East Indies, the treatise confirms a link between gold and hot climates. Eden implicitly reinforces that link when next he describes those lucrative English voyages to Guinea, a region also "where the sonne extendeth his chiefe force and vigour" and where English investors profited from a robust gold trade.⁵⁵

Although forty years separate Ralegh from those first English encounters with West Africa, by the turn of the seventeenth century the English still viewed Africa as a land rich with gold, a view resulting mostly from folklore surrounding the ancient kingdom of Timbuktu, mentioned in chapter 1. A year before Ralegh embarked on his journey to Guiana, an English merchant living in Morocco wrote letters to a merchant-friend in London detailing the immense wealth coming out of the African interior. That merchant, Laurence Madoc, noted the bounty to which Morocco gained access as a result of their conquest of Timbuktu in 1591. Madoc saw "with [his] own eies" caravans of "mules laden with gold" coming into Morocco from Timbuktu.⁵⁶ "It doth appeare," Madoc wrote, "that they have more golde then any other part of the world."⁵⁷ He declares ultimately that the king of Morocco "is like to be the greatest prince in the world for money" because of his recent conquest.⁵⁸

Two decades later, a group of English investors commissioned a series of voyages to find West Africa's version of El Dorado, which those English investors believed existed along the River Gambra (Gambia) in upper Guinea.⁵⁹ The first two expeditions in 1618 and 1619 failed because Portuguese locals, who lived near the river, killed most of the English sailors. A third expedition in 1620 did not find Timbuktu but did confirm reports of the region's golden bounty. In his narrative *The Golden Trade*, published in 1623, the expedition's captain, Richard Jobson, reports encounters with African locals who tell him of "houses covered with gold."⁶⁰ The reports confirm ancient knowledge. According to Jobson, "There is no Historian but will accord, that in all ancient Histories discoursing of the inward parts of Affrica, assurely always called by the name of Ethiopia, it hath beene noted for the golden region."[61] The association between West Africa and gold in English culture was common enough, manifested for example in English money. In the mid-seventeenth century, England began circulating the guinea, a gold coin named for the region from which most of the gold was obtained to make the currency. In an example even more relevant to the present discussion, when Ralegh returned from Guiana equipped with a tiny sample of the region's gold, his detractors readily accused him of having brought back gold from Barbary instead of Guiana (127). Although Barbary is not part of Guinea, the region's gold supply was thought to have had its roots in the African interior, as illustrated by merchant-travelers like Madoc and Jobson. In fact, those expeditions to the River Gambra between 1618 and 1620 were an effort to discover the trade route of Barbary merchants. Jobson writes: "Talke or discourse with any Marchant of this City of London, who have yearely trade and commerse in Barbary . . . and inquire of them, whence the Moore of Barbary hath that rich gold, he makes his Chequens of, and they will tell you, there is no gold growing, within the confines of Morocco, or Fesse . . . but that the great aboundance of that rich gold they have, is fetcht and brought into the Country . . . by the South-parts."[62] Jobson's mission, then, was to establish contact with those communities south of Barbary and establish a golden trade for the English.[63]

The English never found "houses covered with gold" in the African interior. The point, though, is that such a discovery at the time was deemed plausible, a belief driven by science, folklore, eyewitness testimony, and travel. It makes sense, then, that Ralegh would evoke Africa to prove the plausibility of a golden kingdom in Guiana. That association was all the more credible because the two regions were situated near the equator, along the same latitude. The latitudinal similarity matters because of the cosmographical theories, begun by the likes of Ptolemy, that said every place had specific natural properties unique to that place, and the properties manifested themselves in matters of climate, material resources, and the features of the people (or monsters) who lived in that place, an iteration of the climate-based theory discussed earlier. The differences in natural properties of places (or climate) were determined by latitudinal variances, not longitudinal.[64] "It was with latitude in mind," according to Nicolás Wey Gómez, "that Mediterranean geographers had long established meaningful connections between sub-Saharan Africa, or 'Ethiopia,' and the extended basin of the Indian Ocean, or 'India.' Latitude explains why, for instance, geographers thought it natural that gold, cinnamon, crocodiles, elephants, and dragons should flourish in both Ethiopia and India."[65] This association between latitude and the natural properties of place is reflected in a number of early travel texts to the Americas, beginning with Columbus, that articulated the landscape (and its people) within the context of its latitudinal counterparts across the Atlantic. In a letter to King Ferdinand describing his first voyage, Columbus notes of the people he encounters in the Caribbean, "In these islands I have so far found no human monstrosities, as many expected, but on the contrary the whole population is very well-formed, nor are they negroes as in Guinea, but their hair is flowing."[66] Columbus had expected to find monsters and dark-skinned people in an American region that was situated along the same latitude as Africa and India.[67]

Richard Eden notes a similar cosmographical bemusement in 1555. At the end of his discussion of Guinea, Eden describes vividly a hellish heat that blankets the landscape. He marvels that the same kind of climate and people do not exist on the other side of the world though the same distance from the equator:

> This is also to bee consydered as a secreate woorke of nature, that throughout all Afryke under the Equinoctiall line and neare abowt the same on bothe sydes, the regions are extreme hotte and the people very blacke. Whereas contrarily such regions of the West Indies as are under the same line, are very temperate and the people neyther blacke nor with curlde and short woole on theyr heads as have they of Afryke but of the coloure of an olive with longe and blacke heare on theyr heads.[68]

Importantly, Columbus's voyages and those chronicled in Eden's text subvert theories about latitude in much the same way Best's narrative does—through observations of people's somatic features. Refer again to Best's observations about the *olive* skin of the Inuit, which was quite similar to that of people in the Mediterranean. Best notes this as a perplexing commonality given that the Inuit "are at least tenne degrees more towards the north than we in Englande are" (54).

While Columbus, Eden and Best's texts all strain the boundaries of cosmographical theories by contrasting the people who populate Africa and America, Ralegh seemingly confirms those theories. In an essay detailing the history of ship building around the world and assessing England's naval defenses, Ralegh observes similarities between Guinea and America:

> The *West-Indies* and many Nations of the *Africans*, wanting means and materialls, have been taught by their own necessities to passe Rivers in

a Boate of one Tree, and to tye unsquared Poles together, on the top for their houses, which they cover with large leaves, yea the same Boats, and the same buildings, are found in Countries, two thousand miles distant, debarred from all commerce, by unpassable Mountains, Lakes, and Deserts; Nature hath taught them all to choose Kings and Captains for their leaders, And Judges. They all have lighted on the invention of Bowes and Arrowes, All have Tar|gets and wooddeen Swords: All have instruments to encourage them to fight: All that have Corne beate it in Morters, and make Cakes, baking them upon Slatestones: All devised Lawes without any grounds had from the Scriptures, or from *Aristotles Politiques,* whereby they are governed: All that dwell neere enemies impale their villages to save themselves from surprize, yea besides the same inventions, All have the same naturall im|pulsions, They follow nature in the choice of many wives, and there are every where among them, which out of a kind of wolvish ferocitie, eate mans flesh. [69]

Initially in the passage, Ralegh ascribes the regions' similarities to a common necessity and limited access to materials and knowledge. As his rumination progresses, though, he locates the similarity in a shared inherent, "naturall impulsion" reflected in cultural practices, mores, and monstrous behavior, such as anthropophagy. He collapses racial difference.

For Ralegh, Guinea and Guiana exist in the same imaginative space. It is perhaps no accident, then, that Ralegh claims to have found in Guiana, which lies "between 4. And 5. degrees of the Equinoctiall," the same precious metals, climate, and monstrous races that earlier travelers found in Africa.[70] Ralegh's choice to evoke Africa to bolster his claims about gold in Guiana, however, comes at the price of narrative continuity. As the scene with the Negro youth and the lagarto illustrates, Ralegh darkens his landscape through the use of racial rhetoric and imagery that interrupt the course of the narrative, resulting in a series of digressions, contradictions, and self-conscious explanations. This is evident first in his description of the headless people the Guianians call Ewaipanoma.

According to Ralegh, the Ewaipanoma live on a southern tributary of the Orinoco, and they have "their eyes in their shoulders, and their mouths in the middle of their breasts, & . . . a long train of haire groweth backward between their shoulders" (157). Anticipating his readers' disbelief, Ralegh insists that the Ewaipanoma are real. "Though it may be thought a meere fable, yet for mine owne parte I am resolved it is true, because every child in the provinces of Arromaia and Canura affirme the same" (155–57). To make the report more credible, Ralegh tells readers he would have returned with an Ewaipanoma—similar to the Inuit Frobisher brought back to London—except that he had already "come away" from that region in which they lived. He says, "If I had but spoken one word of it while I was there, I might haue brought one of them with me to put the matter out of doubt" (157).

As with the gold of Guiana, Ralegh cannot provide tangible evidence of the Ewaipanoma. He validates both through association with John Mandeville, in whose text "such a nation was written" (157). In his *Travels,* Mandeville describes an acephalous race of people for whom "theyr eyen are in theyr shulders and theyr mouth is on theyr brest. An other ile are men that have no heed ne eye and theyr mouth is behynde in theyr shulds."[71] Although it is impossible to pinpoint exactly where Mandeville locates this nation in his travels through the Middle East and across North Africa, most important is his belief that the acephali are descendants of Noah's cursed son Ham. According to Mandeville, from Ham "come the paen folke & dyuers maner of men of the yles / *some hedles* / & other men dysfygured" (italics my emphasis).[72] Mandeville's acephali, and by extension Ralegh's, are of the same lineage as those black Africans about whom Best theorized. As Best's narrative illustrates, this biblical story assumed a new racial significance by the end of the sixteenth century by linking cultural differences to inherent qualities of sinfulness. Ralegh's inclusion of this monstrous race, then, and his insistence on placing them in Mandeville's tradition suggest that the periphery of Guiana, just like Africa, is plagued by dark races, whose cultural differences and innate depravity appear as somatic deformities.[73]

Ralegh's discussion of Ewaipanoma and the issue of credibility is microcosmic, reflecting his larger claims about the discovery of an El Dorado in Guiana.[74] He encourages readers to approach his account about headless men—and about El Dorado—with an open mind, reminding them that Mandeville's "reports were held for fables many years, and yet since the East Indies were discouered, we finde his relations true of such things as heeretofore were held incredible"(157).[75] Ralegh's reference to the "East Indies" should be read in its larger context to include Africa, as both regions were the focus of Mandeville's travels and treated interchangeably as symbolic of exotic and exorbitant wealth. What is more, the "things" that were "held incredible" included reports not just of monstrous races but also of gold and other riches that *were* discovered in the East Indies and Africa and brought back to England through overseas trade.

The certainty with which Ralegh discusses the Ewaipanoma gives way to a measure of skepticism. He ends the report by declaring, "Whether it be true or no the matter is not great, neither can there be any profit in the imagination, for mine owne part I saw them not, but I am resolved that so many people did not all combine, or forethinke to make the report" (157). Here, Ralegh derives credibility by emphasizing the various eyewitness testimonies from which he got his reports of the Ewaipanoma. In addition to the village children mentioned earlier, eyewitnesses include the son of a tribal leader and an unidentified Spanish "man of great travell" who had observed Ewaipanoma on a number of occasions (159). Ralegh moderates his tone, first dismissing the issue of credibility and then rearticulating it as a matter of logic.[76] For sure, Ralegh's ultimate goal is not to convince readers that headless people live on the Orinoco River; "Whether it be true or no the matter is not great." In this moment, Ralegh makes use of a larger sign system that linked the idea of monsters with gold in equatorial regions—the East Indies, Africa, and now Guiana. The irony of the associative strategy, though, is that his references to a headless race both establish and threaten his credibility, creating tension in the text. As Oldenburg notes, Ralegh dedicates much of his narrative "to precisely that which would call its veracity into question" (43).[77] On the one hand, the evocation of Mandeville and headless men reminds readers that Guiana shares the same geographical properties, and presumably resources, as Africa and the East Indies. On the other hand, he strives for credibility by representing the incredible, which he, himself, struggles to accept—"for mine owne part I saw them not." Despite Ralegh's efforts to link Guiana with its counterparts across the Atlantic, doubt frames his discussion of the Ewaipanoma and, by extension, his discovery of El Dorado. Ultimately, as Fuller points out, he fails to establish credibility. "None of his claims stood up or were believed," Fuller maintains, because he could only offer "the proof of things," rather than the things themselves.[78] It is no accident, however, that an essential part of that proof-making depends on establishing a relationship between Africa and Guiana despite the destabilizing effect of that relationship.

Even more overtly, Ralegh links Guiana to Africa in his descriptions of the violent and dark Aroras. He calls his discussion of this nation a "digression" that is "not unnecessary" as it emphasizes Ralegh's mastery of the people and lands bordering Manoa (135). At the same time, the Aroras cast the landscape as hostile and dangerous, reflecting the same potential for death that Europeans associated with West Africa, which would eventually become known as "The White Man's Grave."[79] According to Ralegh, the Aroras are "blacke as

Negros, but haue smooth haire, and these are very valiant, or rather desperate people, and haue the most strong poison on their arrows, and [are] most dangerous of all nations" (135). While the Aroras are not monstrous in the sense of physical deformities, their incongruent somatic features, the dark skin with smooth hair, render them anomalous. Their dark skin is the product of indigo body paint, a detail Ralegh omits.[80] He often describes Native Americans physically, but usually those descriptions are in opposition to Europeans.[81] In this case, he evokes sub-Saharan Africa through what I would argue is both a literal and symbolic use of "black." In order to magnify the threat the Aroras pose, Ralegh withholds the crucial detail about their dye-tinted skin, taking advantage of the cultural association between blackness and evil or danger, which has its roots in medieval Christian discourses in which the description of a person as "black" was a commentary on moral depravity. As Peter Fryer notes, "Blackness, in England, traditionally stood for death, mourning, baseness, evil, and sin and danger."[82] By the sixteenth century, black more often became a literal somatic descriptor for those people in the sub-Saharan region of Africa. Inside the figure of the sub-Saharan African, the religious and the somatic combined, and black Africans came to symbolize a host of negative character traits, among them immorality, evil, and violence. That Ralegh takes advantage of this discourse is suggested by his commentary on the Aroras' physical blackness, coupled with the extreme language he employs to describe them as "the most dangerous of all nations" with the "most strong poison" in their arrows.

Once he establishes them as a dark, foreboding menace, he constructs himself as a mediating force that mitigates the danger. Once a victim has been shot with a poison arrow, according to Ralegh, he "indureth the most insufferable torment in the world, and abideth a most uglie and lamentable death, somtimes dying starke mad, sometimes their bowels breaking out of their bellies, and are presently discolored, as blacke as pitch, and so unsauery, as no man can endure to cure, or to attend them" (135). The arrow's poison creates a monstrous effect in the victim. The antidote for this potent poison is known by only a select few "southsaiers and priests, who do conceale it, and onely teach it but from the father to the sonne" (135). The gruesome effect of the poison and the secrecy veiling the cure dramatize Ralegh's success in obtaining knowledge of the proper treatment, a feat resulting apparently from his own charm. "I was more beholding to the *Guianians* than any other," he writes. "They taught me the best way of healing as wel therof, as of al other poisons" (137). He then proves his newfound medicinal knowledge by revealing the cure, made with the juice of a root called tupara. Ralegh brings South American medicine to his English readers, ripping the veil away from what had been sacred knowledge.

Although the Aroras remain a dark, menacing presence along the river, Ralegh neutralizes their threat through knowledge that is as valuable as Guianian gold. The scene, however, also complicates representations of Guiana as an easy, simple conquest as it harkens back to the same kinds of violent, life-threatening ordeals English traders experienced in their first encounters with West African nations, many of whom also wielded poisonous arrows. Among the events that made Hawkins's 1568 voyage so troublesome was the attack by inhabitants off the Guinea coast; he nearly died from a poisonous arrow. The mystique and monstrous effects on the body that Ralegh notes in his description of the Arora's poisonous arrows matches Hawkins's description of those in Guinea.[83] "Although in the beginning it seemed to be but small hurts," Hawkins marvels about the injuries he and his men suffered, "yet there hardly escaped any that had blood drawn of them, and dyed in strange sort with their mouths shut some ten day before he died, and after their wounds were whole."[84] As with the Ewaipanoma, the Aroras illustrate a commonality in people and natural resources between Guiana and Guinea. This rhetorical move suggests that also in Guiana would-be English voyagers are susceptible to the same dangers. Guiana is not simply a passive virgin opening her arms to English arrival.

The representation of Guiana as dark and dangerous finds confirmation finally in Ralegh's description of that monstrous, war-like race of women whose kingdom along the Amazon River juxtaposes Manoa. His initial description of Amazons is rendered as yet another aside. "And though I digresse from my purpose," he warns readers, "yet I will set downe what hath been deliuered me for truth of those women" (63). He says of the Amazons:

> The memories of the like women are very ancient as well in Africa as in Asia: In Africa those that had Medusa for Queene: others in Scithia neere the riuers of Tanais and Thermadon: we find also that Lampedo and Marthesia were Queens of the Amazones: in many histories they are verified to haue been, and in diuers ages and Provinces . . . they are said to be very cruell and bloodthirsty, especially to such as offer to inuade their territories. These Amazones haue likewise great store of these plates of golde, which they recouer by exchange chiefly for a kinde of greene stones, which the Spaniards call Piedras Hijadas, and

we vse for spleene stones, and for the disease of the stone we also esteeme them. (63–65)

To prove the existence of this female warrior nation, Ralegh locates them within an Old World, classical context. Note that he refers first to that race of African Amazons who worshipped the snake-headed Medusa. His reference to African Amazons appears to be more than an incidental historical marker if we consider that Herodotus originally situated them near Scythia, a region of present-day Ukraine.[85] Subsequent accounts, including those from Pliny, Mandeville, and Ralegh's near-contemporary Andre Thevet, placed them in regions throughout the Middle East and Asia. Ralegh very well could have situated his South American Amazons into a historical context without mentioning Africa at all. That he does so suggests Africa is performing a specific rhetorical function. Other important aspects of his description here include the Amazons' aggressive nature, their wealth, and the amount of power they wield because of that wealth is in the form of gold and spleen-stones, life-saving medicine. The Amazons cohere with Stephen Greenblatt's understanding of the function of marvels in early exploration accounts as "not only . . . a source of fascination but of authentication."[86] Like the Ewaipanoma, the Amazons do not signify new knowledge but confirm old knowledge—the belief that the Torrid Zone produces monsters and gold.

Although Ralegh calls this moment a digression, it does, as Louis Montrose points out, allow him to discuss "the circulation of gold and other commodities among the people situated between the Orinoco and Amazon rivers."[87] The Amazons are a metonymic meditation on the wealth existing in Guiana. They also evoke through implied analogy Queen Elizabeth I's own power and strength. At the level of analogy their representation subverts Ralegh's larger imperial vision. At the end of his narrative Ralegh urges the queen to claim Guiana. He appeals to her pride by assuring her that her greatness would resonate not only with other European powers but also "where the south border for Guiana reacheth to the Dominion and Empire of the Amazones, those women shall hereby heare the name of a virgin, which is not only able to defend her owne territories and her neighbors, but also to inuade and conquere so great Empyres and so farre remoued" (221). He emphasizes a race of women who are strong, rich, and rulers over a "Dominion and Empire." Potentially, Elizabeth could be the Amazon of all Amazons in South America. This association is problematic, however, because it threatens to render the Queen as powerful but also monstrous. By linking the queen to those positive attributes of the Amazons (power, wealth), Ralegh also necessarily associates her with those negative attributes. Recall his initial description of the Amazons as "very cruell and bloodthirsty" and their genealogical origins in Africa and Asia. Then, there is the evocation of the serpent-headed Medusa, who finds her way into the text specifically because Ralegh references African Amazons. She is a monstrous figure of indiscriminate killing that African Amazons worship precisely because of her destructive powers, which reminds readers that the Amazons are not friendly neighbors but conquerors themselves. If we follow the analogy through to completion, Ralegh's use of the Amazons threatens to align the queen with a gendered and racial monstrosity. The same way African Amazons worship Medusa, those in South America would worship the queen. Ralegh, though, does not complete the analogy. He ends the comparison—and the narrative—abruptly, writing, "To speake more at this time, I feare would be but troublesome" (221). This self-consciously terse ending is suggestive of the anxieties that package Ralegh's narrative alongside the promises of immense wealth and opportunities. Similar to the serpent-like lagarto, the Amazons invade Ralegh's Edenic Guiana, interrupting his narrative of an easy, peaceful conquest.

In some regards, my reading here echoes Montrose, who also sees the comparison between Elizabeth and the Amazons as ambiguous, primarily because Ralegh establishes the queen as an Amazon, evoking "tropes of feminine self-empowerment."[88] Then he dissociates her from the Amazons, according to Montrose, when he suggests that she "invade and conquer" all those regions surrounding Manoa, including Amazon, which realigns her instead with the conquering Spanish. I disagree with Montrose that Ralegh's call for invasion moves her out of the realm of Amazon imagery because conquest and invasion were fundamental tropes of Amazon lore. By calling on the queen to become a great conqueror, Ralegh is not dissociating but elevating her in his analogy, imagining her as the ultimate Amazon.

Despite the strategies Ralegh employed to prove the existence of an El Dorado in South America, which included evoking images of Africa, the queen remained unimpressed with his reports. She refused to fund a military force to claim the region. I should note that there were a number of reasons Ralegh failed to gain royal support for a Guiana invasion, including the fact that the queen remained more focused on securing her existing realm than on expanding it.[89] Ralegh's efforts to position Guiana as the prime frontier for English imperial expansion ultimately led to his execution in 1618. After Queen Elizabeth's death in 1603, Ralegh was convicted of treason in a plot to overthrow the newly crowned King James I.[90] Although the king issued a stay of execution, Ralegh remained confined in the Tower of London until 1616. By then he had managed to convince King James that he could find Manoa. As Lorimer and Fuller point out, Ralegh hoped that the discovery of Manoa would result in his freedom and his restoration to a favored place in the royal court.[91] A follow-up expedition had the opposite result. On a second voyage, Ralegh's men, who he claims acted without his authority, attacked the Spanish settlement of San Thomé along the Orinoco River. To mollify the Spanish, enraged by the act of aggression, King James promptly re-imprisoned Ralegh and executed him in 1618.

Despite Ralegh's failed efforts to drum up excitement for his Guiana project and save his own life, his narrative is a useful counterpoint to Best's, offering an alternative perspective on how and why sub-Saharan Africa was employed to promote English imperial expansion. Through his descriptions of Hametically cursed Ewaipanoma, black Aroras, and African-like Amazons, Ralegh populates Guiana with the same kind of nonhumans that were said to exist in Africa. Through his dehumanization of the populations in Guiana he sets up the region for the same level of commercial exploitation and disregard for human life that was increasingly defining the trade relationship between Africa and Europe at the turn of the seventeenth century and that fueled European imperial expansion. Consider his final declaration that "Guiana is a Countrey that hath yet her Maydenhead, never sackt, turned, nor wrought, the face of the earth hath not beene torne, nor the virtue and salt of the soyle spent by manurance, the graves have not been opened for gold.... It hath never been entred by any armie of strength, and never conquered or possessed by any Christian Prince" (211). His image of a vacant, pristine land is the ultimate—and ironic—effacement of his allies, the Orenoqueponi, and those very same monstrous races and violent Native American nations he assured readers existed in Guiana.

Both Best and Ralegh employ racial rhetoric to contemplate and order human difference and lend credibility to their commercial visions in the arctic northwest and South America. That rhetoric, however, obfuscates what it intends to clarify. In Best's narrative, he constructs a racial theory that designates African blackness the product not of climate but of a biblically generated, immutable, and observable curse. The theory, though, fails to account for Inuit difference or predict the effect of an Arctic climate on potential English travelers to the northwest. As for Ralegh, he portrays his discovery as the equivalent of Spain's gold mines in Peru and Mexico and Portugal's monopoly of Guinea gold, but in evoking Africa, Ralegh creates a Guiana landscape that is not a passive virgin awaiting English arrival. Rather it is a hostile environment, full of dangers at every turn. The risks undermine the potential commercial benefits, especially when coupled with Ralegh's lack of physical proof.

Reading Best and Ralegh's narratives within the context of sub-Saharan Africa expands discussions of how and why early modern English travel writers manipulated racial discourses and the stakes involved in that manipulation, not only in how the English conceived of black Africans but also in how those conceptions informed their interactions with Native Americans and indigenous populations. Even more important, I emphasize the challenges they faced in attempting to translate ideologies about Africa and human difference into their encounters with unfamiliar cultures. Granted, my work is more suggestive than conclusive in that I see Best and Ralegh's narratives, together with the narratives discussed in previous chapters, as a starting point to larger conversations about the extent to which Africa informed—and disrupted—English encounters with the Americas. For Best and Ralegh, Africa is an essential but problematic mediatory tool that hinders their efforts to articulate the foreign in familiar terms and find value in new and "marvelous" discoveries.

AFTERWORD

Beyond the Mediation

My primary goal in this book has been to re-orientate readers to colonial contact literature by reading narratives against the grain while accounting for the material presences of black Africans. Rather than mining the literature for clues about European imperial ambitions, I have isolated a series of mediated moments that tell us something about black Africans' experiences and engagement with English colonial projects and literature. Through a triangulated strategy of textual analysis, perception, and speculation, I interrogate what those mediated moments mean, how they mean it, and why they mean it. Such readings illuminate the extent to which black Africans, materially and literarily, undermined the rhetoric and representations that were so crucial for how the English understood national identity and imperial ambitions in Spanish America.

Specifically, conceptions of and contact with sub-Saharan Africa and its people fueled English literary imaginations in the sixteenth and seventeenth centuries, consequently complicating English efforts to articulate anti-Spanish sentiment and to justify their own imperial desires. By ending this book with an examination of George Best and Sir Walter Ralegh, the argument comes full circle, as the very racial ideologies on which Best and Ralegh depend to articulate their imperial visions are indebted to the experiences of those first English travelers to Guinea, discussed in chapter 1. Reading Best and Ralegh's narratives within the context of sub-Saharan Africa helps to explain why early modern English travel writers manipulated racial discourses and to explain the stakes involved in that manipulation—in terms of how the English conceived of black Africans and how those conceptions informed their interactions with Native Americans. In addition to bodies and material goods, Europeans also took from their Guinea encounters strategies for navigating cultural interactions that would inform how they thought about and wrote about their experiences in the Americas. I emphasize the challenges they faced in attempting to translate ideologies into narratives.

The narrative disruptions I have traced throughout this book are the product of material-world interactions among black Africans, Europeans, and Native Americans, which is a conclusion that might appear self-evident to some scholars invested in early Atlantic and colonial discursive studies. As David Read notes, "The fact that colonial texts are intellectually, politically, and aesthetically problematic requires no great skill to ferret out; it is a given—a point of departure."[1] This "point of departure" usually leads scholars to conclusions about European ideologies and imperial/colonial enterprises. I take this point of departure to arrive at observations about black Africans, their activity in the early Americas, and their effect on the literature produced in the Americas. When we position black African mediations at the center of early Atlantic literature and utilize the tools of textual analysis, speculation, and perception to re-create their possible material world experiences, we see that the literature derives its energy not only from the rhetorical prerogatives of the author but also from the author's interactions outside the text. I conclude ultimately that black Africans were integral to the shaping of early Atlantic literature.

Beyond identifying the narrative disruptions and the mediated moments that convey them, this project presents an occasion to re-assess early African American literary studies. In their introduction to the volume of essays titled *Beyond Douglass: New Perspectives on Early African-American Literature*, editors Michael Drexler and Ed White criticize what they call a "streamlined artificially constructed canon."[2] They describe it as one in which the individual, distinct experiences of early African American writers have been subsumed into or disregarded by central moments and/or texts deemed paradigmatic of a unified African American experience. As such, the canon, in its current state, creates a false sense of narrative unity, a limited number of national narratives against which every text is evaluated. Their aim in the volume, they explain, is to contemplate new ways of reading and teaching early African American literature to account for the many varied experiences and discursive formulations of those experiences that appear in the literature. They want to "make space" for texts previously deemed "minor variants" of a larger tradition, so those texts are no longer beholden to "representational" figures like Frederick Douglass to derive their meaning (14). Drexler and White call for a canon expansion, one that incorporates more themes, more discourses, more texts, more approaches to established texts. *Black Africans in the British Imagination* pushes even further Drexler and White's charge by challenging the very process through which we define the canon.

Traditionally, the texts we define as African American literature adhere to understandings of authorship as synonymous with writer (or speaker in the case of early slave narratives and oral folktales), a lone figure who creates and therefore owns the text. We pinpoint the origins of this literature based on when African Americans started creating their own narratives. Most studies locate the origins of African American literature in the mid-eighteenth century.[3] A few studies look to "Adam Negro's Tryall" in 1701–3, a compilation of court documents that provide a narrative of one enslaved man's efforts to secure his freedom from his master in Boston.[4] No studies consider texts appearing before the eighteenth century because the American literary archive has not yet yielded any narratives—in English—written by African-descended people before then. In 1987 John Sekora first dismisses those early slave narratives written through amanuenses as black messages wrapped inside white envelopes, because of this issue of authorship—or more precisely the absence of clearly defined authors.[5] He understands the texts as the creation of white editors and publishers whose political agendas overwrite the particular, unique life experiences of the slave-authors. The texts, therefore, lack the authority to be labeled African American literature, according to Sekora. Since then, a number of studies have complicated Sekora's perspective[6] while reaffirming authorship as ownership, transferring possession from white publishers to black speakers who render their narratives orally. Authorship remains the primary mode for designating African American literature.

We have been seduced by what Michel Foucault calls the author function, the ideology of authorship that allows us to categorize texts, in this specific case as African American, and create systems of inclusion and exclusion. According to Foucault, the author "is a certain functional principle by which, in our culture, one limits, excludes, and chooses; in short, by which one *impedes* the free circulation, the free manipulation, the free composition, decomposition, and recomposition of fiction."[7] He argues specifically about the author's effect on fiction what Roland Barthes argues about text more broadly conceived. "The image of literature to be found in ordinary culture is," according to Barthes, "tyrannically centred on the author, his person, his life, his tastes, his passions."[8] "To give a text an Author," Barthes insists, "is to impose a limit on that text, to furnish it with a final signified, to close the writing."[9] Both Foucault and Barthes advocate modes of reading that divorce texts from authors, understanding the writers of those texts as regulators (Foucault) or interlocutors (Barthes) who do not create single meanings or discourses but compile multiple discourses in texts.

Granted, Foucault and Barthes entertain notions of authorship that speak to certain privileges and luxuries unavailable to those who study African American literature and culture, who for decades have been engaged in the crucial task of recovering African American voices and experiences within a larger American culture. This task has been imperative given centuries of social and political mechanisms that conspired to make those voices silent, their presences invisible. Especially in the eighteenth and nineteenth centuries, African Americans who were engaged in the process of writing—just like critics analyzing those texts today—were inherently participating in political activities with profound consequences for the daily lives of African Americans.[10] To conceive discursively of the "death of the author," as Barthes does, is to undermine the embodied efforts of writers like Phillis Wheatley, Frederick Douglass, and Anna Julia Cooper who, through the process of writing, created social, cultural, and political life. In other words, the production and study of what we call African American literature is a prolonged recovery project, a move from cultural erasure toward visibility.

We cannot, then, afford to dismiss authorship as a strictly theoretical or discursive apparatus in discussions of early African American literature. I insist, rather, that we expand those classificatory systems, to reference Foucault again, that have for too long allowed us to claim certain texts as African American, based on the identity of the writer, while disregarding others.[11] Because of this essentialist approach to authorship, we have missed opportunities to recover black voices and experiences.[12] We have overlooked the ways in which black Africans, to use Drexler and White's turn of phrasing, were intervening in American literature (broadly conceived) long before the first slave narratives and poems by black writers appeared in print. They were actively involved in adapting to the Americas. As such, their actions get read and recorded by European-descended writers and appear in the texts as counter-narratives that prove theirs was no simple process of mediation, no more than it was a simple process for an amanuensis to mediate Briton Hammon's life story in 1760 or that of the other numerous as-told-to slave narratives printed in the eighteenth and nineteenth centuries. Mediation is, in fact, a defining feature of many early African American texts; even Wheatley's poetry is filtered through her master's preface. This book, then, offers new strategies for reading mediation. Those new ways of reading mediation make clear the relationship between the earliest representations of black Africans in colonial contact narratives and an African American literary tradition.

If we ignore the mediated presences of black Africans prior to 1760, we offer up what is at best a truncated African American literary history. We ignore the ways in which African-descended people were negotiating their lives and constructing identities that survive in the literary record. We overlook figures like the Cimarrón leader Pedro from Drake's narrative and the acculturated mulatto Lewis from Gage's narrative. Many of the details of these earliest black African lives in the Americas have been long lost to us. However, they all maintained some degree of self-possession that—in ways we will never be able to understand fully—marked the texts in which they appear. Even if we cannot offer specific conclusions about their actions and motivations, we can at least begin to ask questions about how black Africans might have taken an active part in forging multicultural relationships, helping to shape both the landscape and the literature produced as a consequence of cultural encounters in the early Americas. To broaden conversations about African American literature, we can look not only beyond Douglass but also look before 1700.

NOTES

INTRODUCTION

1. Please note that throughout this book the term "black African" refers to those people who descended from or who share somatic and cultural traits with those who in turn descended from the sub-Saharan region of Africa. The terminology, which might appear at first to be redundant, is intended to differentiate the figures examined in this book from their mostly lighter-skinned neighbors to the north and east. "Black African" carries political, geographical, and racial significance. I elaborate on this point later.

2. For studies that have examined the ways in which England formulated its American imperial project in response to Spain, see Jonathan Hart's *Comparing Empires: European Colonialism from Portuguese Expansion to the Spanish-American War* (New York: Palgrave Macmillan, 2003), and *Representing the New World: The English and French Uses of the Example of Spain* (New York: Palgrave Macmillan, 2001). See also Elizabeth Mancke's "Empire and State," in *The British Atlantic World, 1500–1800*, ed. David Armitage and Michael J. Braddick (New York: Palgrave Macmillan, 2002), 175–95; and the essays in Anne J. Cruz, ed., *Material and Symbolic Circulation between Spain and England, 1554–1604* (Burlington, VT: Ashgate, 2008). Also see Barbara Fuchs's *The Poetics of Piracy: Emulating Spain in English Literature* (Philadelphia: University of Pennsylvania Press, 2013), which examines the ways in which English culture appropriated Spanish literature, rather than forming in opposition. These studies all emphasize the tense and problematic relationship between England and Spain that fueled England's literary production. I am interested in how black Africans factor into that imperial tension.

3. For a more specific discussion and survey of such literature, see William Maltby's *The Black Legend in England* (Durham, NC: Duke University Press, 1971).

4. See Ira Berlin, *Generations of Captivity: A History of African-American Slaves* (Cambridge, MA: Belknap Press of Harvard University Press, 2003); John Kelly Thornton, *Africa and Africans in the Making of the Atlantic World, 1400–1800* (Cambridge: Cambridge University Press, 1998); and Stephanie E. Smallwood, *Saltwater Slavery: A Middle Passage from Africa to American Diaspora* (Cambridge, MA: Harvard University Press, 2008). Several literary studies focus on black literary production in later periods, beginning usually with the eighteenth century and those texts written or as-told by black voices. See Vincent Carretta, *"Genius in Bondage": The Literature of the Early Black Atlantic* (Lexington: University Press of Kentucky, 2001), and *Unchained Voices: An Anthology of Black Authors in the English-Speaking World of the Eighteenth Century* (Lexington: University Press of Kentucky, 2003); and Nicole N. Aljoe, *Creole Testimonies: Slave Narratives from the British West Indies, 1709–1838* (New York: Palgrave MacMillan, 2011). Aljoe's book perhaps comes closest to what I do here by turning our attention toward another form of mediation—the as-told-to narratives of slaves in the Caribbean.

5. *Documents Concerning English Voyages to the Spanish Main, 1569–1580*, trans. I. A. Wright (London: Hakluyt Society, 1932), 9.

6. See Drake, *Sir Francis Drake Reuiued . . . Reviewed also by Sr. Francis Drake himselfe before his death, & much holpen and enlarged, by diuers notes, with his owne hand here and there inserted* (London 1626), 8: *Early English Books Online*, Web,. March 10, 2007.

7. Ibid., 56.

8. Ibid.

9. Joyce Chaplin, *Subject Matter: Technology, the Body, and Science on the Anglo-American Frontier, 1500–1676* (Cambridge, MA: Harvard University Press, 2001), 27.

10. Stephen Greenblatt, "Invisible Bullets: Renaissance Authority and Its Subversion, *Henry IV* and *Henry V*," in *Political Shakespeare: New Essays in Cultural Materialism*, ed. Jonathan Dollimore and Alan Sinfield (Manchester: Manchester University Press, 1985), 18–47, 27. For a more recent perspective on English colonial ventriloquism, see Cristobal Silva's *Miraculous Plagues: An Epidemiology of Early New England Narrative* (Oxford: Oxford University Press, 2011), which is informed by Chaplin and Greenblatt's perspectives. In *Miraculous Plagues,* Silva presents a method for reading colonial New England narratives about illness, health, and epidemics that illuminates the ways in which epidemiological rhetoric implicated and was implicated by colonial theological, legal, and political discourses, shaping the cultural landscape of colonial New England. Silva acknowledges that Native Americans and black Africans possessed their own understandings about sickness and health, or "counter-epidemiologies." He determines, though, that such counter-narratives were ultimately subsumed by or "ventriloquized through English voices, and printed in English texts" (18). Those moments in colonial texts that seemingly reflect black African and Native American voices are instead appropriations and sites of "erasure" that tell us more about colonial representational practices than about the material presences of natives and black Africans (181).

11. Ibid., 35.

12. Ibid., 27.

13. For examples of such studies, in addition to Chaplin and Silva, see Stephen Greenblatt, *Marvelous Possessions* (Chicago: University of Chicago Press, 1991). See also Mary B. Campbell, *The Witness and the Other World: Exotic European Travel Writing, 400–1600* (Ithaca, NY: Cornell University Press, 1988); Anthony Pagden, *European Encounters with the New World from Renaissance to Romanticism* (New Haven, CT: Yale University Press, 1993); Peter Hulme, *Colonial Encounters: Europe and the Native Caribbean, 1492–1797* (London: Methuen, 1986); Mary Louise Pratt, *Imperial Eyes: Travel Writing and Transculturation* (New York: Routledge, 1992); Mary Fuller, *Voyages in Print: English Travel to America, 1576–1624* (Cambridge: Cambridge University Press, 1995); and more recently, Michael Householder, *Inventing Americans in the Age of Discovery: Narratives of Encounter* (Burlington, VT: Ashgate, 2011).

14. See especially Hulme's *Colonial Encounters,* Pratt's *Imperial Eyes,* and Fuller's *Voyages in Print.* See also David Read's *New World, Known World: Shaping Knowledge in Early Anglo-American Writing* (Columbia: University of Missouri Press, 2005); and Susan Castillo's *Colonial Encounters in New World Writing, 1500–1786: Performing America* (New York: Routledge, 2005). Like the sources mentioned above in note 13, these studies understand early colonial texts as products of cultural contact, and they offer especially nuanced discussions about European authors' struggles (and those of indigenous people for Castillo) to account for that contact in their efforts to write

empire. My study interrogates what these struggles mean in terms of how we understand the material presences of black Africans and their effect on the literatures written in and about the early Americas.

15. See Neil Whitehead, "Anthropology and Colonial Text," in his edited version of *Sir Walter Ralegh's The Discoverie of the Large, Rich, and Bewtiful Empyre of Guiana (1596)* (Manchester: Manchester University Press, 1997), 36. Whitehead's notion of texture is fairly broad, manifested, for example, as narrative interruptions and inconsistencies, marginalia, syntactical and semantic anomalies, even multiple editions of the text.

16. See Kelly Wisecup, *Medical Encounters: Knowledge and Identity in Early American Literatures* (Amherst: University of Massachusetts Press, 2013), 199. Even more than Whitehead's, Wisecup's work has informed my thinking about texture, specifically as it relates to black African presences in the early Atlantic world. She defines texture as "the narrative fragmentation and formal inconsistencies that signal colonists' transcriptions of Native and African knowledge and the influence of that knowledge on colonial writing" (197).

17. In this way, my study has much in common with Wisecup's. In *Medical Encounters*, Wisecup argues that colonists, in order to survive in a colonial context, cobbled together medical knowledge not only from Europe but also from Native and African cultures. The cross-cultural nature of those medical practices produced new colonial-specific knowledge and identities that required modes of articulation that strained or broke from established English literary traditions. Wisecup and I understand authorship as a collaborative process. We both argue that interactions among Native Americans, black Africans, and Europeans were vital to how and why narratives took shape in the Atlantic world. We differ in that Wisecup emphasizes the epistemological consequences of those cultural interactions. I emphasize more the mediated forms in which black Africans appear in the literature, and I consider what those mediated forms mean in terms of authorship, early African American literature, and England's imperial ambitions.

18. Drake, *Sir Francis Drake Revived*, 72.

19. Bartolomé de las Casas, *A Short Account of the Destruction of the Indies*, trans. Nigel Griffin (New York: Penguin, 1992), 12. Some scholars, like Anthony Pagden, characterize Las Casas's text as hyperbole and argue that his numbers are exaggerated for rhetorical effect. See Pagden's introduction to *A Short Account of the Destruction of the Indies*, xiii–xliii.

20. Las Casas, *A Short Account*, 12–13.

21. Ibid., 6.

22. Ibid.

23. E. Shaskan Bumas, "The Cannibal Butcher Shop: Protestant Uses of las Casas's Brevisima relacion in Europe and the American Colonies," *Early American Literature* 35, no. 2 (2000): 107–36, 107.

24. Bartolomé de las Casas. *The Spanish colonie, or Briefe chronicle of the acts and gestes of the Spaniardes in the West Indies, called the newe world, for the space of xl. yeeres: written in the Castilian tongue by the reuerend Bishop Bartholomew de las Cases or Casaus, a friar of the order of S. Dominicke. And nowe first translated into English*, Trans. by M.M.S. (London, 1583), 3: *Early English Books Online*, Web, May 18, 2009.

25. Ibid.

26. For a concise discussion of how this motif appears in Renaissance England, see Anu Korhonen's "Washing the Ethiopian White: Conceptualizing Black Skin in Renaissance England,"

in *Black Africans in Renaissance Europe*, ed. T. F. Earle and K. J. P. Lowe (Cambridge: Cambridge University Press, 2005), 94–112.

27. Chaplin, *Subject Matter*, 22.

28. Ibid.

29. Winthrop Jordan, *White over Black: American Attitudes toward the Negro, 1550–1812* (New York: W. W. Norton, 1977), 43.

30. Ibid., 7.

31. See Barbara Fuchs, "A Mirror across the Water: Mimetic Racism, Hybridity, and Cultural Survival," in *Writing Race Across the Atlantic World: Medieval to Modern*, ed. Philip Beidler and Gary Taylor (New York: Palgrave MacMillan, 2005), 9–26, 9. For more perspectives on this side of the debate, see Jonathan Burton and Ania Loomba's introduction to *Race in Early Modern England: A Documentary Companion* (New York: Palgrave Macmillan, 2007). See also Sujata Iyengar's *Shades of Difference: Mythologies of Skin Color in Early Modern England* (Philadelphia: University of Pennsylvania Press, 2005); Benjamin Braude's "Michelangelo and the Curse of Ham: From a Typology of Jew-Hatred to a Genealogy of Racism," in Beidler and Taylor, *Writing Race across the Atlantic World*, 79–92; Kate Lowe's "The Stereotyping of Black Africans in Renaissance Europe," in *Black Africans in Renaissance Europe*, 17–47; and James Sweet's "The Iberian Roots of American Racist Thought," *William and Mary Quarterly*, 3rd ser.. 54, no. 1 (Jan. 1997): 143–66.

32. Roxann Wheeler, *The Complexion of Race: Categories of Difference in Eighteenth-Century British Culture* (Philadelphia: University of Pennsylvania Press, 2000), 289. For other works that also note, for various reasons, the eighteenth and even the nineteenth centuries as central in the development of modern concepts of race, see Barbara J. Fields's "Ideology and Race in American History," in *Region, Race, and Reconstruction*, ed. J. Morgan Kousser and James M. McPherson (Oxford: Oxford University Press, 1982), 143–77; Henry Louis Gates, Jr.'s introduction in "'Race,' Writing, and Difference," *Critical Inquiry* 12, no. 1 (Autumn 1985): 1–20; Ralph Bauer's "The Hemispheric Genealogies of 'Race': Creolization and the Cultural Geography of Colonial Difference across the Eighteenth-Century Americas," in *Hemispheric American Studies*, ed. Caroline Levander and Robert Levine (New Brunswick, NJ: Rutgers University Press, 2008), 36–56. See also Nicholas Hudson's "From 'Nation' to 'Race': The Origin of Racial Classification in Eighteenth-Century Thought," *Eighteenth-Century Studies* 29, no. 3 (1996): 247–64. Hudson traces the changing uses of the term "race" and its applicability in European culture from the Renaissance to the Enlightenment.

33. See Ruth Hill's *Hierarchy, Commerce, and Fraud in Bourbon Spanish America: A Postal Inspector's Expose* (Nashville: Vanderbilt University Press, 2005), in which she argues that modern race, "a cornerstone of biological determinism, was an invention of nineteenth-century scientists, social scientists, poets and historians. Race replaced, or at least came to outweigh, cultural explanations and rationales for difference" (200). See also Michael Banton's "The Idiom of Race: A Critique of Presentism," in *Theories of Race and Racism; A Reader*, ed. Les Back and John Solomos (New York: Routledge, 2000), 51–63, in which Banton argues that some scholars "interpret the racial attitudes of earlier centuries in terms of their own generation's understanding of biological variation. . . . This practice diminishes some of the differences between periods of history" (62).

34. Wheeler, *The Complexion of Race*, 11.

35. The stakes of this debate are perhaps best articulated in a roundtable discussion that appeared in the pages of *Early American Literature* (41, no. 2) in 2006 in which the journal's editor, Sandra Gustafson, and Philip Gould, Joanna Brooks, and David Kazanjian contemplate the theoretical consequences of studying race's historical dimensions.

36. It is worth noting that even in the modern era, racial discourses have fluctuated, exhibiting their own forms of instability as cultural, social, and political landscapes evolve.

37. Burton and Loomba, *Race in Early Modern England*, 10.

38. My discussion of race here is an extension of a point I briefly articulate in "Beyond the Mediation: Esteban, Cabeza de Vaca's *Relaciòn*, and a Narrative Negotiation," *Early American Literature* 47, no. 2 (2012): 267–91. See also Joanna Brook's contribution to that *EAL* roundtable, "Working Definitions: Race, Ethnic Studies, and Early American Literature," *Early American Literature* 41, no. 2 (2006): 313–20.

39. See Phillips's "A discourse written by one *Miles Philips* Englishman, one of the company put on shoare Northward of *Panuco*, in the *West Indies* by M. *Iohn Hawkins* 1568. . . ." *Principal Nauigations*, ed. Richard Hakluyt (London, 1599–1600), 481: *Early English Books Online*, Web, October 2, 2008.

40. Richard Hakluyt, *A Discourse Concerning Western Planting (1584)* (Cambridge, MA: Press of John Wilson and Son (for the Maine Historical Society), 1877), 159: *Google Books Online*, Web, May 5, 2014.

41. Michael Guasco, "'Free from the Tyrannous Spanyard'? Englishmen and Africans in Spain's Atlantic World," *Slavery and Abolition* 29, no.1 (2008): 1–22, 3.

42. Ibid., 14.

43. Ibid.

44. Spivak poses the question in a 1988 essay and further ponders it in *A Critique of Postcolonial Reason: Toward a History of the Vanishing Present* (Cambridge, MA: Harvard University Press, 1999).

45. Stephen Greenblatt expresses this sentiment in a more nuanced engagement with Native American voices in an introduction to the collection of essays *New World Encounters* (Berkeley: University of California Press, 1993), vii–xviii, published several years after his "Invisible Bullets" essay. The effort to communicate between Native Americans and Europeans, according to Greenblatt, resulted ultimately in miscommunication. "But the point," he argues, "is that even failed communication is two-way" (viii).

46. For some examples of studies that examine the "disruptive" qualities of colonial texts, see earlier note 14.

47. Myra Jehlen, "History before the Fact; Or, Captain John Smith's Unfinished Symphony," *Critical Inquiry* 19, no. 4 (1993): 677–92, 687. Jehlen insists that we push through the perceived inaccessibility of mediated moments, or what Hulme calls the 'historical uncertainty,' to contemplate more the human actors beyond the text, whose interactions correlate in essential ways with the discursive formulations. Jehlen and Hulme debate the relationship between discourse and material reality in a 1993 issue of *Critical Inquiry*. While they agree that colonial contact narratives contain disruptive moments resulting from material world interactions, they disagree about what we can do with those moments. Hulme argues that the disruptions can tell us little about the actual historical circumstances of colonial encounters, the "facts" distorted by discourse. Jehlen maintains that the literature yields valuable clues about colonial realities (even if

the "facts" of those realities are uncertain) that shape the discourse. See Jehlen's "History before the Fact"; Peter Hulme's "Making No Bones: A Response to Myra Jehlen," *Critical Inquiry* 20, no. 1 (Autumn 1993): 179–86; and Jehlen's "Response to Peter Hulme," *Critical Inquiry* 20, no. 1 (Autumn 1993): 187–91. See also Jehlen's *Readings at the Edge of Literature* (Chicago: University of Chicago Press, 2000).

48. Jehlin, "History before the Fact," 685.

49. See Paul Gilroy, *The Black Atlantic: Modernity and Double Consciousness* (Cambridge, MA: Harvard University Press, 1993). In his influential study, Gilroy characterizes the culture created by black Africans in the Western world as a transnational phenomenon linking black Africans in all those regions bordering the Atlantic Ocean, shifting the focus in African diaspora studies from Africa (as the central unifying feature of diasporic communities) to the Atlantic and its watery routes that fostered black African mobility and the renegotiating and sharing of cultural identities.

50. For examples of studies that discuss African American literature in a broader Atlantic context, see Vincent Carretta and Philip Gould, *"Genius in Bondage": The Literature of the Early Black Atlantic* (Lexington: University Press of Kentucky, 2001); Joanna Brooks and John Saillant, *"Face Zion Forward": First Writers of the Black Atlantic, 1785–1798* (Boston: Northeastern University Press, 2002); and April Langley, *The Black Aesthetic Unbound: Theorizing the Dilemma of Eighteenth-Century African American Literature* (Columbus: Ohio State University Press, 2008).

51. See, for example, Dickson Bruce, *The Origins of African American Literature, 1680–1865* (Charlottesville: University of Virginia Press, 2001); Rafia Zafar, *We Wear the Mask: African-Americans Write American Literature, 1760–1870* (New York: Columbia University Press, 1997); and Carretta and Gould, *"Genius in Bondage."* They all make various claims for an African American literary tradition that begins in the 18th century. Bruce does, however, recognize that the cultural conditions that made it possible for black writers to write began at the end of the seventeenth century.

52. See also Dana Nelson's *The Word in Black and White: Reading "Race" in American Literature, 1638–1867* (Oxford: Oxford University Press, 1992), in which Nelson examines American literature from 1638 to 1867, focusing on the ways in which literature became a vehicle for *reifying* race. Her study is unique in that she does consider how black Africans in the Americas affected American literature before 1760. My study builds on her work by understanding the ways in which black Africans become not just symbolic matter for Euro-American writing but obstacles. Nelson and Morrison's studies update Jordan's arguments from the 1960s, which posited that the *Negro* was the product of a subjective white (or more precisely English) psyche. See also Winthrop Jordan's contemporaries Milton Cantor, "The Image of the Negro in Colonial Literature," *New England Quarterly* 36, no. 4 (Dec., 1963): 452–77; and Earl Conrad, *The Invention of the Negro* (New York: Paul S. Eriksson, 1966). Note that Jordan's *White over Black* was first published for the Omohundro Institute of Early American History by the University of North Carolina Press in 1968. All in-text citations refer to the Norton edition published in New York in 1977.

53. See Toni Morrison, *Playing in the Dark: Whiteness and the Literary Imagination* (Cambridge, MA: Harvard University Press, 1992).

54. See, for example, Eric Sundquist, *To Wake the Nations: Race in the Making of American Literature* (Cambridge, MA: Belknap Press of Harvard University Press, 1993); Jared Gardner, *Master Plots: Race and the Founding of American Literature, 1787–1845* (Baltimore: Johns Hopkins University Press, 1998); Ezra Tawil, *The Making of Racial Sentiment: Slavery and the Birth of the*

Frontier Romance (Cambridge: Cambridge University Press, 2006); and Joanna Brooks, *American Lazarus: Religion and the Rise of African-American and Native American Literatures* (Oxford: Oxford University Press, 2003). See also Katy L. Chiles, *Transformable Race: Surprising Metamorphoses in the Literature of Early America* (Oxford: Oxford University Press, 2014), in which Chiles examines the ways in which eighteenth-century American culture understood racial difference as surface-level, the result of environmental factors such as climate, diet, and lifestyle. This understanding of race—mirroring the kind of racial thinking Wheeler and Hill argue pervaded Europe before the Enlightenment—deemed race mutable, meaning it had a transformable quality. According to Chiles, American literature at the end of the eighteenth century exhibits anxieties about racial categorization and malleability in an emerging national period.

55. I evoke here Adam Newton's understanding of narrative *as* ethics, that is "the ethical consequences of narrating story and fictionalizing person, and the reciprocal claims binding teller, listener, witness, and reader in that process" (11). See Newton's *Narrative Ethics* (Cambridge, MA: Harvard University Press, 1995). See also Wayne C. Booth, *The Company We Keep: An Ethics of Fiction* (Berkeley: University of California Press, 1988).

56. Booth, *The Company We Keep*, 8.

57. Based on archival work, Warren surmises that the woman was among the first group of enslaved Africans to arrive in the Massachusetts Bay Colony by way of Providence Island in the Caribbean in 1638. Wendy Anne Warren, "'The Cause of Her Grief': The Rape of a Slave in Early New England," *Journal of American History* 93, no. 4 (March 2007): 1031–49.

58. Warren argues, "One story of one rape opens a view into a larger world of Anglican-Puritan rivalries, of gritty colonial aspirations, of settlement and conquest in the early modern Atlantic world, of race and sexuality and how those two constructs combined to determine the shape of many lives. But there are more compelling and more human reasons to tell this story. This woman's life deserves to be reconstructed simply because too many factors have conspired to make reconstruction nearly impossible. Brought against her will to a foreign continent populated by peoples speaking unfamiliar languages, sold as property, raped, and then ignored in the public record. Her story mirrors that of millions" (1033).

59. For examples, in addition to Jehlen's *Readings at the Edge of Literature* and Wisecup's *Medical Encounters*, see Joshua Bellin's *The Demon of the Continent: Indians and the Shaping of American Literature* (Philadelphia: University of Pennsylvania Press, 2001); and Birgit Brander Rasmussen's *Queequeg's Coffin: Indigenous Literacies and Early American Literature* (Durham, NC: Duke University Press, 2012).

60. Bellin, *Demon of the Continent*, 3.

61. Greenblatt, "Invisible Bullets," 30.

62. Ed White, "Invisible Tagkanysough," *PMLA* 120, no. 3 (May 2005): 751–67, 756, which is a response to Greenblatt's "Invisible Bullets" essay. White contemplates the theoretical challenges early American contact narratives pose for literary scholars. Echoing Jehlen, White argues that approaches like Greenblatt's overemphasize the anthropological and foreclose possibilities for historical understandings, rendering it impossible to gain richer, fuller understandings of colonial contact. In Greenblatt's essay, White maintains, "there emerges a streamlined hermeneutic sequence moving from an initial privileging of comprehensive ethnography to a consequent clarification of European discursive systems, concluding with an acknowledgment of an indigenous presence that remains largely inaccessible" (752).

63. White, "Invisible Tagkanysough," 756.

64. In addition to Silva's *Miraculous Plagues* and Householder's *Inventing Americans*, see David Read's *New World, Known World: Shaping Knowledge in Early Anglo-American Writing* (Columbia: University of Missouri Press, 2005).

65. See Greenblatt, *New World Encounters*, xvii.

66. I discuss Pedro's representation in Davenant's *The History of Sir Francis Drake* in more detail in chap. 3.

67. My approach here is inspired by Saidiya Hartman and her effort to "imagine what cannot be verified" when excavating the historical archives for information about enslaved black lives (12). She examines the silences and erasures that circumscribe our access to information about the history of enslaved Africans in the Atlantic. Recognizing the impossibility of recovering those lives, Hartman instead examines the historical (and archival) conditions that coalesced to produce the silence and erasure. Saidiya Hartman, "Venus in Two Acts," *Small Axe, Number 26*, 12, no. 2 (June 2008): 1–14.

68. See note 14.

69. See Chaplin's essay "Race" in *The British Atlantic World, 1500–1800*, ed. David Armitage and Michael J. Braddick (New York: Palgrave Macmillan, 2002), 154–74.

70. Iyengar, *Mythologies of Race*, 11.

71. See Orlando Patterson, *Slavery and Social Death: A Comparative Study* (Cambridge, MA: Harvard University Press, 1982); Patterson specifically defines the phenomenon of social death as the "loss of natality as well as honor and power" (46). He argues that systems of enslavement gain their efficacy from "denying the slave his humanity, his independent social existence" (8).

72. David Armitage, *"Three Concepts of Atlantic History": The British Atlantic World, 1500–1800*, ed. David Armitage and Michael J. Braddick (New York: Palgrave Macmillan, 2002), 11–30, 12.

CHAPTER ONE

1. For biographical information about Towerson, see J. D. Alsop, "The Career of William Towerson"; and John C. Appleby, "Towerson, William (d. 1584)," *Oxford Dictionary of National Biography* (Oxford University Press, 2004): Web, August 29, 2014; Doi:10.1093/ref:odnb/27593.

2. Alsop, "The Career of William Towerson," 45. Although he did not travel again to Guinea after 1558, Towerson actively pushed English overseas trade. In the 1570s and 1580s, he joined the Spanish, Eastland, and Muscovy trading companies and helped establish England's trade with Constantinople.

3. Ibid., 47.

4. According to Hair, the English made some thirty-five voyages to Guinea between 1550 and 1600, not counting voyages for which Guinea was an intermediary stop. They arrived in the region relatively late, and the number of voyages paled in comparison to those of other European nations. By 1550, according to Hair, "several hundred voyages from Portugal [to Guinea] had occurred and several dozen from Spain and France." P. E. H. Hair, "The Experience of the Sixteenth-Century English Voyages to Guinea," *Mariner's Mirror* 83, no. 1 (1997): 3–13, 3: Web, June 5. 2013; DOI: 10.1080/00253359.1997.10656625.

5. Towerson's three narratives were published formally in 1589 in Hakluyt's *Principal Naviga-*

tions. News about the expeditions circulated much earlier, immediately upon Towerson's return. I elaborate on this point later.

6. Eden is writing during the reign of Queen Mary I, who marries Spain's Philip II—before a widespread anti-Spanish sentiment permeates England.

7. Among the sources for Eden's *Decades* is the Spanish historian Peter Martyr, who wrote in Latin his own history of Spanish travels in the Americas in 1530, *De orbe novo decades*. Martyr organizes the history into ten segments or "decades," the first three of which Eden translates and includes in his 1555 collection.

8. As Hair notes, by 1550, the English already had experience in overseas trade, with "regular voyages to Iceland and the Newfoundland Banks, and occasional voyages to Middle America and Brazil" (3). See Hair's "Experience of the Sixteenth-Century English Voyages to Guinea," 3.

9. Kenneth R. Andrews, *Trade, Plunder and Settlement* (Cambridge: Cambridge University Press, 1984), 104. See also J. D. Alsop's "The Career of William Towerson, Guinea Trader," *International Journal of Maritime History* 4, no. 2 (December 1992): 45–82.

10. John W. Blake speculates that this was not the first English voyage to Guinea. The distinction is that it is the first one for which we have a narrative. See Blake's *Europeans in West Africa: 1450–1560*, vol. 2 (London: Hakluyt Society, 1942). Also worth noting: the explorer and merchant William Hawkins stopped along the Sestos River on the Guinea coast in 1530, while en route to South America. See "A briefe relation of two sundry voyages made by the worshipful M. William Hawkins of Plimmouth . . .," in *The principal navigations, voyages, traffiques and discoveries of the English nation . . .*, ed. Richard Hakluyt (London, 1599), 700: *Early English Books Online*,. Web, April 28, 2013.

11. For a description of the voyage's leaders, see John W. Blake, "Petition of Thomas Windham, 3 March 1553," in *Europeans in West Africa*, vol 2, 313.

12. This and all subsequent citations for Eden's narratives of those first two voyages to Guinea are from Richard Eden, *The Decades of the Newe Worlde or West India* (1555), in *The first Three English Books on America*, ed. Edward Arber (Westminster: A. Constable & Co., 1895), 383: *Google Book Search*, Web, August 13, 2012.

13. For examples, see Winthrop Jordan's *White over Black: American Attitudes toward the Negro, 1550–1812* (New York: W. W. Norton, 1977); and Alden T. and Virginia Mason Vaughan's "Before Othello: Elizabethan Representations of Sub-Saharan Africans," *William and Mary Quarterly*, 3rd ser., 54, no. 1 (Jan. 1997): 19–44. See also P. E. H. Hair, "Attitudes to Africans in English Primary Sources on Guinea up to 1650," *History in Africa* 26 (1999): 43–68; Emily C. Bartel, "Imperialist Beginnings: Hakluyt's Navigations and the Place and Displacement of Africa," in *Speaking of the Moor: From Alcazar to Othello* (Philadelphia: University of Pennsylvania 2009); and Mary Floyd-Wilson, *English Ethnicity and Race in Early Modern Drama* (Cambridge: Cambridge University Press, 2003).

14. Eden, *Decades*, 384.

15. Ibid., 386.

16. William Towerson, "William Towerson's First Voyage to Guinea," *Europeans in West Africa: 1450–1560*, vol. 2, ed. John William Blake (London: Hakluyt Society, 1942): 360-430, 367. Blake reprints and annotates all three narratives of Towerson's voyages based on Hakluyt's 1589 edition. Subsequent citations refer to Blake's reprint and appear in text.

17. Towerson, with his descriptions of black women's bodies, participates in a larger racial and gendered discourse. See Jennifer Morgan's "'Some Could Suckle over Their Shoulder': Male Travelers, Female Bodies, and the Gendering of Racial Ideology, 1500–1770," *William and Mary Quarterly*, 3rd ser., 54, no. 1 (Jan. 1997): 167–92. See also Jennifer Morgan, *Laboring Women: Reproduction and Gender in New World Slavery* (Philadelphia: University of Pennsylvania Press, 2004). I discuss Morgan's work and representations of black African women more specifically in chap. 4.

18. For a discussion of the ways in which racial discourse and the Atlantic world emerge in tandem, see Kim Hall, *Things of Darkness: Economies of Race and Gender in Early Modern England* (Ithaca, NY: Cornell University Press, 1995); and Joyce Chaplain, "Race," in *The British Atlantic World, 1500–1800*, ed. David Armitage and Michael J. Braddick (New York: Palgrave Macmillan, 2002), 154–74.

19. See Leo Africanus, *A Geographical Historie of Africa*, trans. John Pory (London: Eliot's Court Press, 1600): Early English Books Online, Web, April 3, 2013; and John Mandeville, *Here Begynneth a Lytell Treatyse . . . [and] Speketh of the Wayes of the Holy Londe Towarde Jherusalem, of Marueyles of Ynde of other Dyuerse Cou[n]trees* (1499): Early English Books Online, Web, April 3, 2013.

20. For a discussion of how these monstrous races developed into textual and visual discourses throughout the Middle Ages and early modern period, see Rudolf Wittkower, "Marvels of the East. A Study of the History of Monsters," *Journal of the Warburg and Courtauld Institutes* 5 (1942): 159–97; and John Block Friedman, *The Monstrous Races in Medieval Art and Thought* (Syracuse, NY: Syracuse University Press, 2000). See also Suzanne Conklin Akbari, "The Diversity of Mankind in the Book of John Mandeville." in *Eastward Bound: Travel and Travellers, 1050–1550*, ed. Rosamund Allen (Manchester: Manchester University Press, 2004), 156–76.

21. For those in early American and African American literary studies, this moment probably looks familiar. Technology and native wonder were common tropes in the writings of European travelers to the Americas such as Thomas Harriot, John Smith, Samuel de Champlain, and Christopher Columbus and in the accounts of enslaved black Africans such as Olaudah Equiano and Ukawsaw Gronniosaw, who describe their initial reactions upon seeing slave ships, books, and other modes of technology.

22. The Spanish, or more precisely Castilians, also traded in the region, initially. In the mid-fifteenth century, both Castile and Portugal claimed exclusive rights to trade in Guinea, the Portuguese on the grounds of first discovery. The Castilians claimed exclusive rights on the grounds that they had established a robust trading network with Guinea and that the cessation of trade would unduly strain the Crown financially. Papal bulls issued in 1455 and 1456 granted exclusive trading rights to Portugal, establishing a tenuous monopoly. For more on the Portuguese-Spanish rivalry, see John William Blake, *Europeans in West Africa 1450–1560*, vol. 1 (London: Hakluyt Society, 1942), 16–25.

23. A. Teixeira Da Mota and P. E. H. Hair, *East of Mina: Afro-European Relations on the Gold Coast in the 1550s and 1560s* (Madison: University of Wisconsin-Madison, 1988), 59. Other administrators at El Mina wrote similar letters.

24. For more on the Portuguese response to English Guinea trade, see John William Blake, "Triple Rivalry in West Africa," in his *West Africa: Quest for God and Gold, 1454–1578* (London: Curzon Press, 1977), 138–60.

25. See "The Claim of the English Merchants to Pursue Free Trade with Guinea, 1555," in Blake, *Europeans in West Africa*, vol. 2, 356.

26. Ibid. For more on Portuguese occupation and control of Guinea, or the lack thereof, see Andrews, *Trade, Plunder and Settlement*, 103. He argues that the Portuguese claim to possession of Guinea was tenuous at best. "Apart from the Cape Verde Islands and the islands in the Gulf of Guinea, which were effectively occupied and formed the strategic centres of an extremely dispersed commerce with the mainland, the say of the Portuguese was confined to the immediate vicinity of a handful of coastal forts. . . . The numerous tribes, varying in power and all more or less independent, continually jostled with each other and often with the Portuguese, who could only maintain a modicum of security by mixing favours with brute force according to the shifting circumstances."

27. Interactions were made even more complex by the Anglo-French War in 1557. The Anglo-French War was part of a larger decade-long conflict between France and Spain, fighting for territory in Italy. In 1557, England joined the war as an ally for Spain because of Queen Mary I's marriage to Spain's Philip II.

28. See Aristotle's "Book IV, Part 2," *Meteorology* (350 B.C.E.), trans. E. W. Webster: Internet Classics Archive (MIT), Web, May 14, 2012.

29. For more information about gold's centrality in early European voyages to Africa, see John William Blake, *West Africa: Quest for God and Gold 1454–1578* (London: Curzon Press, 1977). See also Frank T. Kryza, *The Race for Timbuktu: In Search of Africa's City of Gold* (New York: Ecco, 2006).

30. Africanus, *A Geographical Historie of Africa*, 288.

31. Raymond E. Dumett, *El Dorado in West Africa: The Gold-mining Frontier, African Labor, and Colonial Capitalism in the Gold Coast, 1875–1900* (Athens: Ohio University Press, 1998), 1. For more on the precolonial trade relationship between Africa and Europe, see Blake, *West Africa: Quest for God and Gold*; John Thornton, *Africa and Africans in the Making of the Atlantic World 1400–1800* (Cambridge: Cambridge University Press, 1998); and Philip D. Morgan, "Africa and the Atlantic, 1450–1820," in *Atlantic History: A Critical Appraisal*, ed. Jack D. Greene and Philip D. Morgan (New York: Oxford University Press, 2009), 223–48.

32. Thornton, *Africa and Africans*, 45.

33. In his narrative of Lok's 1554 voyage, Eden expresses his wonder in seeing a huge elephant's head on display in the home of English merchant Andrew Judde. Eden proclaims that he beheld the sight "not only with my bodily eyes, but much more with the eyes of my mynde and spirite considered by the woorke, the cunnynge and wysdome of the woorke master." Eden, *Decades*, 383.

34. Don John's Town was a smaller, coastal town of the larger polity Fetu that lay just east and slightly north of El Mina. The coastal town was named for the ruler of Fetu, Don John. For more information about the geographical landscape of Guinea, especially the lower region, see J. D. Fage, "A Commentary on Duarte Pacheco Pereira's Account of the Lower Guinea Coastlands in His 'Esmeraldo de Situ Orbis,' and on Some Other Early Accounts," *History in Africa* 7 (1980): 47–80.

35. While his men wait at Don John's Town, Towerson sails with a small crew to a town about a mile away, Don John de Viso. He is greeted by the same kind of stalled trading tactics that end with town residents and Portuguese soldiers attacking him and his men. They flee back to their ships anchored off Don John's Town.

36. See Da Mota and Hair, *East of Mina*, 12.

37. Ibid., 66.

38. Ibid., 60–66.

39. Often, Towerson refers to the leaders in these coastal towns as *capitane*. The term, according to Tarikhu Farrar, corresponds with the political structure of the region, which was populated by a series of "states," each stretching inland to varying distances. States consisted of smaller settlements, or what Towerson calls *towns*. The more powerful towns were usually situated farther inland, often closer to gold supplies. Originally established for fishing and boat building, the coastal towns Towerson visited were outliers, the equivalent of frontiers for the state. In calling the leaders of those coastal towns *capitane* (as opposed to *king* or *chief*), Towerson, according to Farrar, recognized "both the important local status of the individual as well as his subordination to a greater authority elsewhere." See Farrar's "When African Kings Became 'Chiefs': Some Transformations in European Perceptions of West African Civilization, c. 1450–1800," *Journal of Black Studies* 23, no. 2 (Dec. 1992): 258–78, 265.

40. Eden, *Decades*, 386.

41. Voyages to Barbary were also ongoing. For evidence of Barbary voyages, see Blake, *Europeans in West Africa*, 347–54.

42. See Towerson, "The Second Voyage Made by Maister William Towrson to the Coast of Guinea," in Blake, *Europeans in West Africa, vol 2*, 406.

43. Note that only five of Hawkins's original six ships traveled together to San Juan de Ulúa. One ship separated from the fleet and traveled back to England before the storm hit near Florida. Also, Hawkins seized additional vessels from the Portuguese and Guineans before traveling to the Caribbean, bringing the number of ships in his fleet to ten. In the battle at San Juan de Ulúa, the Spanish either sank or captured the majority of Hawkins's ships. See Harry Kelsey, "San Juan de Ulúa," in *Sir John Hawkins* (New Haven, CT: Yale University Press, 2003), 70–93; and James A. Williamson, "San Juan de Ulúa," *Hawkins of Plymouth: A New History of Sir John Hawkins and of the other Members of his Family Prominent in Tudor England* (London: Adam & Charles Black, 1949), 132–46.

44. See Kelsey, *Sir John Hawkins*, 105.

45. Here, the number of estimated survivors does not include those who sailed with Drake and escaped from San Juan de Ulúa. The count also does not include the fifteen or so who were aboard a sixth ship in Hawkins's fleet, the *William and John*, which separated from the fleet before they arrived at San Juan de Ulúa. See Kelsey, *Sir John Hawkins*, 105–6.

46. I echo Da Mota and Hair, who argue specifically, "The voyages of Hawkins are usually thought to mark a turning point, since . . . his activities in Guinea extended no further East than Sierra Leone" shifting the focus from gold to slaves." See, Da Mota and Hair, *East of Mina*, 18.

47. Hawkins claimed a loss worth about £30,000. According to Kelsey, though, "If the valuations given by Hawkins were reduced by 80 percent, the total might be nearly correct." See Kelsey, *Sir John Hawkins*, 105.

48. At the same time that Hawkins is negotiating the aftermath of events at San Juan de Ulúa, Spain is attempting to undermine Elizabeth's reign by covertly pressing the claims to the throne of Elizabeth's Catholic cousin, Mary Queen of Scots. For their part, the English are subverting Spain's military efforts to impose colonial reign over England's Netherland neighbors, uneasy with Spanish troops so close to their own borders. For more on the political environment

into which Hawkins returns in 1568, see Kelsey, *Sir John Hawkins*. See also Williamson, "The Narrow Seas," in *Hawkins in Plymouth*, 159–72.

49. See John Hawkins, *A True Declaration of the Troublesome Voyage of John Hawkins to the Parties of Guinea and the West Indies, in the Years of Our Lord 1567 and 1568* (London, 1569): *Early English Books Online*, Web, March 10, 2007. Note: All page citations appear in text. Also, Hawkins's reference here to the late time of year reflects a common fear about tropical climates, a fear that pervaded English expeditions to both Guinea and the Caribbean. For a concise discussion of these English anxieties, see Karen Ordahl Kupperman, "Fear of Hot Climates in the Anglo-American Colonial Experience," *William and Mary Quarterly*, 3rd ser., 41, no. 2 (Apr., 1984): 213–40.

50. Andrews, *Trade, Plunder, and Settlement*, 114.

51. Mary Louise Pratt, *Imperial Eyes: Travel Writing and Transculturation* (New York: Routledge, 1992), 64.

52. Here I evoke Chaplin's viewpoint that racial discourses were already taking form and solidifying in conjunction with the transatlantic slave trade. See Chaplin's "Race" in *The British Atlantic World, 1500–1800*, 154–74.

53. James A. Williamson transcribed what he could of the manuscript, badly damaged in a fire in 1731, and included it as an appendix to his 1927 biography of Hawkins. See Williamson, "An Account of Hawkins's Third Slaving Voyage," in his *Sir John Hawkins: The Time and the Man* (Oxford: Clarendon Press, 1927), 491–534.

54. Minus the normalizing discourse, Phillips describes the town leader's actions similarly to Hawkins: "The *Negro* King which requested our ayde, falsifying his word and promise, secretly in the night conueyed himselfe away with as many prisoners as he had in his custodie." See Phillips's "A discourse written by one *Miles Philips* Englishman, one of the company put on shoare Northward of *Panuco*, in the *West Indies* by *M. Iohn Hawkins* 1568." in *Principal Nauigations*, ed. Richard Hakluyt (London, 1599–1600), 470: *Early English Books Online*, Web, October 2, 2008. As Hair has pointed out, Phillips's version of events "tends to echo [that of Hawkins] (at some points suspiciously) and says little more." He suggests that because of Phillips's youth at the time of the events, "he may have learned little" and therefore relied on other accounts for his memories. See P. E. H. Hair, *Hawkins in Guinea, 1567–1568* (Leipzig: Universität Leipzig, 2000), 2.

55. Both narratives also mention several kings, not just one, with whom Hawkins allies in the assault on the town named Conga.

56. See Hortop's "The Travailes of Job Hortop, which Sir John Hawkins Set on Land Within the Bay of Mexico, after His Departure from the Haven of S. John de Ulúa in Nueva Espanna, the 8 of October 1568," In Hakluyt, *Principal Nauigations*, 488–95, 488. Hortop also mentions that five Portuguese found in the town readily surrendered.

57. See Williamson, "An Account of Hawkins's Third Slaving Voyage," *Sir John Hawkins*, 513.

58. Ibid.

59. See Hair, *Hawkins in Guinea*, 77.

60. In calling himself a *frend* of the king's, Hawkins might be attempting to evoke an old alliance. Hawkins claimed on more than one occasion to have established a special relationship with King Philip when he was married to Mary I. There are even reports, unsubstantiated, that the king knighted Hawkins during a trip to England. See Kelsey, *Sir John Hawkins*, 27.

61. Only Hortop's text can provide useful context for Hawkins's rhetorical strategies. For reasons mentioned earlier, Phillips's account mimics Hawkins, and the Cotton manuscript does not

include the battle scene. It ends several days before the battle—at the point where the Spanish fleet enters the harbor.

62. Hortop, "Travailes," 489.

63. Ibid., 490.

64. Ibid.

65. Ibid.

66. Ibid.

67. Of course, the differences between Hortop's rendition of the battle and Hawkins's reflect divergent rhetorical aims. Hortop is relating information thirty-plus years after the fact. There are none of the immediate stakes that were present in Hawkins's text, and the political landscape has changed due in large part to England's defeat of the Spanish Armada in 1588.

68. This reference to John Foxe and his *Book of Martyrs,* which is a catalog of those Protestants persecuted (or *martyred*) by the Catholic Church, is a final, and perhaps sensational, rhetorical flourish that casts Hawkins's ordeal within a religious, not simply political, context.

69. Emphasizing the links between Hawkins's narrative and those of Eden/Towerson is not designed to undermine the difference. Guinea figures into Hawkins's overseas activities in radically different ways than the accounts of Towerson and Eden, not the least of which is that his primary quest is for slaves, not gold, which limits his travels and interactions to the upper regions of the Guinea coast. Despite these differences, it is important to note how those encounters coalesce into a common language, a pattern of articulation that reappears in English accounts of America.

CHAPTER TWO

1. According to biographer John Cummins, the incident at San Juan de Ulúa "remained an obsession with Drake; he complained repeatedly in conversations with captured Spaniards of the viceroy's duplicity" (31). See Cummins, *Francis Drake: The Lives of a Hero* (London: Weidenfeld & Nicolson, 1995).

2. The link between Drake's narrative and Hawkins's is self-evident. The link between Drake and Towerson is more tenuous. In linking the texts, I do not intend specific claims that Drake read Towerson's accounts although Towerson's narratives were published three years prior to Drake's commissioning his own narrative in 1592. It is not a stretch to think that Drake, having traveled to Guinea himself, was at least aware of Towerson's ventures even if he did not read the narratives. Ultimately, even if Drake never had a conversation with Towerson and was completely ignorant of Towerson's rhetoric, my larger point in comparing the texts is to remind readers that Drake's strategy of creating a "pathetic" black African presence to validate England's overseas commercial interests was not new.

3. E. Shaskan Bumas offers a nice, concise discussion of Black Legend rhetoric and iconography in his essay "The Cannibal Butcher Shop: Protestant Uses of las Casas's 'Brevísima relación' in Europe and the American Colonies," *Early American Literature* 35, no. 2 (2000):107–36.

4. For more on Drake's Protestant identity and England's imperial activity in the Americas, see Christopher Hodgkins, *Reforming Empire: Protestant Colonialism and Conscience in British Literature* (Columbia: University of Missouri Press, 2002).

5. There has been little discussion of the rhetorical relationship between Drake and the

Cimarrones of Panama. Edmund Morgan offers a rare exception. In his study of the paradoxical relationship between slavery and freedom in the forming of what would become the United States, he argues specifically about the Cimarrones that Drake and his men "had cast themselves as liberators and had allied with blacks against whites. They had taught the Cimarrones their own religious views and engaged them in piracy and pillage flavored with righteousness and revolution" (13). Liberation is a key theme in Drake's narrative—despite the fact that the Cimarrones were not in need of rescue. Morgan, a historian, stops short of contemplating what this rhetorical conflict does for Drake's narrative. Edmund Morgan, *American Slavery, American Freedom: The Ordeal of Colonial Virginia* (New York: Norton, 1975).

6. I acknowledge the potential drawbacks in linking Drake's sixteenth-century English narrative to Morrison's argument. Morrison focuses only on white American writers and mostly fiction, primarily in the nineteenth and twentieth centuries. A larger issue is the very notion of race, central to the lens through which Morrison examines American literature. The term "race" in sixteenth-century England did not articulate human difference in quite the same manner that the term would post-eighteenth century, a point I discuss in more detail in this book's Introduction. Morrison's study of American literature is useful for understanding the rhetorical design of Drake's narrative because it highlights the ways in which a writer's imagination can be informed by larger racial (or more precisely cultural) factors.

7. I discuss Pedro's representation in more detail later in this chapter.

8. See John Hawkins, *A True Declaration of the Troublesome Voyage of John Hawkins to the Parties of Guinea and the West Indies, in the Years of Our Lord 1567 and 1568* (London, 1569), sig. B v, recto: *Early English Books Online*, Web, March 10, 2007.

9. See John H. Parry, "Drake and the World Encompassed," in *Sir Francis Drake and the Famous Voyage, 1577–1580: Essays Commemorating the Quadricentennial of Drake's Circumnavigation of the Earth*, ed. Norman J. W. Thrower (Berkeley: University of California Press, 1984), 1–11, 3.

10. Richard Frohock, *Heroes of Empire: The British Imperial Protagonist in America, 1596–1764* (Newark: University of Delaware Press, 2004), 40.

11. Hodgkins, *Reforming Empire*, 81.

12. Ibid. Hodgkins's *Reforming Empire* is largely an examination of the extent to which religion galvanized England's imperial energies. He argues that England's manipulation of Black Legend rhetoric illustrates "the degree to which the British were able to transmute their own daunting imperial liabilities into ideological advantages and virtues, and even their anti-imperialist impulses into a divine mandate for a reforming empire" (56).

13. In *Principal Nauigations,* Hakluyt includes a brief summary, a couple of paragraphs, provided by a Portuguese eyewitness of the raid. See Lopez Vaz, "The First voyage, attempted and set foorth by the expert, and valiant Captain M. Francis Drake himself, with a ship called the Dragon, and another ship, and a pinnesse, to Nombre de Dios, and Dariene, about the year 1572," in Hakluyt, *Principal Nauigations*, 594–95: *Early English Books Online*, Web, October 10, 2008.

14. The younger Drake oversaw publication of several narratives detailing his uncle's expeditions. Drake the nephew hoped the publications would, as he states it on the title page, revive and call "upon this dull or effeminate age, to folowe his [the elder Drake] noble steps" for the expansion and glory of England. In chap. 3, I discuss in more detail the literary and cultural legacy of Drake's narrative in the seventeenth century.

15. See Drake's *Sir Francis Drake Revived, ed.* Philp Nichols (London, 1626): *Early English*

Books Online, Web, March 10, 2007. Note: all subsequent page citations for the narrative appear in text.

16. The full title reads: *Sir Francis Drake Revived: Calling upon this Dull and Effeminate Age, to folowe his Noble Steps for Golde & Silver, By this Memorable Relation, of the Rare Occurrances (never yet declared to the World) in a Third Voyage, made by him into the West-Indies, in the Yeares 72. & 73. When Nombre de Dios was by him and 52. Others only in his Company, surprised. Faithfully taken out of the Reporte of M Christofer Ceely, Ellis Hixon, and others, who were in the same Voyage with him. By Philip Nicoles, Preacher. Reviewed also by Sr Francis Drake himselfe before his Death, and Much hoplen and enlarged, by divers notes, with his owne hand here and there Inserted. Set forth by Sr Francis Drake Baronet (his Nephew) now living.*

17. See Roland Barthes, "The Death of the Author," in his *Image Music Text*, trans. Stephen Heath (New York: Hill & Wang, 1977), 146.

18. Ibid.

19. Note: although Drake takes ownership of the text, it is written in third person, referring to Drake as "Our Captain," a reflection of the narrative's complex composition.

20. Drake traveled to Panama twice between 1569 and 1571. He does not offer any great detail about either expedition, only that the two trips were instrumental in scouting the Panama isthmus for his 1573 raid. According to Wade Dudley, that 69/70 voyage might have been a slaving expedition. See Dudley's *Drake: For God, Queen, and Plunder* (Washington, DC: Brassey's Inc., 2003), 30.

21. William Maltby, *The Black Legend in England* (Durham, NC: Duke University Press, 1971), 29.

22. Edmund Campos, "West of Eden: American Gold, Spanish Greed, and the Discourses of English Imperialism," in *Rereading the Black Legend: The Discourses of Religious and Racial Difference in the Renaissance Empires*, ed. Margaret Greer et al. (Chicago: University of Chicago Press, 2007), 247–69, 268.

23. For more on the queen's policies regarding Drake, see Cummins, *Francis Drake*, 164. Cummins notes that the queen made a show of attempting to curtail Drake's Spanish raids. Hers was an "ambiguous policy of letting Drake have his head while covering herself against accusations of encouraging him."

24. Although the image existed for centuries, the actual term "black legend" is a twentieth-century neologism, coined in 1914 by a Spanish official, Julián Juderías, complaining of Spain's unfair reputation in Europe. For a critical discussion of the terminology, see Benjamin Keen, "The Black Legend Revisited: Assumptions and Realities," *Hispanic American Historical Review* 49, no. 4 (Nov. 1969): 703–19.

25. For examples, see Dudley's *Drake* and Cummins's *Francis Drake*. See also Kenneth R. Andrews, *The Spanish Caribbean: Trade and Plunder 1530–1630* (New Haven, CT: Yale University Press, 1978); Erin Mackie, "Welcome the Outlaw: Pirates, Maroons, and Caribbean Countercultures," *Cultural Critique* 59 (Spring 2005): 24–62. Richard Price's understanding of the collaboration is an exception. He deems it an "alliance of convenience . . . based on opportunism by both sides" (14). See Price's introduction to *Maroon Societies: Rebel Slave Communities in the Americas*, ed. Richard Price (Baltimore: Johns Hopkins University Press, 1996), 1–32.

26. For more specifics about the mule train routes, see Cummins, "Reconnaissance," in his *Francis Drake*, 33–43. See also Dudley, *Drake*.

27. See Document No. 4 in I. A. Wright's *Documents Concerning English Voyages to the Spanish Main 1569–1580* (London: Hakluyt Society, 1932), 9–10.

28. According to Harry Kelsey, Drake's insistence that his men walked away from massive treasure was exaggerated. The storehouses were all but empty, Kelsey points out, and the "small amount of booty that the pirates managed to take away was not of sufficient value for the citizens to make a claim" (56). See Kelsey, *Sir Francis Drake: The Queen's Pirate* (New Haven, CT: Yale University Press, 1998).

29. Like Kelsey, Cummins (*Francis Drake*) argues that Drake's claims about the amount of treasure at Nombre de Dios are likely inflated. He points out that any significant treasure had already been collected by the treasure fleet several weeks before. "Drake must have had reason to believe the town was worth raiding," Cummins argues, "and he may well have found some silver, but it may be that the pile of bars gleaming in the light from the courtyard was somewhat inflated in *Sir Francis Drake Revived*, and the gravity of Drake's injury overstated, as a way of depicting the raid on Nombre de Dios as a heroic near-miss, rather than a misguided muddle based on poor information" (49–50).

30. Although we cannot know with any certainty Diego's fate after Drake leaves Panama, a figure named Diego and working as a servant for Drake appears in accounts of Drake's 1577 circumnavigation. If this is the same Diego, he dies on that circumnavigation voyage.

31. It should be noted that those images, like those of the black Africans under examination here, are the product of European(-American) rhetorical machinations. See Robert Berkhofer, *The White Man's Indian: The Image of the Indian from Columbus to the Present* (New York: Vintage Books, 1979).

32. Note that the details of this initial encounter and the exchange of hostages follow exactly that of English traders establishing trade alliances with Guinea traders, emphasized in chap. 1. It suggests a mutual respect, not a hierarchical relationship.

33. Not all was lost for the French pirates. In their retreat, they happened upon a richly stocked Spanish ship on the Chagre River that was loaded with silks and wines. After claiming those treasures, they raided along the coast of Central America en route back to France. See the introduction in Wright's *Documents Concerning English Voyages*, xxxi–xxxii. See also Kelsey, *Sir Francis Drake*, 46–47; and Cummins, *Francis Drake*, 38.

34. Refer again to Eden's descriptions of Africa that bookend the first English voyages to Guinea, discussed in chap. 1. The narratives of those voyages provide an occasion for Eden to rehearse prior conceptions of Africa as a region occupied by "people of beastly living, without a God, lawe, religion, or common wealth" (*Decades*, 384).

35. See Walter D. Mignolo, "What Does the Black Legend Have to Do with Race?" in Greer et al., *Rereading the Black Legend*, 312–24, 313–14.

36. See Kim Hall, *Things of Darkness: Economies of Race and Gender in Early Modern England* (Ithaca, NY: Cornell University Press, 1995), 4.

37. It should be noted that for Hall racialized bodies take on a gendered significance, an aspect of her argument I engage more fully elsewhere in this book. For now, I only point out the relationship she outlines between physical, somatic features and ideologies of inferiority within early modern English culture.

38. Hall, *Things of Darkness*, 2.

39. See Las Casas's "Memorial of Remedies for the Indies (1516)," in *Bartolome de Las Casas and Thomas More's Utopia: Connections and Similarities*, ed. and trans. Victor N. Baptiste (Culver City, CA: Labyrinthos, 1990), 25.

40. Mignolo, "What Does the Black Legend Have to Do with Race?" 315.

41. Because of an illness that swept through Drake's camp in December killing almost thirty of his men, including a younger brother, a number of those who survived were too weak to travel. The expedition began with seventy-three men, all but one younger than thirty.

42. See Cummins, *Francis Drake*, 38.

43. See Bartolomé de las Casas, *A Short Account of the Destruction of the Indies*, trans. Nigel Griffin (New York: Penguin Books, 1992), 15.

44. See Document nos. 24, 26, and 28 in Wright, *Documents Concerning English Voyages*.

45. Wright, *Documents Concerning English Voyages*, 50.

46. The Spanish also feared that the English intended to establish a permanent settlement, a base from which to contest Spanish control of the West Indies. See Document nos. 25, 43, and 44 in Wright, *Documents Concerning English Voyages*.

47. There was a second option for accessing the Pacific. It required pirates to sail around the southern tip of South America and navigate the dangerously narrow and windy Strait of Magellan; Drake pursued this course during his famed 1577 circumnavigation.

48. The Spanish spared the lives of the five youngest crew members, who were made slaves.

49. For details about Oxenham's voyage, see "A discourse of the West Indies and South sea written by *Lopez Vaz* a Portugal, borne in the citie of *Eluas*. . . . Wherein among diuers rare things not hitherto deliuered by any other writer, certaine voyages of our Englishmen are truly reported," in Hakluyt, *Principal Nauigations*, 779–80: *Early English Books Online*, Web, April 28, 2013. See also Sir Richard Hawkins's *The observations of Sir Richard Hawkins Knight, in his voiage into the South Sea*, Anno Domini 1593 (London, 1622), 164–66: *Early English Books Online*, Web, March 4, 2014. See also Document nos. 52 and 70 in Wright, *Documents Concerning English Voyages*, which provide testimony from Oxenham himself.

50. See Document nos. 4, 21, 25, 38, 42, 43, and 66 in Wright, *Documents Concerning English Voyages*.

51. Assessments of the military campaign's effectiveness against the Cimarrones were not uniform. Another official reported in February 1578 that the Spanish "have captured twenty-two blacks, negroes and negresses, and this, and the state of alarm in which they are keeping them, have brought punishment home to these cimarrones, who do not show themselves as they did formerly. Therefore this country rests quieter than heretofore" (Wright, *Documents Concerning English Voyages*, 203).

52. According to Price (introduction to *Maroon Societies*), concessions between maroon cultures and European colonists were common and illustrated the efficacy of maroon liberation strategies. He argues that maroon cultures presented "military and economic threats that often taxed the colonists to their limits. In a remarkable number of cases throughout the Americas, the whites were forced to bring themselves to sue their former slaves for peace. In their typical form, such treaties . . . offered maroon communities their freedom, recognized their territorial integrity, and made some provision for meeting their economic needs, demanding in return an agreement to end all hostilities toward the plantations, to return all future runaways and, often, to aid the whites in hunting them down" (3–4).

53. Similar to Price, Lauren Benton recognizes the extent to which marronage threatened American colonial order. From a legal perspective, according to Benton, maroon cultures strained an already fragmented legal order that denied Europeans complete and total dominance. The very legal system demanded negotiation and accommodation. She points out that maroon concessions, like the fugitive slave agreement, were not merely acts of submission and resignation. "Though the treaties did implicitly recognize colonial sovereignty, the relation must be understood in the context of a concept of the state as less than completely dominant. Certainly sixteenth- and seventeenth-century maroons, like the Europeans they negotiated with, were accustomed to a world in which fragmented authority was a normal part of the political order, easily understood and not necessarily unstable" (53). See Benton. "The Legal Regime of the South Atlantic World, 1400–1750: Jurisdictional Complexity as Institutional Order," *Journal of World History* 11, no. 1 (2000): 27–56.

54. For more on the pacification of Cimarrones on the Panama isthmus, see Document nos. 71 and 73 in Wright, *Documents Concerning English Voyages*; and Ruth Pike, "Black Rebels: The Cimarrons of Sixteenth-Century Panama," *The Americas* 64, no. 2 (2007): 243–66.

CHAPTER THREE

1. Thomas Gage, *The English-American, His Travail by Sea and Land, or, A New Survey of the West-India's* (London, 1648), 130: *Early English Books Online*, Web, February 21, 2014. Note: subsequent references to Gage's narrative appear in text.

2. *Discourse Concerning Western Planting* is the commonly accepted shorthand for the text's much longer title: *A particular discourse concerning the greate necessitie and manifold comodyties that are like to growe to this Realme of Englande by the Westerne discoveries lately attempted, written in the yere 1584 by Richarde Hackluyt of Oxforde*. The text is one of Hakluyt's less often discussed works.

3. The title page of the *Discourse* tells readers that Hakluyt wrote the text at the "requeste and direction" of Ralegh. In his own narrative about his experiences along the Orinoco River in South America, Ralegh expects to collaborate with native populations to wrest control of the region from Spain. In chap. 5, I discuss in detail Ralegh's imperial vision.

4. Richard Hakluyt, *A Discourse Concerning Western Planting (1584)* (Cambridge, MA: Press of John Wilson and Son [for the Maine Historical Society], 1877), 57: *Google Books Online*, Web, May 5. 2014.

5. Ibid.

6. Ibid.

7. Ibid.

8. Ibid., 47. Hakluyt echoes Miles Phillips's assessment of the Chichimici, who Phillips encountered during his decade-long ordeal in Mexico after Hawkins's departure. See Phillips's "A discourse written by one *Miles Philips* Englishman, one of the company put on shoare Northward of *Panuco*, in the *West Indies* by *M. Iohn Hawkins* 1568" in Hakluyt, *Principal Nauigations*, 474–76: *Early English Books Online*, Web, October 2, 2008.

9. Hakluyt, *Discourse Concerning Western Planting*, 47.

10. Ibid. Later in the *Discourse Concerning Western Planting*, Hakluyt declares "that those contries whereof the Spaniarde is lorde are partely ruinated, dispeopled, and laid waste by their

incredible, and more then barbarous, and savage, endeles cruelties, and partely grievously infested by the Indians, Symerons, Moores, Chichimici revolted; and consequently he is easie to be driven thence, and turned out of all with moche lesser force then is commonly imagined" (80). As I will argue shortly, Gage echoes this assessment of a volatile political climate in New Spain that the English could exploit through collaboration.

11. Ibid., 48.

12. I discuss this struggle in more detail later.

13. William Davenant, *The History of Sir Francis Drake* (London, 1659), 17: *Early English Books Online*, Web, January 4, 2014.

14. Ibid., 5.

15. Ibid., 6.

16. Ibid., 12.

17. Ibid.

18. Ibid., 13.

19. Ibid., 12.

20. Ibid., 37.

21. Elsewhere during his travels, Gage notes "in deeds" the Creoles "come short of them, who are borne in Spain" (111).

22. Gage never reaches the Philippines. He changes course while in Mexico City after hearing about the harsh living conditions in the Philippines. He heads to Guatemala instead.

23. According to J. Eric Thompson, Gage's real crime was not his refusal to join the Jesuit order; instead, the father's actions, Thompson surmises, were a response to the fact that Gage openly criticized the order, propagating a number of charges and accusations. "It would seem," Thompson argues, "that Thomas left the Jesuits with a grievance, justified or irrational, and he had not kept it to himself" (xxix). Gage's recriminations would have carried a certain weight, Thompson notes, coming from a member of an influential English family that had long remained faithful to the church, which would have left the Jesuit order—the entire church—vulnerable to "enemies of the Papacy" (xxix). Gage's father, then, saw his son's disavowal of the Jesuits as a move that undermined the church. See Thompson's introduction to *Thomas Gage's Travels in the New World,* ed. J. Eric S. Thompson (Norman: University of Oklahoma Press, 1958).

24. For another perspective on Lewis's representation, see Kristina Bross's coda "Animating Absence" in *Journeys of the Slave Narrative in the Early Americas,* ed. Nicole N. Aljoe and Ian Finseth (Charlottesville: University of Virginia Press, 2014). Bross reads Lewis's story as an embedded slave narrative. She and I approach Lewis's story with a similar sensibility; we both appreciate the potential of this mediated moment to yield significant clues about not just Gage's life in New Spain but also about the lives of those people he encountered. My reading goes one step further by examining the ways in which Gage's encounter with Lewis shaped the narrative.

25. Gage offers an extended discussion of chocolate and often in the text extols its virtues. He consumes it as a beverage several times per day. For a discussion of chocolate's cultural work in Gage's narrative, see Edmund Campos, "Thomas Gage and the English Colonial Encounter with Chocolate," *Journal of Medieval and Early Modern Studies* 39, no. 1 (2009): 183–200.

26. In 1641/42, Gage renounces his Catholic faith and joins the Church of England. According to Thompson, though, the recantation was not the act of a man who found religious certainty in Puritanism. A spiritual ambiguity, Thompson argues, "rent [Gage] for the last fifteen years

of his life" (li). Thompson maintains that Gage's conversion was rooted in "genuine religious doubts" that combined with political expediency, which led him to testify against former Catholic seminary classmates. His testimony caused the death of several English Catholic priests and close friends of the Gage family (xxxvii). See Thompson, *Thomas Gage's Travels*.

27. In fact, the point of this lengthy anecdote is not only to illustrate his missionary zeal but also to criticize the Catholic practice of saint worship.

28. See Richard Eden, *The Decades of the Newe Worlde or West India* (1555), in *The First Three English Books on America*, ed. Edward Arber (Westminster: A. Constable & Co., 1895), 55: *Google Book Search*, Web, August 13, 2012. In addition to casting Spain's conquistadors as "heroes" who "may so much the more for theyr just desertes and good fortune be compared to those goddes made of men . . . as theyr famous factes so farre excel al other," Eden praises their missionary efforts (49). He credits Spain with expanding Christendom into the New World. Recall that Eden is writing during the reign of Queen Mary I, who marries Spain's Philip II—before a widespread anti-Spanish sentiment permeates England.

29. Ibid.

30. See, for example, Jonathan Hart, *Representing the New World: The English and French Uses of the Example of Spain* (New York: Palgrave Macmillan, 2001); and Barbara Fuchs, *The Poetics of Piracy: Emulating Spain in English Literature* (Philadelphia: University of Pennsylvania Press, 2013).

31. Complicating the political milieu of this decade were tensions between the English and the Dutch, fighting for sea dominance and access to trade routes. The tensions escalated into a two-year war that concluded with the signing of a peace treaty in 1654. For more on this Anglo-Dutch war, and the two others that would follow later in the seventeenth century, see David Roger Hainsworth and Christine Churches, *The Anglo-Dutch Naval Wars 1652–1674* (Stroud, Gloucestershire: Sutton Publishing, 1998).

32. In some respects, Cromwell's plan culminates decades of English efforts to weaken Spanish power in the Caribbean. As Karen Kupperman notes, thirty years earlier a handful of powerful English investors founded an English colony—Providence Island—right in the heart of the Spanish Caribbean in 1629. They imagined the colony would serve as a base from which the English would branch out to take over the rest of the West Indies. According to Kupperman, the colony's three goals were "constructing a godly society, striking at Spanish support for the Antichrist of Rome, and enriching the planters and their backers by providing materials essential to the English economy." Karen Kupperman, "Errand to the Indies: Puritan Colonization from Providence Island through the Western Design," *William and Mary Quarterly*, 3rd ser., 45, no. 1 (1988): 70–99, 75.

33. Hakluyt, *Discourse Concerning Western Planting*, 59.

34. See Carla Gardina Pestana, "English Character and the Fiasco of the Western Design," *Early American Studies: An Interdisciplinary Journal* 3, no. 1 (Spring 2005): 1–31, 2.

35. The 1655 reprint of his narrative was designed, as Nicole Greenspan argues, "to set the stage for what was supposed to be news of a spectacular victory." The reprinted edition includes a map of New Spain, presumably so readers could more easily visualize English conquest. See Greenspan's "News and the Politics of Information in the Mid Seventeenth Century: The Western Design and the Conquest of Jamaica," *History Workshop Journal* 69 (2010): 1–26, 7.

36. See Thomas Gage, "Some briefe and True Observations Concerning the West-Indies,

Humbly Presented to His Highnesse, Oliver, Lord Protector of the Commonwealth of England, Scotland, and Ireland, [by Mr. Thomas Gage]," in *A collection of the state papers of John Thurloe, Esq; secretary, first, to the Council of State, and afterwards to the two Protectors, Oliver and Richard Cromwell. In seven volumes. Containing Authentic Memorials of the English Affairs from the Year 1638, to the Restoration of King Charles II. . . .*, vol. 3 (London, 1742), 59: *Eighteenth Century Collections Online*, Web, August 25, 2014.

37. Gage, "Briefe and True Observations," 60.

38. Ibid.

39. Ibid.

40. See Oliver Cromwell's "Instructions Unto Generall Penn, Collonell Venables . . . for the Manageing the Southerne Expedicion," in *The Narrative of General Venables*, ed. C. H. Firth (London: Longmans, Green & Co. [for the Royal Historical Society], 1900), 107–115, 112.

41. Gage, "Briefe and True Observations," 60.

42. See anonymous "Letter Concerning the English Expedition into the Spanish West Indies in 1655," in *The Narrative of General Venables*, 127–43, 130.

43. See "Extracts from Henry Whistler's Journal of the West India Expedition," in *The Narrative of General Venables*, 144–69, 156.

44. Ibid.

45. Anonymous, "Letter Concerning the English Expedition," 134.

46. See Venables's *The Narrative of General Venables* (1655), ed. C. H. Firth (London: Longmans, Green & Co. [for the Royal Historical Society], 1900), 35.

47. For a historical account of events, including casualties, see S. A. G. Taylor, *The Western Design: An Account of Cromwell's Expedition to the Caribbean* (Kingston: Institute of Jamaica, 1969), 36.

48. Pestana, "English Character," 3. See also David Armitage, "The Cromwellian Protectorate and the Languages of Empire," *Historical Journal* 35, no. 3 (1992): 531–55. Armitage argues that the defeat unsettled the kind of divine providence that had insulated Cromwell against critics' concerns about his expansionist, imperial leanings, which were deemed antithetical to the republican ideals that had just fueled a civil war. "The response to the western design among both the self-searching godly and the critical commonwealthmen," he notes, "was to prove a turning-point for Cromwell as it opened up the question of the godly basis of the republic and the motives for its expansion" (541).

49. See Pestana, "English Character."

50. Ironically, Venables, not his soldiers, became the figurehead for the kind of weak, effeminate soldier that those back in England believed plagued the Western Design. Accounts represent him as quarrelsome, cowardly, and indecisive, characteristics that were, as Pestana argues, "the antithesis of all the godly, heroic English man should be." See Pestana, "English Character," 31.

51. Greenspan, "News and the Politics of Information in the Mid Seventeenth Century," 7.

52. Ibid.

53. Venables, *Narrative of General Venables*, 34.

54. Julian deCastilla, *The English Conquest of Jamaica: An Account of What Happened in the Island of Jamaica, from May 20 of the Year 1655, When the English Laid Siege to It, Up to July 3 of the Year 1656*, trans. and ed. Irene A. Wright, Camden Miscellany Vol. XIII (London: Royal Historical Society, 1923), 19.

55. Ibid., 23–24.

56. Ibid., 28. Marronage would remain a problem for the English in Jamaica for almost two centuries. They sought various means to pacify those populations, including treaties similar to those the Spanish employed in Panama after Drake's 1573 raids. For more on maroon resistance and government policy, see Mavis Christine Campbell, *The Maroons of Jamaica, 1655–1796: A History of Resistance, Collaboration and Betrayal* (Granby, MA: Bergin & Garvey, 1988).

57. Gage joined some five thousand English soldiers who perished during that first year of English occupation of Jamaica. Illness, worsened by poor diet, caused most of those deaths. See Taylor, *The Western Design*, 90–92.

58. Taylor, *The Western Design*, 186.

59. Despite a rather inauspicious beginning, English colonization of Jamaica over time proved lucrative. A little more than a century after English invasion, the historian Edward Long insisted, "It is easy to conceive . . . how vastly profitable [Jamaica] is to the mother-country in every view." He catalogs the financial benefits, which include trade expansion and the employment of artisans, such as ship builders, and merchants, sailors, and "all the trades and occupations dependent upon them." He proclaims ultimately that it would be an "enormous and irreparable" loss "should [Jamaica] ever devolve into the hands of any other power." Edward Long, *The History of Jamaica; Or, General Survey of the Antient and Modern State of That Island: With Reflections on Its Situation, Settlements, Inhabitants, . . . In three volumes. Illustrated with copper plates*, vol. 2 (London, 1774), 228: Eighteenth Century Collections Online, Web, August 22, 2014. See also Long's discussion of Jamaica's role in expanding English trade in vol. 1, bk. 2, chap. 5 of the *History of Jamaica*.

CHAPTER FOUR

1. See "A Proclamation Giving Encouragement to Such as Shall Transplant Themselves to Jamaica," in Charles Brigham's *British Royal Proclamations Relating to America, 1603–1783* (New York: B. Franklin, 1911), 96–100. See also Timothy Venning, *Cromwellian Foreign Policy* (New York: St. Martin's Press, 1995); and S. A. G. Taylor, *The Western Design: An Account of Cromwell's Expedition to the Caribbean* (Kingston: Institute of Jamaica and Jamaica Historical Society, 1965).

2. See Richard Ligon, *A true & exact history of the island of Barbados illustrated with a map of the island, as also the principall trees and plants there, set forth in their due proportions and shapes, drawne out by their severall and respective scales : together with the ingenio that makes the sugar, with the plots of the severall houses, roomes, and other places that are used in the whole processe of sugarmaking* (1657): Early English Books Online, Web, October 12, 2009. Subsequent citations appear in text.

3. I borrow again the term "imperial eye" from Mary Louise Pratt. In *Imperial Eyes: Travel Writing and Transculturation* (New York: Routledge, 1992), she examines the discursive function of ethnography and travel writing in creating and re-creating empires. She looks at certain strategies of representation that European travel writers employ to make themselves appear innocent observers of foreign landscapes and peoples while at the same time deploying certain European ideologies of superiority. According to Pratt, the European travel writer is invested with imperial eyes that both "passively look out" and "possess" all that he sees (7).

4. Catherine Bates, *The Rhetoric of Courtship in Elizabethan Language and Literature* (Cambridge: Cambridge University Press, 1992), 2.

5. The most popular example is, of course, John Smith's "romance" with Pocahontas. Also common is the legend of "Inkle and Yarico," an oft-repeated tale in eighteenth-century England about a young Indian woman who saves an English castaway on the coast of South America. They fall in love. After a few months, an English ship arrives and rescues the Englishman. He takes his Indian lover aboard ship with him and sells her as a slave upon his arrival in Barbados. Ligon tells a version of this story in his narrative. See Ligon, *History*, 54–55.

6. My understanding of imperial consumption has been informed by Mimi Sheller's *Consuming the Caribbean: From Arawaks to Zombies* (London: Routledge, 2003), in which she explores "the myriad ways in which Western European and North American publics have unceasingly consumed the natural environment, commodities, human bodies, and cultures of the Caribbean over the past five hundred years" (3). For Sheller, consumption involves various aspects of use and exploitation. I engage her work more later on.

7. Howard Marchitello, *Narrative and Meaning in Early Modern England: Browne's Skull and Other Histories* (New York: Cambridge University Press, 1997), 95.

8. See Kim Hall, *Things of Darkness: Economies of Race and Gender in Early Modern England* (Ithaca, NY: Cornell University Press, 1995), 29.

9. See Kupperman's introduction to *A True and Exact History of the Island of Barbados*, ed. Karen Ordahl Kupperman (Indianapolis: Hackett, 2011), 33.

10. See Thomas Gage, "Some briefe and True Observations Concerning the West–Indies, Humbly Presented to His Highnesse, Oliver, Lord Protector of the Commonwealth of England, Scotland, and Ireland, [by Mr. Thomas Gage]," in *A collection of the state papers of John Thurloe, Esq; secretary, first, to the Council of State, and afterwards to the two Protectors, Oliver and Richard Cromwell. In seven volumes. Containing Authentic Memorials of the English Affairs from the Year 1638, to the Restoration of King Charles II*, vol. 3 (London, 1742), 61: Eighteenth Century Collections Online, Web, August 25, 2014.

11. Oliver Cromwell, "Instructions Unto Generall Penn, Collonell Venables . . . for the Manageing the Southerne Expedicion," in *The Narrative of General Venables*, ed. C. H. Firth (London: Longmans, Green and Co. (for the Royal Historical Society), 1900), 107–15, 108.

12. Thomas Modyford, "A Paper of Col. Muddiford Concerning the West Indies," in *A collection of the state papers of John Thurloe, Esq.*, 62–63, 62: Eighteenth Century Collections Online, Web, August 25, 2014.

13. Ibid., 63.

14. See Venables's *The Narrative of General Venables* (1655), ed. C. H. Firth (London: Longmans, Green & Co. [for the Royal Historical Society], 1900), 8.

15. Carla Gardina Pestana, "English Character and the Fiasco of the Western Design," *Early American Studies: An Interdisciplinary Journal* 3, no. 1 (Spring 2005): 1–31, 2.

16. Interestingly, by referring to his narrative as "Grotesco" and "Drolorie," Ligon concedes that it might appear a bit fantastic—incredulous, a flip piece of art. That he defends the earnestness of his work becomes all the more crucial when he describes the wonder, the marvel of his encounters with black African women.

17. John Smith and Samuel Clark are among those writing early accounts of the history and resources of Barbados.

18. Barbados had a reputation for producing unusually bad tobacco. Even Barbadians didn't use their own product, importing it from Virginia because, as Ligon explains, "theirs at *Barbadoes* is the worst I think that growes in the world" (113).

19. For more on the growth of sugar plantations in Barbados, see Russell R. Menard, *Sweet Negotiations: Sugar, Slavery, and Plantation Agriculture in Early Barbados* (Charlottesville: University of Virginia Press, 2006). Importantly, Menard revises conventional historical narratives that argue Barbados's was a floundering economy before the arrival of sugar in the 1640s.

20. See George Gardyner's *A description of the New World, or, America islands and continent : and by what people those regions are now inhabited : and what places are . . .* (London, 1651), 78–79: *Sabin Americana*, Web, August 26, 2009.

21. See John Smith's *The generall historie of Virginia, New-England, and the Summer Isles : with the names of the adventurers, planters, and governours from their . . .* (London, 1627), 55: *Sabin Americana*, Web, August 26, 2009.

22. In 1644 William Castell compared Barbados to other islands in the Caribbean and deemed it among the "most spacious and in all respects fitter for plantation." See William Castell's *A short discoverie of the coasts and continent of America from the equinoctiall northward and the adjacent isles* (London, 1644), 42: *Sabin Americana*, Web, August 26, 2009.

23. For an introduction to the history of Santiago and all of the Cape Verde islands, see T. Bentley Duncan, *Atlantic Islands: Madeira, the Azores and the Cape Verdes in Seventeenth-Century Commerce and Navigation* (Chicago: University of Chicago Press, 1972).

24. See again Duncan's *Atlantic Islands*. See also A. R. Disney, *A History of Portugal and the Portuguese Empire: From Beginnings to 1807*, Vol. 2, *The Portuguese Empire* (New York: Cambridge University Press, 2009); and William D. Phillips, *Slavery from Roman Times to the Early Transatlantic Trade* (Manchester: Manchester University Press, 1985).

25. For a survey of such literature, see Jennifer Morgan, "'Some Could Suckle over Their Shoulder': Male Travelers, Female Bodies, and the Gendering of Racial Ideology, 1500–1770," *William and Mary Quarterly*, 3rd ser., 54, no. 1 (Jan. 1997): 167–92.

26. See Towerson's account of his first voyage in *Europeans in West Africa: 1450–1560*, vol. 2, ed. John William Blake (London: Hakluyt Society, 1942), 367.

27. Jennifer Morgan, *Laboring Women: Reproduction and Gender in New World Slavery* (Philadelphia: University of Pennsylvania Press, 2004), 8.

28. The mistress and the virgins at the well function a lot like Oroonoko, the title character of Aphra Behn's 1688 novel that tells the story of an African prince, Oroonoko, who is tricked into slavery in the English colony of Surinam. As a slave, he leads a revolt and is executed. In the novel, Behn generates sympathy for Oroonoko by emphasizing the incongruity and injustice between his social status as an African prince and his enslavement. At one point the narrator expresses her dismay upon hearing that as punishment for the failed revolt and as a public example, Oroonoko is "taken and whipt like a common slave" (57). The slave trade is fine, the novel seems to suggest, so long as the right kind of people are enslaved. Like Ligon portrays the black women in Santiago, Behn romanticizes and elevates Oroonoko above a general black African population in Surinam. See Aphra Behn, *Oroonoko*, ed. Joanna Lipking (New York: W. W. Norton, 1997).

29. Susan Dwyer Amussen, *An Ordered Society: Gender and Class in Early Modern England* (New York: Basil Blackwell, 1988).

30. Anthony Fletcher, *Gender, Sex and Subordination in England 1500–1800* (New Haven, CT: Yale University Press, 1995), 83.

31. Ibid., 345.

32. Hall, *Things of Darkness*, 9.

33. Ibid.

34. Ibid.

35. See Lynda Boose, "The Getting of a Lawful Race: Racial Discourse in Early Modern England and the Unrepresentable Black Woman," in *Women, 'Race,' and Writing in the Early Modern Period*, ed. Margo Hendricks and Patricia Parker (New York: Routledge, 1994), 35–54, 46.

36. Ibid.

37. Bates, *Rhetoric of Courtship*, 4.

38. In 1601 Queen Elizabeth issued the last of several mandates spanning a five-year period that urged the deportation of Africans out of England. She resolved that

> after our hearty commendations; whereas the Queen's Majesty, tendering the good and welfare of her own natural subjects greatly distressed in these hard times of dearth, is highly discontented to understand the great numbers of Negars and Blackamoors which (as she is informed) are crept into this realm since the troubles between Her Highness and the King of Spain, who are fostered and relieved here to the great annoyance of her own liege people that want the relief which those people consume; as also for that the most of them are infidels, having no understanding of Christ or his Gospel, hath given especial commandment that the said kind of people should be with all speed avoided and discharged out of this Her Majesty's dominions. (qtd. in Emily C. Bartels, "Too Many Blackamoors: Deportation, Discrimination, and Elizabeth I," SEL 46, no. 2 [Spring 2006]: 305–22, 316)

The order makes clear that black Africans were outsiders culturally, religiously. The queen first advocated deportation in 1596, which was, as Emily Bartels points out, a kind of prisoner exchange, as those black Africans marked for deportation were those who had been taken prisoners of war during a conflict between the English and Spanish in the West Indies. It would seem then, that black Africans were initially targeted not because of racial differences but because they were seen as Spanish allies. And yet, the diction of the queen's letter makes it clear that the English saw black Africans as being a different "kind of people" separate from England's "own liege people."

39. Stephen Greenblatt, *Marvelous Possessions* (Chicago: University of Chicago Press 1991), 14.

40. I discuss Ralegh's representations of monstrous races in more detail in the next chapter.

41. Greenblatt, *Marvelous Possessions*, 20.

42. Ibid., 22.

43. See Philomusus, *The Academy of Complements Wherin Ladyes Gentlewomen, Schollers, and Strangers May Accomodate Their Courtly Practice with most Curious Ceremonies, Complementall, Amorous, High Expressions, and Formes of Speaking, or Writing. A worke perused and most exactly perfected and most exactly perfected by the author with additions of witty amorous poems. And a table expounding the hard English words* (London, 1640), 132: Early English Books Online, Web, January 12, 2010.

44. Ibid., 137.

45. Bates, *Rhetoric of Courtship*, 2–3.

46. Edward Phillips, *The Mysteries of Love & Eloquence, or, The Arts of Wooing and Complementing as They are Manag'd in the Spring Garden, Hide Park, and the New Exchange, and Other Eminent Places* (London, 1685), 20: Early English Books Online, Web, January 12, 2010.

47. Ibid.

48. Kate Aughterson, *The English Renaissance: An Anthology of Sources and Documents* (New York: Routledge, 1998), 166.

49. Susan Vincent, *Dressing the Elite: Clothes in Early Modern England* (New York: Berg Publishers, 2003), 143.

50. I refer here to a moment in the book of Jeremiah 13:23 where the speaker muses "Can the Ethiopian change his skin, or the leopard his spots? Then may ye also do good, that are accustomed to do evil" (KJV). This moment from Jeremiah, in which the image of the Ethiopian is used to illustrate the immutability of (bad) character, was a common evocation for those in England contemplating the (im)mutable nature of black skin. I discuss this point in more detail in the Introduction.

51. Here, once again, Ligon seems to be evoking language from courtship manuals that instruct suitors to articulate a mistress's beauty using classic allusions and to specifically compare her teeth to pearls. *The Academy of Complements* manual offers two examples a suitor can employ to properly compliment a woman's smile: "Her lips nere part, but that they show / of precious pearle a double row" and "Within the compasse of this holow sweet, / Those orient rankes of silver pearles doe meet" (133).

52. For more on the tignon laws, see Kimberly Hanger, "Coping in a Complex World: Free Black Women in Colonial New Orleans," in *Devil's Lane: Sex and Race in the Early South* (New York: Oxford University Press, 1997), 218–31; and Sybil Kein, *Creole: The History and Legacy of Louisiana's Free People of Color* (Baton Rouge: Louisiana State University Press, 2000).

53. Philomusus, *Academy of Complements*, 73.

54. Ibid.

55. See Barbara Bush, *Slave Women in Caribbean Society* (Bloomington: Indiana University Press, 1990), 11–12: *ACLS Humanities E-Book*, Web, September 4, 2013.

56. Ibid., 13.

57. See Myra Jehlen, "History beside the Fact: What We Learn from a True and Exact History of Barbadoes," in her *Readings at the Edge of Literature* (Chicago: University of Chicago Press, 2000), 179–91, 189.

58. Ibid.

59. Here are the lines from the manual *Mysteries of Love*, published a few years after Ligon's narrative: "She comprehends whatsoever can be imagin'd, or wish'd for in the Idea of a Woman; She is so heavenly a piece, that when Nature had wrought her, she lost her needle, like one that never hop'd to work again any so fair and lively a creature" (22). The female object here is very similar to Ligon's virgins in that Nature has bestowed an unusual beauty, one that cannot be reproduced.

60. My understanding of Ligon's representation evokes again Pratt's theory about normalizing discourse and early English travel narratives, discussed more specifically in chap. 1.

61. Phillips, *Mysteries of Love*, 56–57.

62. Mimi Sheller, *Consuming the Caribbean: From Arawaks to Zombies* (London: Routledge, 2003), 47.

63. Ibid.

64. Ibid., 14.

65. Ibid., 52.

CHAPTER FIVE

1. For perspectives on either side of the debate, see this book's Introduction.

2. My understanding of Best's and Ralegh's texts as manifesting moments of cognitive dissonance that they struggle to reconcile resonates with other studies of early modern European travel narratives. For some examples, see Mary B. Campbell, *The Witness and the Other World: Exotic European Travel Writing, 400–1600* (Ithaca, NY: Cornell University Press, 1988); Stephen Greenblatt, *Marvelous Possessions* (Chicago: University of Chicago Press, 1991); and Michael Householder, *Inventing Americans in the Age of Discovery: Narratives of Encounter* (Burlington, VT: Ashgate, 2011).

3. See George Best, *A True Discourse of the Late Voyages of Discoverie for Finding of a Passage to Cathaya, By the North-west, under the conduct of* Martin Frobisher *General* [1578], in *The Three Voyages of Martin Frobisher*, ed. Sir Richard Collinson (London: Hakluyt Society, 1867). There are several versions and reprints of Best's accounts of the voyages. Richard Hakluyt includes the accounts in his *Principal Nauigations* (1589, 99). Please note that Collinson's reprint is based on an edition first published in London in 1578 by Henry Bynnyman. Subsequent citations for Best's narrative refer to the Collinson reprint and appear in text.

4. See Mary Floyd-Wilson, *English Ethnicity and Race in Early Modern Drama* (Cambridge: Cambridge University Press, 2003).

5. Alden T. Vaughan and Virginia Mason Vaughan, "Before Othello: Elizabethan Representation of Sub-Saharan Africans," *William and Mary Quarterly*, 3rd ser., 54, no. 1 (Jan. 1997): 19–44, 27.

6. Imtiaz H. Habib, *Black Lives in the English Archives, 1500–1677: Imprints of the Invisible* (Burlington, VT: Ashgate, 2008), 104.

7. My approach shares similarities with Householder's *Inventing Americans*. We both use Best's narrative to emphasize the problems of building empire. But his emphasizes the ways in which Best imagines indigenous peoples; I am more interested in how Best imagines black Africans and the degree to which that imagination drives his interpretations of the Inuit.

8. For more on England's efforts to find a northwest passage, see James McDermott's *Martin Frobisher: Elizabethan Privateer* (New Haven, CT: Yale University Press, 2001).

9. For a discussion of Frobisher's privateering (or pirating) activity, see McDermott, *Martin Frobisher*, 48–78.

10. Thomas H. B. Symons, "Introduction: The Significance of the Frobisher Expeditions of 1576–1578," in *Meta Incognita: A Discourse of Discovery*, vol. 1, ed. Thomas H. B. Symons (Hull, Quebec: Canadian Museum of Civilization, 1999), xix–xxxiv, xxvi.

11. David Quinn, "Frobisher in the Context of Early English Exploration," in *Meta Incognita: A Discourse of Discovery*, vol. 1, ed. Thomas H. B. Symons (Hull, Quebec: Canadian Museum of Civilization, 1999), 7–18, 8.

12. Nearly a decade after his release, Frobisher testified before the Privy Council, offering details about his captivity and the political and cultural structures of the Portuguese and surrounding African communities. See "The Declaration of Martyne Frubishere," in *Calendar of State Papers . . . Public Record Office, Volume 5*. Cambridge, MA: Harvard University, 1867), 53: *Google Books*, Web, April 24, 2013.

13. Frobisher's parents died when he was relatively young. As a result, he moved to London, where his mother's relative York raised and educated him. York, an investor and trader in those

Guinea expeditions, orchestrated Frobisher's participation in the voyages. For more on Frobisher's experiences in Guinea, see McDermott, *Martin Frobisher*, 28–47.

14. Richard Willes, *The History of Travayle in the West and East Indies. . . . Gathered in Parte and Done into Englyshe by Richarde Eden. Newly Set in Order, Augmented, and Finished by Richarde Willes* (London, 1577), 233.

15. Michael Lok was a traveling merchant who inherited the trade from his father. He spent most of the 1550s trading throughout southern Europe and the Mediterranean before returning to England. Between 1571 and 1576, he served as the London agent for the Muscovy Company, whose originating mission was to find a northeast route to Asia. With Lok's help, Frobisher found the political and financial resources to support his expedition. For more detailed biographical information about Lok, see McDermott, *Martin Frobisher*, 103–19. See also McDermott's "Michael Lok, Mercer and Merchant Adventurer," in *Meta Incognita: A Discourse of Discovery*, vol. 1, ed. Thomas H. B. Symons (Hull, Quebec: Canadian Museum of Civilization, 1999), 119–46.

16. For a detailed discussion of the Inuit Frobisher brought back to England, see Neil Cheshire et. al., "Frobisher's Eskimos in England," *Archivaria* 10 (Summer 1980): 23–50. See also the introduction to Alden T. Vaughan, *Transatlantic Encounters: American Indians in Britain, 1500–1776* (London: Cambridge University Press, 2006), 1–20.

17. The expedition's financial strain created tension between Frobisher and Lok, eventually ending their partnership. Each man accused the other of financial irregularities and poor management.

18. Importantly, Best does not write the first account of Frobisher's expeditions, nor does he write the only firsthand account. Other written accounts include Dionyse Settle's 1577 *A True Report of the Last Voyage into the West and Northwest Regions*. Settle was a gentleman passenger aboard the second voyage's flagship, the *Ayde*. In his narrative, he details the events of only that second voyage. We are provided a number of accounts of the third voyage—from Thomas Ellis, a sailor; Edward Selman, appointed the voyage's official recorder; and Thomas Wiars, a passenger on one of the ships. For annotated versions of accounts from the third voyage, including several journals and logs, see James McDermott, *The Third Voyage of Martin Frobisher to Baffin Island 1578* (London: Hakluyt Society, 2001).

19. See "The Abuses of Captayn Furbusher Agaynst the Companye, 1578," in Collinson, *The Three Voyages of Martin Frobisher*.

20. For a more detailed discussion of the accusations both men faced, in addition to "The Abuses of Captayn Furbusher Agaynst the Companye, 1578," see "The Slanderous Clamors of Captaine Furbusher against Michael Lok 1578," both supplemental documents in Collinson, *The Three Voyages of Martin Frobisher*, 359.

21. The voyages' *scientific* discoveries also, implicitly, challenged Aristotle's ideas about excessive heat and the production of gold: Collinson, *The Three Voyages of Martin Frobisher*, 363.

22. David Whitford, *The Curse of Ham in the Early Modern Era: The Bible and the Justifications for Slavery* (Burlington, VT: Ashgate, 2009), 115.

23. Ibid., 109.

24. It is not beyond the realm of possibility that Frobisher would have shared information with Best about his Guinea experiences. His debriefing before the Privy Council in 1562 illustrates that he came away from the Gold Coast with specific information that England could

exploit—information about Portugal defenses at El Mina, about interactions between those Portuguese stationed at Mina and surrounding African communities, about the amount of ship traffic along the coast, and about failed alliances between the Portuguese and African kings who refused to swear allegiance. Apparently, Frobisher recognized the value of his experiences and shared the knowledge.

25. For a more detailed discussion of how European cultures understood the Hamitic curse in its early stages, see Whitford, *Curse of Ham;* and David Goldenberg, "The Curse of Ham: Race and Slavery," in his *Early Judaism, Christianity, and Islam: Jews, Christians, and Muslims from the Ancient to the Modern World* (Princeton, NJ: Princeton University Press, 2003).

26. Benjamin Braude, "Michelangelo and the Curse of Ham: From a Typology of Jew-Hatred to a Genealogy of Racism," in *Writing Race across the Atlantic World: Medieval to Modern*, ed. Philip Beidler and Gary Taylor (New York: Palgrave MacMillan, 2005), 79–92, 88.

27. William H. Sherman, "Stirrings and Searchings (1500–1720)," in *The Cambridge Companion to Travel Writing*, ed. Peter Hulme and Tim Youngs (Cambridge: Cambridge University Press, 2002), 17–36, 31.

28. See Dionyse Settle, *A true reporte of the laste voyage into the west and northwest regions, &c. 1577* (London: Henrie Middleton, 1577), 18: *Early English Books Online*, Web, April 30, 2013.

29. Greenblatt, *Marvelous Possessions*, 22.

30. This act of possession becomes literal when Frobisher's men actually detach the animal's horn and transport it back to England as a present for Queen Elizabeth. Ironically, Lok points to that exotic relic as evidence of Frobisher's arrogance and misdeeds during the expeditions. In his own written testimony, primarily defending himself against charges of financial impropriety, Lok complains of the "Jewell," intended as a gift for the Queen, that Frobisher "did present it in his owne name and not in the Companyes name to whome it did belonge" (McDermott, *The Third Voyage*, 82).

31. Not incidentally, Best's description of the fish parallels Eden's description of beasts Lok's crew encountered in that 1554 Guinea voyage. Amid the descriptions of monsters and anthropomorphic beings said to inhabit West Africa, Eden describes abnormally large elephants. To articulate the magnitude of their size, he writes of their teeth, "I sawe and measured sum of ix[nine] spannes in length as they were croked. Sum of them were as bigge as a mans thigh above the knee: and weyed abowte foure score and ten pound weyght a piece" (383). Lok and his men manage to secure the head of one of those elephants and to transport it back to London. After declaring that the head "coulde wey little lesse then five hundredth weight," Eden marvels, "This heade dyvers have sene in the house of the worthy marchaunt Sir Andrewe Judde, where also I sawe it, and beheld it not only with my bodily eyes, but much more with the eyes of my mynde and spirite considered by the woorke, the cunnynge and wysdome of the woorke master: withowt which consideration, the sight of such straungne and woonderfull thynges may rather seeme curiosities then profitable contemplations" (Richard Eden, *The Decades of the Newe Worlde or West India* [1555], in *The First Three English Books on America*, ed. Edward Arber [Westminster: A. Constable & Co., 1895], 383: *Google Book Search*, Web, August 13, 2012, 383). The elephant assumes a divine quality not unlike Best's fish with the tapered horn. Both Eden and Best imbue the monstrous with elements of wonder.

32. Robert A. Williams, Jr., *The American Indian in Western Legal Thought: The Discourses of Conquest* (New York: Oxford University Press, 1990).

33. Ibid., 59.

34. Ibid., 130.

35. This is not the first time Best implies the Inuit are cannibals. For example, after the five Englishmen are taken hostage on the 1576 voyage, Best believes it is possible that the men were "slaine and eaten," by the Inuit. On another occasion, Frobisher's men discover a tomb with human remains inside. According to Best, they ask an Inuk man they had just captured "whether his countreymen had not slain this man and eat his flesh so from the bone." Best, *A True Discourse,* 139, 136.

36. This idea would resonate more in the seventeenth century among New England Puritans. For example, Puritan minister John Eliot, known as "apostle to the Indians" because of his missionary work in colonial Massachusetts, argued that Indians in America were descendants of Jews, part of the lost tribes that God "dispersed and scattered into other nations," including America (Thorowgood 19). Thomas Thorowgood included Eliot's theory in his larger work *Jews in America, or Probabilities that Those Indians are Judaical* (London: 1660): Early English Books Online, Web, January 9, 2013.

37. Gordon M. Sayre, "Prehistoric Diasporas: Colonial Theories of the Origins of Native American Peoples," in Beidler and Taylor, *Writing Race across the Atlantic World,* 51–76, 63.

38. "Instructions Given to Martyne Furbisher, Gent., for Orders to be Observed in the Viage Nowe Recommended to Him for the North West Parts and Cathay," in Collinson, *The Three Voyages of Martin Frobisher,* 117–20, 120.

39. Unless otherwise noted, this and all subsequent textual references to Ralegh's narrative are based on Joyce Lorimer's annotated edition. Citations appear in text. See Sir Walter Ralegh, *Discoverie of Guiana,* ed. Joyce Lorimer (London: Hakluyt Society, 2006).

40. The evidence on which Whitehead determines this moment is fabricated seems a bit tenuous; early American written records often exclude references to black African presences or record those presences unevenly; that is to say that a ship manifesto might neglect to list a black sailor among its crew even if a particular captain or sailor's journal notes the presence of several black crewmen. The "negro" sailor to whom Ralegh refers, then, could have been one of his men, or as Lorimer postulates, "it is possible that the man came from the Port of Spain or San Josef [in Trinidad]. He may have been one of Berrío's household," taken after Ralegh attacked a Spanish settlement on the island of Trinidad and captured the Spanish governor, Antonio de Berrío, before heading on to the South American mainland (113 fn 3). The factuality of the episode notwithstanding, it performs specific rhetorical work, which is the emphasis of my discussion. Neil Whitehead, *The Discoverie of the Large, Rich, and Bewtiful Empyre of Guiana by Sir Walter Ralegh* (Manchester: Manchester University Press, 1997), 163.

41. Ibid., 104.

42. See V. S. Naipaul's re-creation of this moment in his novel *A Way in the World* (London: Heinemann, 1994), 175.

43. See John Sparke's account, "The voyage made by M. Iohn Hawkins Esquire, and afterward knight, Captaine of the *Iesus* of *Lubek,* one of her Maiesties shippes, and Generall of the *Salomon,* and other two barkes going in his companie, to the coast of *Guinea,* and the *Indies* of Noua Hispania, begun in An. Dom. 1564," in Hakluyt, *Principal Nauigations,* 512: Early English Books Online, Web, April 10, 2014.

44. Ibid.

45. Mary Fuller, *Voyages in Print: English Travel to America, 1576–1624* (Cambridge: University of Cambridge Press, 1995), 73.

46. Indeed Ralegh never actually *discovered* Guiana and its golden capital. During his expedition, he accumulated evidence—testimony, geological observation, and a tiny sample of gold—to prove the empire's existence. For more on Ralegh's struggles to produce physical proof about Guiana and gold, see Fuller's *Voyages in Print*.

47. Joyce Lorimer, "Introduction," in *Sir Walter Ralegh's Discoverie of Guiana* (London: Hakluyt Society, 2006), xvii–lxxvi, xxii.

48. As Fuller points out, Ralegh uses the narrative as an occasion figuratively to correct his own sexual transgression at court. She argues that those moments in which Ralegh genders Guiana as a virginal female landscape "allowed him to represent at the symbolic level as well as the literal . . . the withholding of [his] male desire," reserving the ultimate discovery and conquest of Manoa for the queen (75). In other words, Ralegh does not pillage—or rape—the landscape (as evident by the absence of material wealth he brought back), exhibiting a measure of restraint and prudence he did not exhibit in his courtship with the queen's lady-in-waiting. See Fuller's *Voyages in Print*.

49. Ralegh is reciting, not creating, an origins story. Spanish conquistadors first linked the myth of El Dorado to the fallen Inca empire in the 1560s. For a summary of this history, see Lorimer's "Introduction," in *Sir Walter Ralegh's Discoverie of Guiana*, xxxviii and 6, fn 3.

50. Like Ralegh, Berrío staged several expeditions from his base at Trinidad to find El Dorado. Upon his arrival in the region in 1595, Ralegh seized Berrío, forcing him to travel with Ralegh as an informant. The captivity also prevented Berrío from organizing his own expedition and finding Manoa before Ralegh.

51. Scott Oldenburg, "Headless in America: The Imperial Logic of Acephalism," in *The Mysterious and the Foreign in Early Modern England*, ed. Helen Ostovich, Mary V. Silcox, and Graham Roebuck (Cranbury, NJ: Associated University Presses, 2008), 39–57, 49.

52. Lorimer, "Introduction," in *Sir Walter Ralegh's Discoverie of Guiana*, xl.

53. See Ralegh's *History of the World*. 1617, sig. E 2, verso: *Early English Books Online*, Web, June 10, 2012.

54. Eden, *Decades*, 363.

55. Mary Fuller offers a similar conclusion about Eden's rhetorical intent. See Fuller's "Making Something of It: Questions of Value in the Early English Travel Collection," in *Bringing the World to Early Modern Europe: Travel Accounts and Their Audiences*, ed. Peter Mancall (Boston: Brill, 2007), 11–38, 21.

56. Laurence Madoc, "A briefe relation concerning the estate of the cities and prouinces of Tombuto and Gago written in Marocco the first of August 1594, and sent to M. Anthony Dassel marchant of London," in Hakluyt, *Principal Nauigations*, 192.

57. Laurence Madoc, "Another briefe relation concerning the late conquest and the exceeding great riches of the cities and prouinces of *Tombuto* and *Gago*, written from *Marocco* the 30 August 1594. to M. *Anthony Dassel* marchant of *London* aforesaid," in Hakluyt, *Principal Nauigations*, 193.

58. Ibid.

59. These English voyages to the River Gambra were unique in their efforts to explore Guinea inland. In fact, Richard Jobson, who led that 1620 expedition, claimed that the black

Africans he and his men encountered had never seen white faces before. Those earliest voyages to West Africa, including those of Towerson and Hawkins, traveled along the coast.

60. Richard Jobson, *The Golden Trade: Or a Discovery of the River Gambra, and the Golden Trade of the Aethiopians* (1623), 102: *Early English Books Online*, Web, March 10, 2014.

61. Ibid., 2.

62. Ibid., 3–4.

63. For more on the material and cultural value of gold in early modern England, see Fuller, "Making Something of It"; and Peter L. Bernstein, *The Power of Gold: The History of an Obsession* (New York: John Wiley & Sons, 2000).

64. In revising the work of earlier cartographer Marinos of Tyre, Ptolemy rejected certain computations of his predecessor on the grounds that Marinos had not accounted for the fact that "all animals and plants that are on the same parallels or equidistant from either pole ought to exist in similar combinations in accordance with the similarity of their environments." See Ptolemy's *Geography*, trans. J. Lennart Berggren and Alexander Jones (Princeton, NJ: Princeton University Press, 2000), 69.

65. Nicolás Wey Gómez, *The Tropics of Empire: Why Columbus Sailed South to the Indies* (Cambridge, MA: MIT Press, 2008), 49.

66. See "First Voyage of Columbus: Letter of Columbus (1493)," in *The Four Voyages of Columbus: A History in Eight Documents. Including Five by Christopher Columbus, in the Original Spanish, with English Translations*, ed. Cecil Jane, 2 vols. bound in 1 (New York: Dover Publications, 1988), 1–19, 14.

67. That expectation, according to Wey Gómez, informed the design of Columbus's voyages. He maintains that Columbus's goal was not simply to travel west across the Atlantic but also to travel south in search of gold. Articulating the long-standing intellectual history underpinning Columbus's voyages, Wey Gómez argues that latitude "explains why Ptolemy, the most influential geographer of antiquity, should have assumed that 'black' peoples equally flourished in sub-Saharan Africa, the Arabian Peninsula, and the very confines of the Indian Ocean, and why many centuries later Columbus should have been perturbed not to find them in the Caribbean basin." Wey Gómez, *Tropics of Empire*, 49.

68. Eden, *Decades*, 387–88.

69. See Ralegh's "A Discourse of the invention of Ships, Anchors, Compasse, &c," in *Sir Walter Ralegihs Judicious and Select Essayes and Observations Upon the First Invention of Shipping, Invasive War, the Navy Royal and Sea-Service : With His Apologie for His Voyage to Guiana* (London, 1667), 7–8: *Early English Books Online*, Web, March 21, 2014. Interestingly, Ralegh notes a unity in all mankind, recognizing "that all Nations how remote soever" are all "reasonable creatures, and enjoy one and the same Imagination and fantasie, having devised according to their means and materialls the same things" (6). The passage comparing Africa and America is particularly interesting, though, because he notes commonalities not simply in technological inventions, which are driven by necessity and the availability of resources at hand, but also in cultural mores.

70. Ralegh, *Discoverie of Guiana*, 145. Whitehead argues that the European myth of El Dorado is based largely on European observations and hearsay about native cultural practices, but the myth gains its credence from a "general expectation, partly deriving from the encounter with Africa, that gold was especially engendered as a geophysical property of the 'torrid zone,' or equatorial latitudes." Whitehead, *Discoverie of the Large … Guiana*, 71.

71. Sir John Mandeville, *Here Begynneth a Lytell Treatyse . . . [and] Speketh of the Wayes of the Holy Londe Towarde Jherusalem, of Marueyles of Ynde of other Dyuerse Cou[n]trees* (1499), lxiiii: *Early English Books Online*, Web, April 3, 2013.

72. Ibid., lxxix.

73. According to Whitehead, Ralegh is not simply inserting European monsters into an American landscape. Whitehead points out that Ralegh's description of the Ewaipanoma is an illustration of cultural commensurability between European and Native belief systems. "A trope of the monstrous," according to Whitehead, "was already present in native thought before the European arrival. . . . Equally the 'men-with-heads-in-their-chests' have a number of analogues within native idioms." In Ralegh's rhetorical hands and his evocation of Mandeville, whatever culturally specific references might have produced the Ewaipanoma are subsumed—but not completely obscured—by larger European traditions. My reading of this moment emphasizes the consequences of Ralegh's rhetorical choice. See Whitehead, *Discoverie of the Large . . . Guiana*, 93.

74. I note that there are a number of factors guiding Ralegh's decision to include this discussion of Ewaipanoma in his narrative. Those factors include readers' expectations that authentic, faraway travel experiences will be marked by sightings of the monstrous and exotic. There is also the fact that Ralegh's text is a scouting report, designed to inform the Crown about the landscape and its resources and people.

75. Even in Ralegh's day, European readers approached Mandeville's text with mixed measures of fascination, credulity, and skepticism—even those explorers, like Frobisher, who carried copies of Mandeville's tales with them during their own travels.

76. According to Whitehead, "Ralegh engages in the collection of reports of these marvels with a firm scepticism as to their literal existence but a definite appreciation of the importance of establishing the bounds of the possible." Whitehead, *Discoverie of the Large . . . Guiana*, 91.

77. Oldenburg examines the veracity of Ralegh's narrative and his representation of Ewaipanoma to make a larger argument about the ways in which Ralegh dehumanizes the people who populate Guiana in order to justify England's imperial desires. Oldenburg sees the headless Ewaipanoma as symbolizing uncivilized states of being, cultures without governments or the ability to govern. "Early modern notions of acephalism relate to the idea of the head as the seat of rational thought," Oldenburg argues. "From the imperialist or colonialist point of view, if the inhabitants of a desired piece of land lack rationality, one can more easily explain away their humanity or fantasize that colonization will be a great benefit in that it will bring the advances of European rational thought." Oldenburg, "Headless in America," 50–51.

78. Fuller, *Voyages in Print*, 60.

79. Brian Gardner, *The Quest for Timbuctoo* (London: Cassell, 1968), 5.

80. See Whitehead, *Discoverie of the Large . . . Guiana*, 170, fn 81.

81. For example, see Ralegh's description of those people who live and trade at the confluence of the Barema, Pawroma, and Dissequebe rivers, who "but for their tawnie colour may bee compared to anie of Europe" (85). At another point, he says of a cacique's wife, "In all my life I haue seldom seene a better fauored woman: She was of good stature, with blacke eies, fat of body, of an excellent countenance. . . . I haue seene a Lady in England so like hir, as but for the difference of colour I would haue sworne might haue beene the same" (127). By contrast, the Aroras' physical features are rendered not within an English context, but a sub-Saharan African context.

82. Peter Fryer, *Staying Power: The History of Black People in Britain* (London: Pluto Press, 1984), 135.

83. For other accounts of violent English clashes with bow-wielding West Africans, see Robert Baker's poetic rendition of his 1562 voyage, "The First Voyage of Robert Baker," in *A Selection of Curious, Rare and Early Voyages. . . .*, vol. 2 (London: R. H. Evans, 1810), 518–31; and Walter Wren's account of George Fenner's 1566 voyage to Guinea: "The Voyage of M. *George Fenner to Guinie*, and the Islands of *Cape Verde*, in the Yeere 1566," in *A Selection of Curious, Rare and Early Voyages*, 2:533–41.

84. John Hawkins, *A True Declaration of the Troublesome Voyage of John Hawkins to the Parties of Guinea and the West Indies, in the Years of Our Lord 1567 and 1568* (London, 1569), A iii, recto: *Early English Books Online*, Web, March 10, 2007.

85. Herodotus, *The Histories*, trans. Robin Waterfield (Oxford: Oxford University Press, 1998), 271–73.

86. Greenblatt, *Marvelous Possessions*, 30.

87. Louis Montrose, "The Work of Gender in the Discourse of Discovery," in *New World Encounters*, ed. Stephen Greenblatt (Berkeley: University of California Press, 1993), 177–217, 202.

88. Ibid., 205.

89. Lorimer offers a useful catalog of reasons for Ralegh's failure: "Economic distress at home, the ruinous drain of the war on the Crown's finances, the distraction and expense of simultaneously maintaining troops in France, Ireland, and the Netherlands, the cost of Drake's last expedition, Ralegh's own reports of rumours that a Spanish armada was preparing against Ireland and his support of maturing plans to attack Cadiz precluded any possibility of a state-funded conquest of Guiana." Joyce Lorimer in her introduction to Sir Walter Ralegh's *Discoverie of Guiana*, xxxviii. In other words, England was already spread thin, and Ralegh was unable to present a convincing case that the nation should spread itself thinner.

90. Ralegh's connection to what was called the Main Plot is tenuous at best, based primarily on hearsay testimony. For a concise discussion of the plot and its connection to Ralegh, see Mark Nicholls and Penry Williams, "Ralegh, Sir Walter (1554–1618)," in *Oxford Dictionary of National Biography* (Oxford University Press, 2004), Web, April 9, 2014.

91. Mary Fuller argues, "The criminalization of Ralegh under James pressured his claims in a particularly intense way" and the fact that he couldn't find Guiana, even after insisting that he could in a second voyage, gave his discovery the appearance of being a "hidden space in which treason and defection could be hoarded up and concealed." The only way to alleviate that taint, to clear himself of the suspicion of treason and duplicity, was to locate a nonexistent El Dorado. Fuller, *Voyages in Print*, 57. With that second expedition, as Lorimer notes, "Ralegh once gain offered more than he could hope to accomplish and paid for this failure with his head." Lorimer in her introduction to Sir Walter Ralegh's *Discoverie in Guiana*, xcvi.

AFTERWORD

1. David Read, *New World, Known World: Shaping Knowledge in Early Anglo-American Writing* (Columbia: University of Missouri Press, 2005), 8.

2. Michael Drexler and Ed White, *Beyond Douglass: New Perspectives on Early African-American Literature* (Lewisburg: Bucknell University Press, 2008), 10.

3. For sure, the mid- to late eighteenth century marked an epoch in African American literature, an age of firsts. Briton Hammon published his account of captivity by Native Americans and Spaniards off the coast of Florida. Phillis Wheatley, Jupiter Hammon, and Lucy Terry wrote poetry. Olaudah Equiano, in 1789, published his slave narrative, shaping his life into the self-made man archetype that would become a popular motif in American literature. Henry Louis Gates, Jr., and Frances Smith Foster have expounded upon the importance of this era. See Gates's *Signifying Monkey: A Theory of Afro-American Literary Criticism* (New York: Oxford University Press, 1988); and Frances Smith Foster, *Witnessing Slavery: The Development of Ante-bellum Slave Narratives*, 2nd ed. (Madison: University of Wisconsin Press, 1994). For more recent studies, see April Langley, *The Black Aesthetic Unbound: Theorizing the Dilemma of Eighteenth-Century African American Literature* (Columbus: Ohio State University Press, 2008); Cedrick May's *Evangelism and Resistance in the Black Atlantic, 1760–1835* (Athens: University of Georgia Press, 2008); and Rafia Zafar, *We Wear the Mask: African-Americans Write American Literature, 1760–1870* (New York: Columbia University Press, 1997).

4. See Foster's *Witnessing Slavery*, in which she argues about the significance of Adam's court case that "it is a precursor of the slave narratives, for it emerges as the first American writing to depict clearly the actions and circumstances under which a black slave rejected the role of chattel or permanent bondsman" (32). See also John Sekora, "Black Message/White Envelope: Genre, Authenticity, and Authority in the Antebellum Slave Narrative," *Callaloo* 32 (Summer 1987): 482–515; Marion Wilson Starling, *The Slave Narrative: Its Place in American History* (Washington, DC: Howard University Press, 1998); and Raymond Hedin, "The American Slave Narrative: The Justification of the Picaro," *American Literature* 53, no. 4 (Jan. 1982): 630–45.

5. See Sekora's "Black Message/White Envelope."

6. For examples, see Zafar, *We Wear the Mask*; Dickson Bruce, *The Origins of African American Literature, 1680–1865* (Charlottesville: University of Virginia Press, 2001); and Nicole N. Aljoe, *Creole Testimonies: Slave Narratives from the British West Indies, 1709–1838* (New York: Palgrave Macmillan, 2012).

7. Michel Foucault, "What Is an Author," in *The Foucault Reader*, ed. Paul Rabinow (New York: Pantheon, 1984), 101–20, 119.

8. Roland Barthes, "The Death of the Author," in his *Image Music Text*, trans. Stephen Heath (New York: Hill & Wang, 1977), 143.

9. Ibid., 147.

10. For a discussion of the political contours of African American literature, see Kenneth Warren, *What Was African American Literature?* (Cambridge, MA: Harvard University Press, 2011). Warren links the advent of African American literature to the rise of Jim Crow legislation in the wake of the Civil War. According to Warren, when legal Jim Crow ended in the 1960s, so, too, did the impetus for an "African American literature." Although I find Warren's primary argument problematic because it essentializes the literature in ways that threaten to diminish the literary contributions of African-descended people prior to 1865 and after 1965, his study does offer a useful reminder of the stakes involved whenever a person of black African descent participates in American literary culture.

11. One exception to this is Aljoe's work on early Caribbean slave narratives. In *Creole Testimonies*, she uncovers a body of slave narratives from the Caribbean in the eighteenth and nineteenth centuries, making more prominent the voices of black enslaved populations whose

narratives often appeared first in oral forms, as fragments, or as embedded texts in larger narratives written by Europeans. Aljoe and I both address the issue of mediation in early Atlantic texts and call for a broader understanding of authorship. According to Aljoe, when we reconceptualize authorship, a body of slave narratives in the early Caribbean emerges, which expands a slave narrative tradition we usually associate with an antebellum United States. I argue that the benefit of broadening conceptions of authorship is that it makes more visible the literary contributions of black Africans in the Americas from the beginning of English, African, Native American encounters.

12. I note that we have begun already to think in less essentialist ways about what it means to be "African American" producing literature in the colonial period. A number of studies, beginning with Paul Gilroy's, have located early African American literature within a larger Atlantic circuit of ideas and sociopolitical influences. For examples, see Gilroy, *The Black Atlantic: Modernity and Double Consciousness* (Cambridge, MA: Harvard University Press, 1993); April Langley, *The Black Aesthetic Unbound;* Philip Gould and Vincent Carretta, *Genius in Bondage: The Literature of the Early Black Atlantic* (Lexington: University Press of Kentucky, 2001); Vincent Carretta, *Unchained Voices: An Anthology of Black Authors in the English-Speaking World of the Eighteenth Century* (Lexington: University Press of Kentucky, 2003); and Joanna Brooks and John Saillant, *"Face Zion Forward": First Writers of the Black Atlantic, 1785–1798* (Boston: Northeastern University Press, 2002).

INDEX

acephali, 167, 214n77

Africa, in the English imagination: and theory of gold, 37–38, 163–64; and theories of monsters, 33, 168, 210n31. *See also* Guinea

Africa, sub-Saharan, 140–41, 174

Africanist presence, 15, 60. *See also* Morrison, Toni

Africans, black: definition of, 26; English attitudes toward, 33, 142–43

Africanus, Leo, 34

agenda (imperial), 7, 87

alliances: failed, 17, 49, 52, 55, 73–74, 82, 105, 106; fantasy of, 11, 12–13, 105; trade, 37, 39, 41–43. *See also* collaboration

Alsop, J. D., 29

Amazons, 170–73

Andrews, Kenneth, 52, 53, 191n26

apparel. *See* laws, sumptuary

Aristotle, 37, 162

Atlantic world. *See* world, Atlantic

Arora, 168–70

Audiencia, 66, 74

authorship: in African American literature, 5, 177, 178, 183n17, 216n11; and autonomy, black African, 39, 66, 100, 105; agency and, 5, 39, 46, 65, 78, 100, 133, 136; as collaboration, 24, 62

Aztec, 96–97

Baffin Island, 145–46

Barbados: resources of, 19, 119–20, 138, 204n18, 205n22; in the western design, 117–18.

Barbary, English travels to, 32, 164

Barthes, Roland, 62, 177–78

Bates, Catherine, 115, 127

Best, George: biography of, 146; imperial vision of, 140–41, 146–48

Black Atlantic, theory of, 14, 27, 186n49

black legend: and descriptions of Spanish cruelty, 2, 12, 80, 161; English uses of, 6, 8; representations of Portugal as, 16–17

blackness discourse, 76, 138; definition of, 25–27

Boose, Lynda, 122–23

breasts, 33–34, 120–21, 138. *See also* monsters

Campos, Edmund, 64

canon, African American literary, 176–77

Cape Verde (Islands), 113, 119

captive: Frobisher as, 144; Guinea trader as, 39–43; Inuit as, 145, 151, 154–55

Carib, 92–95

Castilla, Julian de, 110

Chagre, River, 65, 73

Chichimici, 87, 88

Cimarrones: black legend rhetoric, 17, 18, 66, 75, 80; blackness discourse, 76–77, 79; descriptions of, 2–4, 58, 64, 65, 66, 98, 99, 196n5; racialization of war rituals, 78, 99

civil war (English), 106; in Sierra Leone, 49

class: sartorial laws and, 128, 129; as social order, 91, 12

clothing. *See* laws, sumptuary

collaboration: as authorship, 24, 65; expectations for African-English, 3, 87, 88; necessity of, 90, 96, 11; viability of, 103, 199n10; political. *See also* alliances

Columbus, Christopher, 36, 165, 213n67
consumption: bodies as commodities for, 115, 137, 138, 159; of material goods, 19, 20, 137–39
Cortés, Hernán, 96, 97, 86, 106
cosmography. *See* race
Cotton manuscript, 53, 54, 71
counter-narrative: as product of colonial encounter, 43, 85–86, 182n10; as reading strategy, 48, 178
courtship, discourse of: the courtly romance and, 115, 121; courtship manuals, 125, 128, 131; discursive disruptions in, 115, 125, 127; role of the suitor in, 115, 123
cow killers, 109
creole, Spanish, 91, 97
Cromwell, Oliver, 19, 86, 106, 107, 108, 110, 113, 117
Cuba, 108
curse of Ham, 141, 150. *See also* race

Dalva, Miguel, 100–105
Davenant, William, 23, 88–90
Diego, 67–71, 73, 197n30
discourse: of the black legend, 59, 60, 68, 74–75; colonial, 4, 13; gendered, 127, 138; normalizing, 52, 126, 135; racial, 8, 11, 25, 34, 53, 74. *See also* black legend
disruption (narrative), 2, 5, 6, 13–14, 23, 24, 176, 185n47
Don John, 40–43
Don John's Town, 41–44, 191n34
Drake, Sir Francis: biography of, 60–62
Drake, Francis (nephew), 62
Drexler, Michael, 176–77

Eden, Richard, *Decades of the New World*, 32, 33, 46, 106, 144, 163, 165, 189n7, 191n33, 201n28, 210n31
Elizabeth, Queen, 49, 62–64, 123, 171–72, 206n38
El Dorado: in Guinea, 38, 163; myth of, 158, 160, 162, 167, 212n50, 213n70. *See also* Manoa

el Mina. *See* São Jorge da Mina
encounter, colonial, as discursive phenomenon, 2, 4, 5, 13, 124, 185n47
Enlightenment Movement, 10–11, 140. *See also* race
Enriquez, Martin, 50–51, 55, 63
Equator, 37–38, 142, 164, 165
Ethiop(ia), 9, 129, 149, 156, 164, 207n50
ethnicity. *See* race
evidence, circumstantial, 21–24, 30, 41, 94
Ewaipanoma, 166–68, 214n73, 214n77

fantasy (imperial), 3, 18, 90, 111, 131
Floyd-Wilson, Mary, 142
Foucault, Michel, 177–78
Frobisher, Martin: biography of, 144; as captive, 144, 209n24; voyages of, 142–44, 145–46
Frohock, Richard, 61
Fuller, Mary, 159, 168, 173, 212n48, 215n91

Gage, Thomas: as advisor to Cromwell, 19, 86, 108–11, 117; biography of, 92, as chaplain, 108
Gambia, River, 163
gaze, imperial, 19, 115, 132
gender: and its intersections with race, 122, 138, 139, 154, 172; as social practice, 121, 122, 154
geohumoralism, 142
Ghana, 38
gold: fever, 38, 162, 213n67; formation of, 37–38, 162–63; kingdoms of, 38, 159, 160–61, 163–64; trade in, 31, 33, 38
Gold Coast, 38, 48
Greenblatt, Stephen, 4, 22–23, 124, 171
Guatemala, 86, 97–100
Guiana: descriptions of, 159, 160; historical narratives of, 160–61; voyage to, 158–59
Guinea: descriptions of 33–34, 43; English voyages to, 31, 32–33, 188n4; social and political structures in, 35–38
Guinea king, 53, 71

Habib, Imtiaz H., 143
Hair, P. E. H., 42, 54
Hakluyt, Richard: *Discourse Concerning Western Planting*, 12, 86, 87–88, 107; *Principal Navigations*, 32
Hall, Kim, 25, 74, 116, 122, 197n37
Hametic curse. *See* curse of Ham; race
Hanta, 34, 46
Hawkins, John: condemnation of Spain, 55–57; as England's first slave-trader, 31; *Troublesome Voyage*, 17, 31, 51; voyages through Guinea, 48, 49–50
Hispaniola, 108–110
Hispanophobia, 6. *See also* black legend
Hodgkins, Christopher, 61, 195n12
Hortop, Job, 53–56

Imagination (imperial), 30, 61, 85, 149
Inca, 160, 162
Inuit, 143, 145, 148–49, 151–56, 165; theories of origin, 150–51, 155–56
iron pyrite. *See* ore
ivory, 31, 33

Jamaica, 88, 110–11, 113, 117, 203n59
Jehlen, Myra, 13–14, 133, 185n47
Jesuits, 92–95
Jesus of Lubeck (ship), 49–50
Judith (ship), 61

lagarto, 98, 158–59, 166
Largartos (river), 158
Las Casas, Bartolomé de, 1, 75; descriptions of Spanish cruelty, 7–8, 80
laws, sumptuary, 128, 130
Lewis, 91–95, 105, 106, 200n24
liberation, rhetoric of, 3, 16, 17, 48, 59, 71
Ligon, Richard: biography of, 113, 116–18; as courtier, 114, 125–36
Lok, John, 33, 36, 40, 45, 48–49
Lok, Michael, 144–47, 209n15
Lorimer, Joyce, 160, 162, 173
Lubolo, Juan, 111

maiden: Ligon's encounters with, 114–15, 133–37; Ralegh's descriptions of Guiana as, 159, 171, 174
Mali, 38
Maltby, William, 64
Mandeville, John, 34, 38, 167–68
Mandinga, Pedro, 73–74, 78
Manoa, 158, 160–62
Mansa Musa, 38
Marchitello, Howard, 116
maroons, 85, 98, 107, 110, 199n53. *See also* Cimarrones
material reality. *See* reality, material
mediation: of black Africans, 7, 15, 23, 178; definition of, 22, 178; problems of 4, 14, 21, 23; strategies for reading, 5, 176, 216n11
Melegueta Coast, 33
Meta Incognita. *See* Baffin Island
Mignolo, Walter, 74–75
mistress (Padre's). *See* negro, Padre's mistress
Miwok, 61
Modyford, Thomas, 117
monsters: rhetoric of, 159, 162, 168; theory of, 162, 164, 165, 171
Montrose, Louis, 172
Morrison, Toni, 15, 60, 195n6
mulatto pirate. *See* pirate, mulatto
mule train, 3, 58, 76
Muscovy Company, 32–33, 146, 209n15

narrative: compromise, 2, 24; disruption, 2, 5, 6, 13–14, 23, 24, 176, 185n47; dissonance, 5, 21; as ethical dilemma, 16, 187n55; negotiation and accommodation, 7, 15, 24; rupture, 5, 30; texture, 5, 183n15, 183n16
negro: Padre's mistress, 114–15, 121, 124–33; virgins at the well, 114–15, 133–37. *See also* Africans, black
Nichols, Philip, 62
Nombre de Dios: mule train routes to, 58, 65, 73; Drake's raid of, 58, 61, 63, 66–68
northwest, Arctic, 141, 147
Northwest Passage. *See* passage, northwest

ore (black), 145–47
Orenoqueponi, 161–62
Oxenham, John, 82, 90, 99

palenques. *See* settlements, Cimarrones
Panama City: Cimarrón attacks of, 2–3, 65–66, 77; mule train routes through, 58, 65
Panama isthmus, 65
passage, northwest, 144–45, 147
Pedro: Drake chastised by, 3–7; Drake sells sword to, 72–73; as fictional character, 89. *See also* Mandinga, Pedro
Penn, William, 108, 110–11
Peru, 160, 162
Philip II, 63, 107
Phillips, Miles, 12, 53, 193n54
Pie de Palo, 105
Pinteado, Antonio Anes, 33
piracy: English raids as, 61, 81, 119; Towerson and charges of, 34, 36, 43
pirate, mulatto, 103–6
Pliny the Elder, *Natural History*, 34
Port Plenty, 70
Pratt, Mary Louise, 52, 203n3
presence (black African). *See* mediation
propaganda, anti-Spanish, 3, 7, 20, 63. *See also* black legend; rhetoric
Ptolemy, 164, 213n64

race: debate about, 8–11; definition of 24, 195n6; study of, 15, 140
race, ideology of: capitalism and economic expansion, 74, 121; and climate theory, 142, 147, 148, 149, 155–56, 164–66; cosmography, 148–49, 155; Curse of Ham, 150, 156; geohumora1, 142; infection of blood, 140–42
racism, 9, 25, 52, 74–75, 140
Ralegh, Sir Walter: biography of, 159; execution of, 172–74; and issues of credibility, 158–59, 160, 167–68
reality, material, 4, 185n47
referent, historical, 4, 60
rhetoric: of alliance, 12–13; anti-Spanish, 16, 18, 56, 161; consumptive, 20; liberatory, 17, 46, 48; monstrosity, 33, 152; racial, 75. *See also* black legend; courtship

San Juan de Ulúa, 63; Spanish attack at, 31, 50, 54–55
Santiago, 113–14, 119–20
São Jorge da Mina, 36
Sekora, John, 177
sentiment: anti-Aztec, 96; anti-English, 39; anti-Portuguese, 31, 41; anti-Spanish, 12, 56, 63, 105
settlements, Cimarrones, 58, 65, 82–83
Shama, 34–35, 47–48
Sheller, Mimi, 137, 204n6
Sierra Leone, 31, 49, 53–57
slave trade: impetus for, 31, 50; link between race and, 11, 24, 26, 74, 121; transatlantic, 11, 38, 113
speculation, 21, 23
subaltern, 13
suitor. *See* courtship
symerons. *See* Cimarrones

texture (narrative), 5, 183nn15–16
Thornton, John, 38
Timbuktu, 38, 163
Towerson, William: and accusations of piracy, 30, 36; biography, 29; as liberator, 16, 34–35, 46, 47, 59
trace, textual, 4, 23, 30
trade: Guinea Coast, 38; Guinea-English, 29–33, 33–34, 35, 36, 48; Guinea-French, 37; Guinea-Portuguese, 16, 36. *See also* slave trade
treasure fleet, 67, 76. *See also* mule train
Treaty of Tordesillas, 36
trope (of alliance), 18, 57, 85

Vaughan, Alden, 142
Vaughan, Virginia Mason, 142
Venables, General Robert, 108–12, 117–18, 202n50
Venta de Cruces, 65, 73, 77–81

voice, 4, 13–14, 22–23, 178, 182n10. *See also* autonomy

West Africa. *See* Guinea
Western Design, 19, 86, 107, 117
West Indies, 90, 118, 158, 165
Whistler, Henry, 109
White, Ed, 22, 176, 187n62
Whitehead, Neil, 5, 158, 183n15, 211n40, 214n73
white legend, 61. *See also* black legend
Whitford, David, 148–49
world, Atlantic, definition of, 26–27
Wyndham, Thomas, 33, 144

zones, theory of five, 147–50, 155. *See also* race

www.ingramcontent.com/pod-product-compliance
Lightning Source LLC
Chambersburg PA
CBHW022012220426
43663CB00007B/1052